Diana J Sweeney
bought by Merril Morrison
in BA
APR '97

brought up by Daphne

PAMPAS GRASS: INDIANS ON THE LOOK-OUT FOR STRAYED HORSES.

[Frontispiece.

The Naturalist in La Plata

The Classic Study of the Argentinian Pampas

by

W. H. HUDSON

27 Illustrations by J. Smit

Dover Publications, Inc., New York

Published in Canada by General Publishing Company, Ltd., 30 Lesmill Road, Don Mills, Toronto, Ontario.
Published in the United Kingdom by Constable and Company, Ltd., 10 Orange Street, London WC2H 7EG.

This Dover edition, first published in 1988, is an unabridged, unaltered republication of the third edition (1895) of the work first published by Chapman and Hall, London, 1892. The subtitle, ''The Classic Study of the Argentinian Pampas,'' has been added to the Dover edition.

Manufactured in the United States of America
Dover Publications, Inc., 31 East 2nd Street, Mineola, N.Y. 11501

Library of Congress Cataloging-in-Publication Data

Hudson, W. H. (William Henry), 1841–1922.
   The naturalist in La Plata.

   Reprint. Originally published: 3rd ed. London : Chapman and Hall, 1895.
   Includes index.
   1. Zoology—Argentina—Pampas. 2. Natural history—Argentina—Pampas. 3. Animal behavior—Argentina—Pampas. I. Title.
QL239.H8   1988   508.82   88-11812
ISBN 0-486-25740-1

PREFACE.

THE plan I have followed in this work has been to sift and arrange the facts I have gathered concerning the habits of the animals best known to me, preserving those only, which, in my judgment, appeared worth recording. In some instances a variety of subjects have linked themselves together in my mind, and have been grouped under one heading ; consequently the scope of the book is not indicated by the list of contents : this want is, however, made good by an index at the end.

It is seldom an easy matter to give a suitable name to a book of this description. I am conscious that the one I have made choice of displays a lack of originality ; also, that this kind of title has been used hitherto for works constructed more or less on the plan of the famous *Naturalist on the Amazons*. After I have made this apology the reader, on his part, will readily admit that, in treating of the Natural History of a district so well known, and often described as the southern portion of La Plata, which has a temperate climate, and where nature is neither exuberant nor grand, a personal narrative would have seemed superfluous.

The greater portion of the matter contained in

this volume has already seen the light in the form of papers contributed to the *Field*, with other journals that treat of Natural History; and to the monthly magazines :—*Longmans'*, *The Nineteenth Century*, *The Gentleman's Magazine*, and others : I am indebted to the Editors and Proprietors of these periodicals for kindly allowing me to make use of this material.

Of all animals, birds have perhaps afforded me most pleasure ; but most of the fresh knowledge I have collected in this department is contained in a larger work (*Argentine Ornithology*), of which Dr. P. L. Sclater is part author. As I have not gone over any of the subjects dealt with in that work, bird-life has not received more than a fair share of attention in the present volume.

CONTENTS.

CHAPTER X.

CHAPTER XI.

CHAPTER XII.

CHAPTER XIII.

CHAPTER XIV.

CHAPTER XV.

CHAPTER XVI.

CHAPTER XVII.

CHAPTER XVIII.

CHAPTER XIX.

CHAPTER XX.

CHAPTER XXI.

Contents.

CHAPTER XXII.

LIST OF ILLUSTRATIONS.

THE NATURALIST IN LA PLATA.

CHAPTER I.

THE DESERT PAMPAS.

DURING recent years we have heard much about the great and rapid changes now going on in the plants and animals of all the temperate regions of the globe colonized by Europeans. These changes, if taken merely as evidence of material progress, must be a matter of rejoicing to those who are satisfied, and more than satisfied, with our system of civilization, or method of outwitting Nature by the removal of all checks on the undue increase of our own species. To one who finds a charm in things as they exist in the unconquered provinces of Nature's dominions, and who, not being over-anxious to reach the end of his journey, is content to perform it on horseback, or in a waggon drawn by bullocks, it is permissible to lament the altered aspect of the earth's surface, together with the disappearance of numberless noble and beautiful forms, both of the animal and vegetable kingdoms. For he cannot find it in his heart to love the forms by which they are replaced ; these are cultivated and domesticated, and have only become useful to man at the cost of

that grace and spirit which freedom and wildness
give. In numbers they are many—twenty-five
millions of sheep in this district, fifty millions in
that, a hundred millions in a third—but how few
are the species in place of those destroyed? and
when the owner of many sheep and much wheat
desires variety—for he possesses this instinctive
desire, albeit in conflict with and overborne by
the perverted instinct of destruction—what is there
left to him, beyond his very own, except the weeds
that spring up in his fields under all skies, ringing
him round with old-world monotonous forms, as
tenacious of their undesired union with him as the
rats and cockroaches that inhabit his house?

We hear most frequently of North America, New
Zealand, and Australia in this connection; but
nowhere on the globe has civilization "written
strange defeatures" more markedly than on that
great area of level country called by English writers
the pampas, but by the Spanish more appropriately
La Pampa—from the Quichua word signifying open
space or country—since it forms in most part one
continuous plain, extending on its eastern border
from the river Paraná, in latitude 32°, to the Patagonian formation on the river Colorado, and comprising about two hundred thousand square miles of
humid, grassy country.

This district has been colonized by Europeans
since the middle of the sixteenth century; but
down to within a very few years ago immigration
was on too limited a scale to make any very great
change; and, speaking only of the pampean
country, the conquered territory was a long, thinly-

settled strip, purely pastoral, and the Indians, with their primitive mode of warfare, were able to keep back the invaders from the greater portion of their ancestral hunting-grounds. Not twenty years ago a ride of two hundred miles, starting from the capital city, Buenos Ayres, was enough to place one well beyond the furthest south-western frontier out-post. In 1879 the Argentine Government determined to rid the country of the aborigines, or, at all events, to break their hostile and predatory spirit once for all ; with the result that the entire area of the grassy pampas, with a great portion of the sterile pampas and Patagonia, has been made available to the emigrant. There is no longer anything to deter the starvelings of the Old World from possessing themselves of this new land of promise, flowing, like Australia, with milk and tallow, if not with honey ; any emasculated migrant from a Genoese or Neapolitan slum is now competent to " fight the wilderness " out there, with his eight-shilling fowling-piece and the implements of his trade. The barbarians no longer exist to frighten his soul with dreadful war cries ; they have moved away to another more remote and shadowy region, called in their own language *Alhuemapú*, and not known to geographers. For the results so long and ardently wished for have swiftly followed on General Roca's military expedition ; and the changes witnessed during the last decade on the pampas exceed in magnitude those which had been previously effected by three centuries of occupation.

In view of this wave of change now rapidly sweeping away the old order, with whatever beauty and grace it possessed, it might not seem inopportune at the present moment to give a rapid sketch, from the field naturalist's point of view, of the great plain, as it existed before the agencies introduced by European colonists had done their work, and as it still exists in its remoter parts.

The humid, grassy, pampean country extends, roughly speaking, half-way from the Atlantic Ocean and the Plata and Paraná rivers to the Andes, and passes gradually into the "Monte Formation," or *sterile pampa*—a sandy, more or less barren district, producing a dry, harsh, ligneous vegetation, principally thorny bushes and low trees, of which the chañar (Gurliaca decorticans) is the most common; hence the name of " Chañar-steppe " used by some writers : and this formation extends southwards down into Patagonia. Scientists have not yet been able to explain why the pampas, with a humid climate, and a soil exceedingly rich, have produced nothing but grass, while the dry, sterile territories on their north, west, and south borders have an arborescent vegetation. Darwin's conjecture that the extreme violence of the *pampero*, or south-west wind, prevented trees from growing, is now proved to have been ill-founded since the introduction of the Eucalyptus globulus; for this noble tree attains to an extraordinary height on the pampas, and exhibits there a luxuriance of foliage never seen in Australia.

To this level area—my " parish of Selborne," or, at all events, a goodly portion of it—with the sea on one hand, and on the other the practically infinite expanse of grassy desert—another sea, not

" in vast fluctuations fixed," but in comparative
calm—I should like to conduct the reader in imagination : a country all the easier to be imagined
on account of the absence of mountains, woods,
lakes, and rivers. There is, indeed, little to be
imagined—not even a sense of vastness; and
Darwin, touching on this point, in the *Journal of a
Naturalist*, aptly says :—" At sea, a person's eye
being six feet above the surface of the water, his
horizon is two miles and four-fifths distant. In
like manner, the more level the plain, the more
nearly does the horizon approach within these
narrow limits; and this, in my opinion, entirely
destroys the grandeur which one would have
imagined that a vast plain would have possessed."

I remember my first experience of a hill, after
having been always shut within " these narrow
limits." It was one of the range of sierras near
Cape Corrientes, and not above eight hundred feet
high; yet, when I had gained the summit, I was
amazed at the vastness of the earth, as it appeared
to me from that modest elevation. Persons born
and bred on the pampas, when they first visit a
mountainous district, frequently experience a
sensation as of " a ball in the throat," which seems
to prevent free respiration.

In most places the rich, dry soil is occupied by a
coarse grass, three or four feet high, growing in
large tussocks, and all the year round of a deep
green; a few slender herbs and trefoils, with long,
twining stems, maintain a frail existence among
the tussocks; but the strong grass crowds out
most plants, and scarcely a flower relieves its

uniform everlasting verdure. There are patches, sometimes large areas, where it does not grow, and these are carpeted by small creeping herbs of a livelier green, and are gay in spring with flowers, chiefly of the composite and papilionaceous kinds ; and verbenas, scarlet, purple, rose, and white. On moist or marshy grounds there are also several lilies, yellow, white, and red, two or three flags, and various other small flowers ; but altogether the flora of the pampas is the poorest in species of any fertile district on the globe. On moist clayey ground flourishes the stately pampa grass, Gynerium argenteum, the spears of which often attain a height of eight or nine feet. I have ridden through many leagues of this grass with the feathery spikes high as my head, and often higher. It would be impossible for me to give anything like an adequate idea of the exquisite loveliness, at certain times and seasons, of this queen of grasses, the chief glory of the solitary pampa. Everyone is familiar with it in cultivation ; but the garden-plant has a sadly decaying, draggled look at all times, and to my mind, is often positively ugly with its dense withering mass of coarse leaves, drooping on the ground, and bundle of spikes, always of the same dead white or dirty cream-colour. Now colour—the various ethereal tints that give a blush to its cloud-like purity—is one of the chief beauties of this grass on its native soil ; and travellers who have galloped across the pampas at a season of the year when the spikes are dead, and white as paper or parchment, have certainly missed its greatest charm. The plant is social, and in some places where

scarcely any other kind exists it covers large areas
with a sea of fleecy-white plumes ; in late summer,
and in autumn, the tints are seen, varying from the
most delicate rose, tender and illusive as the blush
on the white under-plumage of some gulls, to purple
and violaceous. At no time does it look so perfect
as in the evening, before and after sunset, when
the softened light imparts a mistiness to the crowding plumes, and the traveller cannot help fancying
that the tints, which then seem richest, are caught
from the level rays of the sun, or reflected from the
coloured vapours of the afterglow.

The last occasion on which I saw the pampa
grass in its full beauty was at the close of a bright
day in March, ending in one of those perfect sunsets
seen only in the wilderness, where no lines of house
or hedge mar the enchanting disorder of nature,
and the earth and sky tints are in harmony. I had
been travelling all day with one companion, and for
two hours we had ridden through the matchless
grass, which spread away for miles on every side,
the myriads of white spears, touched with varied
colour, blending in the distance and appearing
almost like the surface of a cloud. Hearing a
swishing sound behind us, we turned sharply round,
and saw, not forty yards away in our rear, a party
of five mounted Indians, coming swiftly towards us :
but at the very moment we saw them their animals
came to a dead halt, and at the same instant the
five riders leaped up, and stood erect on their
horses' backs. Satisfied that they had no intention
of attacking us, and were only looking out for
strayed horses, we continued watching them for

some time, as they stood gazing away over the plain
in different directions, motionless and silent, like
bronze men on strange horse-shaped pedestals of
dark stone ; so dark in their copper skins and long
black hair, against the far-off ethereal sky, flushed
with amber light ; and at their feet, and all around,
the cloud of white and faintly-blushing plumes.
That farewell scene was printed very vividly on my
memory, but cannot be shown to another, nor could
it be even if a Ruskin's pen or a Turner's pencil
were mine ; for the flight of the sea-mew is not
more impossible to us than the power to picture
forth the image of Nature in our souls, when she
reveals herself in one of those " special moments "
which have " special grace " in situations where
her wild beauty has never been spoiled by man.

At other hours and seasons the general aspect of
the plain is monotonous, and in spite of the un-
obstructed view, and the unfailing verdure and
sunshine, somewhat melancholy, although never
sombre : and doubtless the depressed and melancholy feeling the pampa inspires in those who are
unfamiliar with it is due in a great measure to the
paucity of life, and to the profound silence. The
wind, as may well be imagined on that extensive
level area, is seldom at rest ; there, as in the forest,
it is a " bard of many breathings," and the strings
it breathes upon give out an endless variety of
sorrowful sounds, from the sharp fitful sibilations
of the dry wiry grasses on the barren places, to the
long mysterious moans that swell and die in the tall
polished rushes of the marsh. It is also curious to
note that with a few exceptions the resident birds

are comparatively very silent, even those belonging to groups which elsewhere are highly loquacious. The reason of this is not far to seek. In woods and thickets, where birds abound most, they are continually losing sight of each other, and are only prevented from scattering by calling often ; while the muffling effect on sound of the close foliage, to which may be added a spirit of emulation where many voices are heard, incites most species, especially those that are social, to exert their voices to the utmost pitch in singing, calling, and screaming. On the open pampas, birds, which are not compelled to live concealed on the surface, can see each other at long distances, and perpetual calling is not needful : moreover, in that still atmosphere sound travels far. As a rule their voices are strangely subdued ; nature's silence has infected them, and they have become silent by habit. This is not the case with aquatic species, which are nearly all migrants from noisier regions, and mass themselves in lagoons and marshes, where they are all loquacious together. It is also noteworthy that the subdued bird-voices, some of which are exceedingly sweet and expressive, and the notes of many of the insects and batrachians have a great resemblance, and seem to be in accord with the æolian tones of the wind in reeds and grasses : a stranger to the pampas, even a naturalist accustomed to a different fauna, will often find it hard to distinguish between bird, frog, and insect voices.

The mammalia is poor in species, and with the single exception of the well-known vizcacha (Lagostomus trichodactylus), there is not one of which it can truly be said that it is in any special way the product of the pampas, or, in other words, that its instincts are better suited to the conditions of the pampas than to those of other districts. As a fact, this large rodent inhabits a vast extent of country, north, west, and south of the true pampas, but nowhere is he so thoroughly on his native heath as on the great grassy plain. There, to some extent, he even makes his own conditions, like the beaver. He lives in a small community of twenty or thirty members, in a village of deep-chambered burrows, all with their pit-like entrances closely grouped together ; and as the village endures for ever, or for an indefinite time, the earth constantly being brought up forms a mound thirty or forty feet in diameter ; and this protects the habitation from floods on low or level ground. Again, he is not swift of foot, and all rapacious beasts are his enemies ; he also loves to feed on tender succulent herbs and grasses, to seek for which he would have to go far afield among the giant grass, where his watchful foes are lying in wait to seize him; he saves himself from this danger by making a clearing all round his abode, on which a smooth turf is formed; and here the animals feed and have their evening pastimes in comparative security : for when an enemy approaches, he is easily seen; the note of alarm is sounded, and the whole company scuttles away to their refuge. In districts having a different soil and vegetation, as in Patagonia, the vizcachas' curious, unique instincts are of no special advantage, which makes it seem probable that they have been formed on the pampas.

How marvellous a thing it seems that the two
species of mammalians—the beaver and the vizcacha
—that most nearly simulate men's intelligent actions
in their social organizing instincts, and their habitations, which are made to endure, should belong to
an order so low down as the Rodents ! And in the
case of the latter species, it adds to the marvel when
we find that the vizcacha, according to Waterhouse, is the lowest of the order in its marsupial
affinities.

The vizcacha is the most common rodent on the
pampas, and the Rodent order is represented by the
largest number of species. The finest is the so-called
Patagonian hare—Dolichotis patagonica—a beautiful animal twice as large as a hare, with ears shorter
and more rounded, and legs relatively much longer.
The fur is grey and chestnut brown. It is diurnal
in its habits, lives in kennels, and is usually met
with in pairs, or small flocks. It is better suited to
a sterile country like Patagonia than to the grassy
humid plain ; nevertheless it was found throughout
the whole of the pampas ; but in a country where
the wisdom of a Sir William Harcourt was never
needed to slip the leash, this king of the Rodentia
is now nearly extinct.

A common rodent is the coypú—Myiopotamus
coypú—yellowish in colour with bright red incisors ;
a rat in shape, and as large as an otter. It is
aquatic, lives in holes in the banks, and where there
are no banks it makes a platform nest among the
rushes. Of an evening they are all out swimming
and playing in the water, conversing together in
their strange tones, which sound like the moans and

cries of wounded and suffering men ; and among
them the mother-coypú is seen with her progeny,
numbering eight or nine, with as many on her back
as she can accommodate, while the others swim after
her, crying for a ride.

With reference to this animal, which, as we have
seen, is prolific, a strange thing once happened in
Buenos Ayres.   The coypú was much more abundant fifty years ago than now, and its skin, which

Coypú.

has a fine fur under the long coarse hair, was largely
exported to Europe.   About that time the Dictator
Rosas issued a decree prohibiting the hunting of
the coypú.   The result was that the animals increased and multiplied exceedingly, and, abandoning
their aquatic habits, they became terrestrial and
migratory, and swarmed everywhere in search of
food.   Suddenly a mysterious malady fell on them,
from which they quickly perished, and became
almost extinct.

What a blessed thing it would be for poor rabbit-worried Australia if a similar plague should visit that country, and fall on the right animal! On the other hand, what a calamity if the infection, wide-spread, incurable, and swift as the wind in its course, should attack the too-numerous sheep! And who knows what mysterious, unheard-of retributions that revengeful deity Nature may not be meditating in her secret heart for the loss of her wild four-footed children slain by settlers, and the spoiling of her ancient beautiful order!

A small pampa rodent worthy of notice is the Cavia australis, called *cuí* in the vernacular from its voice : a timid, social, mouse-coloured little creature, with a low gurgling language, like running babbling waters; in habits resembling its domestic pied relation the guinea pig. It loves to run on clean ground, and on the pampas makes little rat-roads all about its hiding-place, which little roads tell a story to the fox, and such like; therefore the little cavy's habits, and the habits of all cavies, I fancy, are not so well suited to the humid grassy region as to other districts, with sterile ground to run and play upon, and thickets in which to hide.

A more interesting animal is the Ctenomys magellanica, a little less than the rat in size, with a shorter tail, pale grey fur, and red incisors. It is called *tuco-tuco* from its voice, and *oculto* from its habits; for it is a dweller underground, and requires a loose, sandy soil in which, like the mole, it may *swim* beneath the surface. Consequently the pampa, with its heavy, moist mould, is not the tuco's proper place; nevertheless, wherever there

is a stretch of sandy soil, or a range of dunes, there
it is found living ; not seen, but heard ; for all day
long and all night sounds its voice, resonant and
loud, like a succession of blows from a hammer ; as
if a company of gnomes were toiling far down
underfoot, beating on their anvils, first with strong
measured strokes, then with lighter and faster, and
with a swing and rhythm as if the little men were
beating in time to some rude chant unheard above
the surface.   How came these isolated colonies of a
species so subterranean in habits, and requiring a
sandy soil to move in, so far from their proper district—that sterile country from which they are
separated by wide, unsuitable areas?   They cannot
perform long overland journeys like the rat.   Perhaps
the dunes have travelled, carrying their little cattle
with them.

Greatest among the carnivores are the two cat-
monarchs of South America, the jaguar and puma.
Whatever may be their relative positions elsewhere,
on the pampas the puma is mightiest, being much
more abundant and better able to thrive than its
spotted rival.   Versatile in its preying habits, its
presence on the pampa is not surprising ; but probably only an extreme abundance of large mammalian
prey, which has not existed in recent times, could
have tempted an animal of the river and forest-
loving habits of the jaguar to colonize this cold,
treeless, and comparatively waterless desert.   There
are two other important cats.   The grass-cat, not
unlike Felis catus in its robust form and dark colour,
but a larger, more powerful animal, inexpressibly
savage in disposition.   The second, Felis geoffroyi,

is a larger and more beautiful animal, coloured like a leopard ; it is called wood-cat, and, as the name would seem to indicate, is an intruder from wooded districts north of the pampas.

There are two canines : one is Azara's beautiful grey fox-like dog, purely a fox in habits, and common everywhere. The other is far more interesting and extremely rare ; it is called *aguará*, its nearest ally being the *aguará-guazú*, the Canis jubatus or maned wolf of naturalists, found north of the pampean district. The aguará is smaller and has no mane ; it is like the dingo in size, but slimmer and with a sharper nose, and has a much brighter red colour. At night when camping out I have heard its dismal screams, but the screamer was sought in vain ; while from the gauchos of the frontier I could only learn that it is a harmless, shy, solitary animal, that ever flies to remoter wilds from its destroyer, man. They offered me a skin—what more could I want ? Simple souls ! it was no more to me than the skin of a dead dog, with long, bright red hair. Those who love dead animals may have them in any number by digging with a spade in that vast sepulchre of the pampas, where perished the hosts of antiquity. I love the living that are above the earth ; and how small a remnant they are in South America we know, and now yearly becoming more precious as it dwindles away.

The pestiferous skunk is universal ; and there are two quaint-looking weasels, intensely black in colour, and grey on the back and flat crown. One, the Galictis barbara, is a large bold animal that hunts in companies ; and when these long-bodied creatures sit up erect, glaring with beady eyes, grinning and chattering at the passer-by, they look like little friars in black robes and grey cowls ; but the expression on their round faces is malignant and bloodthirsty beyond anything in nature, and it would perhaps be more decent to liken them to devils rather than to humans.

On the pampas there is, strictly speaking, only one ruminant, the Cervus campestris, which is common. The most curious thing about this animal is that the male emits a rank, musky odour, so powerful that when the wind blows from it the effluvium comes in nauseating gusts to the nostrils from a distance exceeding two miles. It is really astonishing that only one small ruminant should be found on this immense grassy area, so admirably suited to herbivorous quadrupeds, a portion of which at the present moment affords sufficient pasture to eighty millions of sheep, cattle, and horses. In La Plata the author of *The Mammoth and the Flood* will find few to quarrel with his doctrine.

Of Edentates there are four. The giant armadillo does not range so far, and the delicate little pink fairy armadillo, the truncated Chlamydophorus, is a dweller in the sand-dunes of Mendoza, and has never colonized the grassy pampas. The Tatusia hybrida, called "little mule" from the length of its ears, and the Dasypus tricinctus, which, when disturbed, rolls itself into a ball, the wedge-shaped head and wedge-shaped tail admirably fitting into the deep-cut shell side by side ; and the *quirquincho* (Dasypus minutus), all inhabit the pampa, are diurnal, and feed exclusively on insects, chiefly ants. Wherever the country becomes settled, these three disappear, owing to the dulness of their senses, especially that of sight, and to the diurnal habit, which was an advantage to them, and enabled them to survive when rapacious animals, which are mostly nocturnal, were their only enemies. The fourth, and most important, is the hairy armadillo, with habits which are in strange contrast to those of its perishing congeners, and which seem to mock many hard-and-fast rules concerning animal life. It is omnivorous, and will thrive on anything from grass to flesh, found dead and in all stages of decay, or captured by means of its own strategy. Furthermore, its habits change to suit its conditions : thus, where nocturnal carnivores are its enemies, it is diurnal; but where man appears as a chief persecutor, it becomes nocturnal. It is much hunted for its flesh, dogs being trained for the purpose; yet it actually becomes more abundant as population increases in any district; and, if versatility in habits or adaptiveness can be taken as a measure of intelligence, this poor armadillo, a survival of the past, so old on the earth as to have existed contemporaneously with the giant glyptodon, is the superior of the large-brained cats and canines.

To finish with the mammalia, there are two interesting opossums, both of the genus Didelphys, but in habits as wide apart as cat from otter. One of these marsupials appears so much at home on the plains that I almost regret having said that the vizcacha alone gives us the idea of being in its habits the *product* of the pampas. This animal—

Didelphys crassicaudata—has a long slender, wedge-shaped head and body, admirably adapted for pushing through the thick grass and rushes; for it is both terrestrial and aquatic, therefore well suited to inhabit low, level plains liable to be flooded. On dry land its habits are similar to those of a weasel; in lagoons, where it dives and swims with great ease, it constructs a globular nest suspended from the rushes. The fur is soft, of a rich yellow, reddish above, and on the sides and under surfaces varying in some parts to orange, in others exhibiting beautiful copper and terra-cotta tints. These lovely tints and the metallic lustre soon fade from the fur, otherwise this animal would be much sought after in the interests of those who love to decorate themselves with the spoils of beautiful dead animals—beast and bird. The other opossum is the black and white Didelphys azaræ; and it is indeed strange to find this animal on the pampas, although its presence there is not so mysterious as that of the tuco-tuco. It shuffles along slowly and awkwardly on the ground, but is a great traveller nevertheless. Tschudi met it mountaineering on the Andes at an enormous altitude, and, true to its lawless nature, it confronted me in Patagonia, where the books say no marsupial dwells. In every way it is adapted to an arboreal life, yet it is everywhere found on the level country, far removed from the conditions which one would imagine to be necessary to its existence. For how many thousands of years has this marsupial been a dweller on the plain, all its best faculties unexercised, its beautiful grasping hands pressed to the ground, and its prehensile tail dragged like an idle rope behind it ! Yet, if one is brought to a tree, it will take to it as readily as a duck to water, or an armadillo to earth, climbing up the trunk and about the branches with a monkey-like agility. How reluctant Nature seems in some cases to undo her own work ! How long she will allow a specialized organ, with the correlated instinct, to rest without use, yet ready to flash forth on the instant, bright and keen-edged, as in the ancient days of strife, ages past, before peace came to dwell on earth !

The avi-fauna is relatively much richer than the mammalia, owing to the large number of aquatic species, most of which are migratory with their " breeding " or " subsistence-areas " on the pampas. In more senses than one they constitute a " floating population," and their habits have in no way been modified by the conditions of the country. The order, including storks, ibises, herons, spoonbills, and flamingoes, counts about eighteen species ; and the most noteworthy birds in it are two great ibises nearly as large as turkeys, with mighty resonant voices. The duck order is very rich, numbering at least twenty species, including two beautiful upland geese, winter visitors from Magellanic lands, and two swans, the lovely black-necked, and the pure white with rosy bill. Of rails, or ralline birds, there are ten or twelve, ranging from a small spotted creature no bigger than a thrush to some large majestic birds. One is the courlan, called " crazy widow " from its mourning plumage and long melancholy screams, which on still evenings may be heard a league away. Another is the graceful variegated *ypicaha*, fond of social gatherings, where the birds perform a dance and make the desolate marshes resound with their insane human-like voices. A smaller kind, Porphyriops melanops, has a night-cry like a burst of shrill hysterical laughter, which has won for it the name of " witch ;" while another, Rallus rythyrhynchus, is called " little donkey " from its braying cries. Strange eerie voices have all these birds. Of the remaining aquatic species, the most important is the spur-winged crested screamer ; a noble bird as large as a swan, yet its favourite pastime is to soar upwards until it loses itself to sight in the blue ether, whence it pours forth its resounding choral notes, which reach the distant earth clarified, and with a rhythmic swell and fall as of chiming bells. It also sings by night, " counting the hours," the gauchos say, and where they have congregated together in tens of thousands the mighty roar of their combined voices produces an astonishingly grand effect.

The largest aquatic order is that of the Limicolæ —snipes, plover, and their allies—which has about twenty-five species. The vociferous spur-winged lapwing; the beautiful black and white stilt; a true snipe, and a painted snipe, are, strictly speaking, the only residents ; and it is astonishing to find, that, of the five-and-twenty species, at least thirteen are visitors from North America, several of them having their breeding-places quite away in the Arctic regions. This is one of those facts concerning the annual migration of birds which almost stagger belief; for among them are species with widely different habits, upland, marsh and sea-shore

birds, and in their great biannual journey they pass
through a variety of climates, visiting many countries
where the conditions seem suited to their requirements. Nevertheless, in September, and even as
early as August, they begin to arrive on the pampas,
the golden plover often still wearing his black
nuptial dress ; singly and in pairs, in small flocks,
and in clouds they come—curlew, godwit, plover,
tatler, tringa—piping the wild notes to which the
Greenlander listened in June, now to the gaucho
herdsman on the green plains of La Plata, then to
the wild Indian in his remote village; and soon,
further south, to the houseless huanaco-hunter in
the grey wilderness of Patagonia.

Here is a puzzle for ornithologists. In summer
on the pampas we have a godwit—Limosa hudsonica ;
in March it goes north to breed ; later in the
season flocks of the same species arrive from the
south to winter on the ·pampas. And besides this
godwit, there are several other North American
species, which have colonies in the southern hemi-
spere, with a reversed migration and breeding
season. Why do these southern birds winter so far
south ? Do they really breed in Patagonia ? If so,
their migration is an extremely limited one compared with that of the northern birds—seven or
eight hundred miles, on the outside, in one case,
against almost as many thousands of miles in the
other. Considering that some species which migrate as far south as Patagonia breed in the Arctic
regions as far north as latitude 82°, and probably
higher still, it would be strange indeed if none of
the birds which winter in Patagonia and on the

pampas were summer visitors to that great austral continent, which has an estimated area twice as large as that of Europe, and a climate milder than the arctic one. The migrants would have about six hundred miles of sea to cross from Tierra del Fuego ; but we know that the golden plover and other species, which sometimes touch at the Ber- mudas when travelling, fly much further than that without resting. The fact that a common Argentine titlark, a non-migrant and a weak flyer, has been met with at the South Shetland Islands, close to the antarctic continent, shows that the journey may be easily accomplished by birds with strong flight ; and that even the winter climate of that unknown land is not too severe to allow an acci- dental colonist, like this small delicate bird, to survive. The godwit, already mentioned, has been observed in flocks at the Falkland Islands in May, that is, three months after the same species had taken its autumal departure from the neighbouring mainland. Can it be believed that these late visitors to the Falklands were breeders in Patagonia, and had migrated east to winter in so bleak a region ? It is far more probable that they came from the south. Officers of sailing ships beating round Cape Horn might be able to settle this ques- tion definitely by looking out, and listening at night, for flights of birds, travelling north from about the first week in January to the end of February ; and in September and October travel- ling south. Probably not fewer than a dozen species of the plover order are breeders on the great austral continent ; also other aquatic birds—ducks and geese; and many Passerine birds, chiefly of the Tyrant family.

Should the long projected Australasian expedition to the South Polar regions ever be carried to a successful issue, there will probably be important results for ornithology, in spite of the astounding theory which has found a recent advocate in Canon Tristram, that all life originated at the North Pole, whence it spread over the globe, but never succeeded in crossing the deep sea surrounding the antarctic continent, which has consequently remained till now desolate, "a giant ash (and ice) of death." Nor is it unlikely that animals of a higher class than birds exist there; and the discovery of new mammalians, differing in type from those we know, would certainly be glad tidings to most students of nature.

Land birds on the pampas are few in species and in numbers. This may be accounted for by the absence of trees and other elevations on which birds prefer to roost and nest; and by the scarcity of food. Insects are few in dry situations; and the large perennial grasses, which occupy most of the ground, yield a miserable yearly harvest of a few minute seeds; so that this district is a poor one both for soft and hard billed birds. Hawks of several genera, in moderate numbers, are there, but generally keep to the marshes. Eagles and vultures are somewhat unworthily represented by carrion-hawks (Polyborinæ); the lordly carancho, almost eagle-like in size, black and crested, with a very large, pale blue, hooked beak—his battle axe: and his humble follower and jackal, the brown and

harrier-like chimango. These nest on the ground,
are versatile in their habits, carrion-eaters, also
killers on their own account, and, like wild dogs,
sometimes hunt in bands, which gives them an
advantage. They are the unfailing attendants of
all flesh-hunters, human or feline; and also furiously
pursue and persecute all eagles and true vultures
that venture on that great sea of grass, to wander
thereafter, for ever lost and harried, " the Hagars
and Ishmaels of their kind."

The owls are few and all of wide-ranging species.
The most common is the burrowing-owl, found in
both Americas. Not a retiring owl this, but all day
long, in cold and in heat, it stands exposed at the
mouth of its kennel, or on the vizcacha's mound,
staring at the passer-by with an expression of grave
surprise and reprehension in its round yellow eyes ;
male and female invariably together, standing stiff
and erect, almost touching—of all birds that pair
for life the most Darby and Joan like.

Of the remaining land birds, numbering about
forty species, a few that are most attractive on
account of their beauty, engaging habits, or large
size, may be mentioned here. On the southern portion of the pampas the military starling (Sturnella)
is found, and looks like the European starling, with
the added beauty of a scarlet breast : among resident pampas birds the only one with a touch of
brilliant colouring. It has a pleasing, careless song,
uttered on the wing, and in winter congregates in
great flocks, to travel slowly northwards over the
plains. When thus travelling the birds observe a
kind of order, and the flock feeding along the

ground shows a very extended front—a representation in bird-life of the " thin red line "—and advances by the hindmost birds constantly flying over the others and alighting in the front ranks.

Among the tyrant-birds are several species of the beautiful wing-banded genus, snow-white in colour, with black on the wings and tail : these are extremely graceful birds, and strong flyers, and in desert places, where man seldom intrudes, they gather to follow the traveller, calling to each other with low whistling notes, and in the distance look like white flowers as they perch on the topmost stems of the tall bending grasses.

The most characteristic pampean birds are the tinamous—called partridges in the vernacular—the rufous tinamou, large as a fowl, and the spotted tinamou, which is about the size of the English partridge. Their habits are identical : both lay eggs of a beautiful wine-purple colour, and in both species the young acquire the adult plumage and power of flight when very small, and fly better than the adults. They have small heads, slender curved beaks, unfeathered legs and feet, and are tailless ; the plumage is deep yellowish, marked with black and brown above. They live concealed, skulking like rails through the tall grass, fly reluctantly, and when driven up, their flight is exceedingly noisy and violent, the bird soon exhausting itself. They are solitary, but many live in proximity, frequently calling to each other with soft plaintive voices. The evening call-notes of the larger bird are flute-like in character, and singularly sweet and expressive.

The last figure to be introduced into this sketch
—which is not a catalogue—is that of the Rhea.
Glyptodon, Toxodon, Mylodon, Megatherium, have
passed away, leaving no descendants, and only pigmy
representatives if any; but among the feathered
inhabitants of the pampa the grand archaic ostrich
of America survives from a time when there were
also giants among the avians. Vain as such efforts
usually are, one cannot help trying to imagine something of the past history of this majestic bird, before
man came to lead the long chase now about to end
so mournfully. Its fleetness, great staying powers,
and beautiful strategy when hunted, make it seem
probable that it was not without pursuers, other
than the felines, among its ancient enemies, long-
winded and tenacious of their quarry; and these
were perhaps of a type still represented by the
wolf or hound-like aguará and aguara-guazú. It
might be supposed that when almost all the larger
forms, both mammal and bird, were overtaken by
destruction, and when the existing rhea was on the
verge of extinction, these long-legged swift canines
changed their habits and lost their bold spirit,
degenerating at last into hunters of small birds and
mammals, on which they are said to live.

The rhea possesses a unique habit, which is a
puzzle to us, although it probably once had some
significance—namely, that of running, when hunted,
with one wing raised vertically, like a great sail—a
veritable " ship of the wilderness." In every way
it is adapted to the conditions of the pampas in a
far greater degree than other pampean birds, only
excepting the rufous and spotted tinamous. Its

commanding stature gives it a wide horizon ; and
its dim, pale, bluish-grey colour assimilates to that
of the haze, and renders it invisible at even a moderate distance. Its large form fades out of sight
mysteriously, and the hunter strains his eyes in vain
to distinguish it on the blue expanse. Its figure
and carriage have a quaint majestic grace, somewhat
unavian in character, and peculiar to itself. There
are few more strangely fascinating sights in nature
than that of the old black-necked cock bird, standing with raised agitated wings among the tall plumed
grasses, and calling together his scattered hens
with hollow boomings and long mysterious suspira-
tions, as if a wind blowing high up in the void sky
had found a voice. Rhea-hunting with the bolas,
on a horse possessing both speed and endurance,
and trained to follow the bird in all his quick
doublings, is unquestionably one of the most fascinating forms of sport ever invented by man. The
quarry has even more than that fair chance of
escape, without which all sport degenerates into
mere butchery, unworthy of rational beings ; moreover, in this unique method of hunting the ostrich
the capture depends on a preparedness for all the
shifts and sudden changes of course practised by
the bird when closely followed, which is like instinct
or intuition ; and, finally, in a dexterity in casting
the bolas at the right moment, with a certain aim,
which no amount of practice can give to those who
are not to the manner born.

This ' wild mirth of the desert,' which the gaucho
has known for the last three centuries, is now passing away, for the rhea's fleetness can no longer

avail him. He may scorn the horse and his rider,
what time he lifts himself up, but the cowardly
murderous methods of science, and a systematic
war of extermination, have left him no chance.
And with the rhea go the flamingo, antique and
splendid; and the swans in their bridal plumage;
and the rufous tinamou—sweet and mournful melo-
dist of the eventide; and the noble crested screamer,
that clarion-voiced watch-bird of the night in the
wilderness. These, and the other large avians, together with the finest of the mammalians, will
shortly be lost to the pampas utterly as the great
bustard is to England, and as the wild turkey and
bison and many other species will shortly be lost to
North America. What a wail there would be in the
world if a sudden destruction were to fall on the
accumulated art-treasures of the National Gallery,
and the marbles in the British Museum, and the
contents of the King's Library—the old prints and
mediæval illuminations! And these are only the
work of human hands and brains—impressions of
individual genius on perishable material, immortal
only in the sense that the silken cocoon of the dead
moth is so, because they continue to exist and shine
when the artist's hands and brain are dust:—and
man has the long day of life before him in which to
do again things like these, and better than these, if
there is any truth in evolution. But the forms of
life in the two higher vertebrate classes are Nature's
most perfect work; and the life of even a single
species is of incalculably greater value to mankind,
for what it teaches and would continue to teach,
than all the chiselled marbles and painted canvases

the world contains; though doubtless there are
many persons who are devoted to art, but blind to
some things greater than art, who will set me down
as a Philistine for saying so. And, above all others,
we should protect and hold sacred those types,
Nature's masterpieces, which are first singled out
for destruction on account of their size, or splendour,
or rarity, and that false detestable glory which is
accorded to their most successful slayers. In
ancient times the spirit of life shone brightest in
these; and when others that shared the earth with
them were taken by death they were left, being
more worthy of perpetuation. Like immortal
flowers they have drifted down to us on the ocean of
time, and their strangeness and beauty bring to our
imaginations a dream and a picture of that unknown
world, immeasurably far removed, where man was
not: and when they perish, something of gladness
goes out from nature, and the sunshine loses something of its brightness. Nor does their loss affect
us and our times only. The species now being
exterminated, not only in South America but everywhere on the globe, are, so far as we know, untouched by decadence. They are links in a chain,
and branches on the tree of life, with their roots in
a past inconceivably remote; and but for our action
they would continue to flourish, reaching outward
to an equally distant future, blossoming into higher
and more beautiful forms, and gladdening innumerable generations of our descendants. But we think
nothing of all this: we must give full scope to our
passion for taking life, though by so doing we " ruin
the great work of time;" not in the sense in which

the poet used those words, but in one truer, and wider, and infinitely sadder. Only when this sporting rage has spent itself, when there are no longer any animals of the larger kinds remaining, the loss we are now inflicting on this our heritage, in which we have a life-interest only, will be rightly appreciated. It is hardly to be supposed or hoped that posterity will feel satisfied with our monographs of extinct species, and the few crumbling bones and faded feathers, which may possibly survive half a dozen centuries in some happily-placed museum. On the contrary, such dreary mementoes will only serve to remind them of their loss ; and if they remember us at all, it will only be to hate our memory, and our age—this enlightened, scientific, humanitarian age, which should have for a motto " Let us slay all noble and beautiful things, for to-morrow we die."

CHAPTER II.

THE Puma has been singularly unfortunate in its biographers. Formerly it often happened that writers were led away by isolated and highly exaggerated incidents to attribute very shining qualities to their favourite animals; the lion of the Old World thus came to be regarded as brave and magnanimous above all beasts of the field—the Bayard of the four-footed kind, a reputation which these prosaic and sceptical times have not suffered it to keep. Precisely the contrary has happened with the puma of literature; for, although to those personally acquainted with the habits of this lesser lion of the New World it is known to possess a marvellous courage and daring, it is nevertheless always spoken of in books of natural history as the most pusillanimous of the larger carnivores. It does not attack man, and Azara is perfectly correct when he affirms that it never hurts, or threatens to hurt, man or child, even when it finds them sleeping. This, however, is not a full statement of the facts; the puma will not even defend itself against man. How natural, then, to conclude that it is too timid to attack a human being, or to defend itself, but scarcely philosophical; for even the most cowardly carnivores we know—dogs and hyænas,

for instance—will readily attack a disabled or
sleeping man when pressed by hunger ; and when
driven to desperation no animal is too small or too
feeble to make a show of resistance.   In such a case
" even the armadillo defends itself," as the gaucho
proverb says.   Besides, the conclusion is in contradiction to many other well-known facts.   Putting
aside the puma's passivity in the presence of man,
it is a bold hunter that invariably prefers large to
small game ; in desert places killing peccary, tapir,
ostrich, deer, huanaco, &c., all powerful, well-armed,
or swift animals.   Huanaco skeletons seen in
Patagonia almost invariably have the neck dislocated, showing that the puma was the executioner.
Those only who have hunted the huanaco on the
sterile plains and mountains it inhabits know how
wary, keen-scented, and fleet of foot it is.   I
once spent several weeks with a surveying party
in a district where pumas were very abundant, and
saw not less than half a dozen deer every day,
freshly killed in most cases, and all with dislocated
necks.   Where prey is scarce and difficult to capture,
the puma, after satisfying its hunger, invariably
conceals the animal it has killed, covering it over
carefully with grass and brushwood ; these deer,
however, had all been left exposed to the caracaras
and foxes after a portion of the breast had been
eaten, and in many cases the flesh had not been
touched, the captor having satisfied itself with
sucking the blood.   It struck me very forcibly that
the puma of the desert pampas is, among mammals,
like the peregrine falcon of the same district among
birds ; for there this wide-ranging raptor only

attacks comparatively large birds, and, after fastidi-
ously picking a meal from the flesh of the head and
neck, abandons the untouched body to the polybori
and other hawks of the more ignoble sort.

In pastoral districts the puma is very destructive
to the larger domestic animals, and has an extraordinary fondness for horseflesh. This was first
noticed by Molina, whose *Natural History of Chili*
was written a century and a half ago. In Patagonia
I heard on all sides that it was extremely difficult
to breed horses, as the colts were mostly killed by
the pumas. A native told me that on one occasion,
while driving his horses home through the thicket, a
puma sprang out of the bushes on to a colt following
behind the troop, killing it before his eyes and not
more than six yards from his horse's head. In this
instance, my informant said, the puma alighted
directly on the colt's back, with one fore foot
grasping its bosom, while with the other it seized
the head, and, giving it a violent wrench, dislocated
the neck. The colt fell to the earth as if shot, and
he affirmed that it was dead before it touched the
ground.

Naturalists have thought it strange that the
horse, once common throughout America, should
have become extinct over a continent apparently so
well suited to it and where it now multiplies so
greatly. As a fact wherever pumas abound the
wild horse of the present time, introduced from
Europe, can hardly maintain its existence. Formerly
in many places horses ran wild and multiplied to an
amazing extent, but this happened, I believe, only
in districts where the puma was scarce or had

already been driven out by man. My own experience is that on the desert pampas wild horses
are exceedingly scarce, and from all accounts it
is the same throughout Patagonia.

Next to horseflesh sheep is preferred, and where
the puma can come at a flock, he will not trouble
himself to attack horned cattle. In Patagonia
especially I found this to be the case. I resided
for some time at an estancia close to the town of
El Carmen, on the Rio Negro, which during my
stay was infested by a very bold and cunning
puma. To protect the sheep from his attacks an
enclosure was made of upright willow-poles fifteen
feet long, while the gate, by which he would have
to enter, was close to the house and nearly six
feet high. In spite of the difficulties thus put in
the way, and of the presence of several large dogs,
also of the watch we kept in the hope of shooting
him, every cloudy night he came, and after killing
one or more sheep got safely away. One dark
night he killed four sheep; I detected him in the
act, and going up to the gate, was trying to make
out his invisible form in the gloom as he flitted
about knocking the sheep over, when suddenly he
leaped clear over my head and made his escape,
the bullets I sent after him in the dark failing to
hit him. Yet at this place twelve or fourteen calves,
belonging to the milch cows, were every night shut
into a small brushwood pen, at a distance from the
house where the enemy could easily have destroyed
every one of them. When I expressed surprise at
this arrangement, the owner said that the puma was
not fond of calves' flesh, and came only for the

sheep. Frequently after his nocturnal visits we found, by tracing his footprints in the loose sand, that he had actually used the calves' pen as a place of concealment while waiting to make his attack on the sheep.

The puma often kills full-grown cows and horses, but exhibits a still greater daring when attacking the jaguar, the largest of American carnivores, although, compared with its swift, agile enemy, as heavy as a rhinoceros. Azara states that it is generally believed in La Plata and Paraguay that the puma attacks and conquers the jaguar; but he did not credit what he heard, which was not strange, since he had already set the puma down as a cowardly animal, because it does not attempt to harm man or child. Nevertheless, it is well known that where the two species inhabit the same district they are at enmity, the puma being the persistent persecutor of the jaguar, following and harassing it as a tyrant-bird harasses an eagle or hawk, moving about it with such rapidity as to confuse it, and, when an opportunity occurs, springing upon its back and inflicting terrible wounds with teeth and claws. Jaguars with scarred backs are frequently killed, and others, not long escaped from their tormentors, have been found so greatly lacerated that they were easily overcome by the hunters.

In Kingsley's American *Standard Natural History*, it is stated that the puma in North California has a feud with the grizzly bear similar to that of the southern animal with the jaguar. In its encounter with the grizzly it is said to be always

the victor ; and this is borne out by the finding
of the bodies of bears, which have evidently
perished in the struggle.

How strange that this most cunning, bold, and
bloodthirsty of the Felidæ, the persecutor of the
jaguar and the scourge of the ruminants in the
regions it inhabits, able to kill its prey with the
celerity of a rifle bullet, never attacks a human
being ! Even the cowardly, carrion-feeding dog
will attack a man when it can do so with impunity ;
but in places where the puma is the only large
beast of prey, it is notorious that it is there perfectly safe for even a small child to go out and
sleep on the plain. At the same time it will not
fly from man (though the contrary is always stated
in books of Natural History) except in places where
it is continually persecuted. Nor is this all : it
will not, as a rule, even defend itself against man,
although in some rare instances it has been known
to do so.

The mysterious, gentle instinct of this ungentle
species, which causes the gauchos of the pampas
to name it man's friend—"amigo del cristiano "—
has been persistently ignored by all travellers and
naturalists who have mentioned the puma. They
have thus made it a very incongruous creature,
strong enough to kill a horse, yet so cowardly
withal that it invariably flies from a human being—
even from a sleeping child ! Possibly its real reputation was known to some of those who have
spoken about it ; if so, they attributed what they
heard to the love of the marvellous and the ro-
mantic, natural to the non-scientific mind ; or else

preferred not to import into their writings matter which has so great a likeness to fable, and might have the effect of imperilling their reputation for sober-mindedness.

It is, however, possible that the singular instinct of the southern puma, which is unique among animals in a state of nature, is not possessed by the entire species, ranging as it does over a hundred degrees of latitude, from British North America to Tierra del Fuego. The widely different conditions of life in the various regions it inhabits must necessarily have caused some divergence. Concerning its habits in the dense forests of the Amazonian region, where it must have developed special instincts suited to its semi-arboreal life, scarcely anything has been recorded. Everyone is, however, familiar with the dreaded cougar, catamount, or panther—sometimes called "painter"—of North American literature, thrilling descriptions of encounters with this imaginary man-eating monster being freely scattered through the backwoods or border romances, many of them written by authors who have the reputation of being true to nature. It may be true that this cougar of a cold climate did occasionally attack man, or, as it is often stated, follow him in the forest with the intention of springing on him unawares; but on this point nothing definite will ever be known, as the pioneers and hunters of the past were only anxious to shoot the cougar and not to study its instinct and disposition. It is now many years since Audubon and Bachman wrote, " This animal, which has excited so much terror in the minds of the ignorant and timid, has been nearly exterminated in all the Atlantic States, and we do not recollect a single well-authenticated instance where any hunter's life fell a sacrifice in a cougar hunt." It might be added, I believe, that no authentic instance has been recorded of the puma making an unprovoked attack on any human being. In South America also the traveller in the wilderness is sometimes followed by a puma; but he would certainly be very much surprised if told that it follows with the intention of springing on him unawares and devouring his flesh.

I have spoken of the comparative ease with which the puma overcomes even large animals, comparing it in this respect with the peregrine falcon; but all predacious species are liable to frequent failures, sometimes to fatal mishaps, and even the cunning, swift-killing puma is no exception. Its attacks are successfully resisted by the ass, which does not, like the horse, lose his presence of mind, but when assaulted thrusts his head well down between its fore-legs and kicks violently until the enemy is thrown or driven off. Pigs, when in large herds, also safely defy the puma, massing themselves together for defence in their well-known manner, and presenting a serried line of tusks to the aggressor. During my stay in Patagonia a puma met its fate in a manner so singular that the incident caused considerable sensation among the settlers on the Rio Negro at the time. A man named Linares, the chief of the tame Indians settled in the neighbourhood of El Carmen, while riding near the river had his curiosity aroused by the

appearance and behaviour of a young cow standing
alone in the grass, her head, armed with long and
exceedingly sharp horns, much raised, and watching
his approach in a manner which betokened a state
of dangerous excitement. She had recently dropped
her calf, and he at once conjectured that it had
been attacked, and perhaps killed, by some animal
of prey. To satisfy himself on this point he began
to search for it, and while thus engaged the cow

Puma killed by Cow.

repeatedly charged him with the greatest fury.
Presently he discovered the calf lying dead among
the long grass ; and by its side lay a full-grown
puma, also dead, and with a large wound in its
side, just behind the shoulder. The calf had been
killed by the puma, for its throat showed the wounds
of large teeth, and the puma had been killed by
the cow. When he saw it he could, he affirmed,
scarcely believe the evidence of his own senses, for
it was an unheard-of thing that a puma should be

injured by any other animal. His opinion was that it had come down from the hills in a starving condition, and having sprung upon the calf, the taste of blood had made it for a moment careless of its own safety, and during that moment the infuriated cow had charged, and driving one of her long sharp horns into some vital part, killed it instantly.

The puma is, with the exception of some monkeys, the most playful animal in existence. The young of all the Felidæ spend a large portion of their time in characteristic gambols; the adults, however, acquire a grave and dignified demeanour, only the female playing on occasions with her offspring; but this she always does with a certain formality of manner, as if the relaxation were indulged in not spontaneously, but for the sake of the young and as being a necessary part of their education. Some writer has described the lion's assumption of gaiety as more grim than its most serious moods. The puma at heart is always a kitten, taking unmeasured delight in its frolics, and when, as often happens, one lives alone in the desert, it will amuse itself by the hour fighting mock battles or playing at hide-and-seek with imaginary companions, and lying in wait and putting all its wonderful strategy in practice to capture a passing butterfly. Azara kept a young male for four months, which spent its whole time playing with the slaves. This animal, he says, would not refuse any food offered to it ; but when not hungry it would bury the meat in the sand, and when inclined to eat dig it up, and, taking it to the water-trough, wash it clean. I have only known one puma kept as a pet, and this animal, in seven

or eight years had never shown a trace of ill-
temper. When approached, he would lie down,
purring loudly, and twist himself about a person's
legs, begging to be caressed. A string or hand-
kerchief drawn about was sufficient to keep him in a
happy state of excitement for an hour ; and when
one person was tired of playing with him he was
ready for a game with the next comer.

I was told by a person who had spent most of
his life on the pampas that on one occasion, when
travelling in the neighbourhood of Cape Corrientes,
his horse died under him, and he was compelled to
continue his journey on foot, burdened with his
heavy native horse-gear. At night he made his
bed under the shelter of a rock, on the slope of a
stony sierra ; a bright moon was shining, and
about nine o'clock in the evening four pumas
appeared, two adults with their two half-grown
young. Not feeling the least alarm at their presence, he did not stir ; and after a while they began
to gambol together close to him, concealing themselves from each other among the rocks, just as
kittens do, and frequently while pursuing one
another leaping over him. He continued watching
them until past midnight, then fell asleep, and
did not wake until morning, when they had left
him.

This man was an Englishman by birth, but
having gone very young to South America he had
taken kindly to the semi-barbarous life of the
gauchos, and had imbibed all their peculiar notions,
one of which is that human life is not worth very
much. "What does it matter?" they often say,

and shrug their shoulders, when told of a comrade's death ; " so many beautiful horses die ! " I asked him if he had ever killed a puma, and he replied that he had killed only one and had sworn never to kill another. He said that while out one day with another gaucho looking for cattle a puma was found. It sat up with its back against a stone, and did not move even when his companion threw the noose of his lasso over its neck. My informant then dismounted, and, drawing his knife, advanced to kill it : still the puma made no attempt to free itself from the lasso, but it seemed to know, he said, what was coming, for it began to tremble, the tears ran from its eyes, and it whined in the most pitiful manner. He killed it as it sat there unresisting before him, but after accomplishing the deed felt that he had committed a murder. It was the only thing he had ever done in his life, he added, which filled him with remorse when he remembered it. This I thought a rather startling declaration, as I knew that he had killed several individuals of his own species in duels, fought with knives, in the fashion of the gauchos.

All who have killed or witnessed the killing of the puma—and I have questioned scores of hunters on this point—agree that it resigns itself in this unresisting, pathetic manner to death at the hands of man. Claudio Gay, in his *Natural History of Chili*, says, " When attacked by man its energy and daring at once forsake it, and it becomes a weak, inoffensive animal, and trembling, and uttering piteous moans, and shedding abundant tears, it seems to implore compassion from a generous

enemy." The enemy is not often generous; but
many gauchos have assured me, when speaking on
this subject, that although they kill the puma readily
to protect their domestic animals, they consider it
an evil thing to take its life in desert places, where
it is man's only friend among the wild animals.

When the hunter is accompanied by dogs, then
the puma, instead of drooping and shedding tears,
is roused to a sublime rage : its hair stands erect;
its eyes shine like balls of green flame ; it spits and
snarls like a furious tom cat. The hunter's presence seems at such times to be ignored altogether,
its whole attention being given to the dogs and its
rage directed against them. In Patagonia a sheep-
farming Scotchman, with whom I spent some days,
showed me the skulls of five pumas which he had
shot in the vicinity of his ranche. One was of an
exceptionally large individual, and I here relate
what he told me of his encounter with this animal,
as it shows just how the puma almost invariably
behaves when attacked by man and dogs. He was
out on foot with his flock, when the dogs discovered
the animal concealed among the bushes. He had
left his gun at home, and having no weapon, and
finding that the dogs dared not attack it where it
sat in a defiant attitude with its back against a
thorny bush, he looked about and found a large dry
stick, and going boldly up to it tried to stun it
with a violent blow on the head. But though it
never looked at him, its fiery eyes gazing steadily at
the dogs all the time, he could not hit it, for with a
quick side movement it avoided every blow. The
small heed the puma paid him, and the apparent

ease with which it avoided his best-aimed blows,
only served to rouse his spirit, and at length striking
with increased force his stick came to the ground
and was broken to pieces. For some moments he
now stood within two yards of the animal perfectly
defenceless and not knowing what to do. Suddenly
it sprang past him, actually brushing against his arm
with its side, and began pursuing the dogs round
and round among the bushes. In the end my
informant's partner appeared on the scene with his
rifle, and the puma was shot.

In encounters of this kind the most curious thing
is that the puma steadfastly refuses to recognize an
enemy in man, although it finds him acting in
concert with its hated canine foe, about whose
hostile intentions it has no such delusion.

Several years ago a paragraph, which reached
me in South America, appeared in the English
papers relating an incident characteristic of the
puma in a wild beast show in this country. The
animal was taken out of its cage and led about the
grounds by its keeper, followed by a large number
of spectators. Suddenly it was struck motionless
by some object in the crowd, at which it gazed
steadily with a look of intense excitement; then
springing violently away it dragged the chain from
the keeper's hand and dashed in among the people,
who immediately fled screaming in all directions.
Their fears were, however, idle, the object of the
puma's rage being a dog which it had spied among
the crowd.

It is said that when taken adult pumas invariably
pine away and die; when brought up in captivity

they invariably make playful, affectionate pets, and are gentle towards all human beings, but very seldom overcome their instinctive animosity towards the dog.

One of the very few authentic instances I have met with of this animal defending itself against a human being was related to me at a place on the pampas called Saladillo. At the time of my visit there jaguars and pumas were very abundant and extremely destructive to the cattle and horses. Sheep it had not yet been considered worth while to introduce, but immense herds of pigs were kept at every estancia, these animals being able to protect themselves. One gaucho had so repeatedly distinguished himself by his boldness and dexterity in killing jaguars that he was by general consent made the leader of every tiger-hunt. One day the comandante of the district got twelve or fourteen men together, the tiger-slayer among them, and started in search of a jaguar which had been seen that morning in the neighbourhood of his estancia. The animal was eventually found and surrounded, and as it was crouching among some clumps of tall pampas grass, where throwing a lasso over its neck would be a somewhat difficult and dangerous operation, all gave way to the famous hunter, who at once uncoiled his lasso and proceeded in a leisurely manner to form the loop. While thus engaged he made the mistake of allowing his horse, which had grown restive, to turn aside from the hunted animal. The jaguar, instantly taking advantage of the oversight, burst from its cover and sprang first on to the haunches of the horse, then seizing the hunter by his poncho dragged him to the earth, and would no doubt have quickly despatched him if a lasso, thrown by one of the other men, had not closed round its neck at this critical moment. It was quickly dragged off, and eventually killed. But the discomfited hunter did not stay to assist at the finish. He arose from the ground unharmed, but in a violent passion and blaspheming horribly, for he knew that his reputation, which he prized above everything, had suffered a great blow, and that he would be mercilessly ridiculed by his associates. Getting on his horse he rode away by himself from the scene of his misadventure. Of what happened to him on his homeward ride there were no witnesses; but his own account was as follows, and inasmuch as it told against his own prowess it was readily believed: Before riding a league, and while his bosom was still burning with rage, a puma started up from the long grass in his path, but made no attempt to run away; it merely sat up, he said, and looked at him in a provokingly fearless manner. To slay this animal with his knife, and so revenge himself on it for the defeat he had just suffered, was his first thought. He alighted and secured his horse by tying its fore feet together, then, drawing his long, heavy knife, rushed at the puma. Still it did not stir. Raising his weapon he struck with a force which would have split the animal's skull open if the blow had fallen where it was intended to fall, but with a quick movement the puma avoided it, and at the same time lifted a foot and with lightning rapidity dealt the aggressor a blow on the face, its unsheathed claws literally dragging down the flesh

from his cheek, laying the bone bare. After inflicting this terrible punishment and eyeing its
fallen foe for a few seconds it trotted quietly away.
The wounded man succeeded in getting on to his
horse and reaching his home. The hanging flesh was
restored to its place and the ghastly rents sewn
up, and in the end he recovered: but he was dis-
figured for life; his temper also completely changed;
he became morose and morbidly sensitive to the
ridicule of his neighbours, and he never again
ventured to join them in their hunting expeditions.

I inquired of the comandante, and of others,
whether any case had come to their knowledge in
that district in which the puma had shown anything
beyond a mere passive friendliness towards man ; in
reply they related the following incident, which had
occurred at the Saladillo a few years before my
visit : The men all went out one day beyond the
frontier to form a *cerco*, as it is called, to hunt
ostriches and other game. The hunters, numbering about thirty, spread themselves round in a vast
ring and, advancing towards the centre, drove the
animals before them. During the excitement of the
chase which followed, while they were all engaged
in preventing the ostriches, deer, &c., from doubling
back and escaping, it was not noticed that one of
the hunters had disappeared; his horse, however, returned to its home during the evening, and on the
next morning a fresh hunt for the lost man was
organized. He was eventually found lying on the
ground with a broken leg, where he had been thrown
at the beginning of the hunt. He related that
about an hour after it had become dark a puma

appeared and sat near him, but did not seem to notice him. After a while it became restless, frequently going away and returning, and finally it kept away so long, that he thought it had left him for good. About midnight he heard the deep roar of a jaguar, and gave himself up for lost. By raising himself on his elbow he was able to see the outline of the beast crouching near him, but its face was turned from him, and it appeared to be intently watching some object on which it was about to spring. Presently it crept out of sight, then he heard snarlings and growlings and the sharp yell of a puma, and he knew that the two beasts were fighting. Before morning he saw the jaguar several times, but the puma renewed the contest with it again and again until morning appeared, after which he saw and heard no more of them.

Extraordinary as this story sounds, it did not seem so to me when I heard it, for I had already met with many anecdotes of a similar nature in various parts of the country, some of them vastly more interesting than the one I have just narrated ; only I did not get them at first hand, and am consequently not able to vouch for their accuracy ; but in this case it seemed to me that there was really no room for doubt. All that I had previously heard had compelled me to believe that the puma really does possess a unique instinct of friendliness for man, the origin of which, like that of many other well-known instincts of animals, must remain a mystery. The fact that the puma never makes an unprovoked attack on a human being, or eats human flesh, and that it refuses, except in some very rare cases, even

PUMA ATTACKING JAGUAR.

[Page 48.

to defend itself, does not seem really less wonderful
in an animal of its bold and sanguinary temper than
that it should follow the traveller in the wilderness,
or come near him when he lies sleeping or disabled,
and even occasionally defend him from its enemy
the jaguar. We know that certain sounds, colours,
or smells, which are not particularly noticed by
most animals, produce an extraordinary effect on
some species; and it is possible to believe, I think,
that the human form or countenance, or the odour
of the human body, may also have the effect on the
puma of suspending its predatory instincts and in-
spiring it with a gentleness towards man, which we
are only accustomed to see in our domesticated
carnivores or in feral animals towards those of their
own species. Wolves, when pressed with hunger,
will sometimes devour a fellow wolf; as a rule,
however, rapacious animals will starve to death
rather than prey on one of their own kind, nor is it
a common thing for them to attack other species
possessing instincts similar to their own. The
puma, we have seen, violently attacks other large
carnivores, not to feed on them, but merely to
satisfy its animosity; and, while respecting man, it
is, within the tropics, a great hunter and eater of
monkeys, which of all animals most resemble men.
We can only conclude with Humboldt that there is
something mysterious in the hatreds and affections
of animals.

The view here taken of the puma's character
imparts, I think, a fresh interest to some things
concerning the species, which have appeared in

historical and other works, and which I propose to discuss briefly in this place.

There is a remarkable passage in Byron's *Narrative of the loss of the Wager*, which was quoted by Admiral Fitzroy in his *Voyage of the Beagle*, to prove that the puma inhabits Tierra del Fuego and the adjacent islands; no other large beast of prey being known in that part of America. " I heard," he says, " a growling close by me, which made me think it advisable to retire as soon as possible: the woods were so gloomy I could see nothing; but, as I retired, this noise followed me close till I got out of them. Some of our men did assure me that they had seen a very large beast in the woods. . . I proposed to four of the people to go to the end of the bay, about two miles distant from the bell tent, to occupy the skeleton of an old Indian wigwam, which I had discovered in a walk that way on our first landing. This we covered to windward with seaweed; and, lighting a fire, laid ourselves down in hopes of finding a remedy for our hunger in sleep; but we had not long composed ourselves before one of our company was disturbed by the blowing of some animal at his face; and, upon opening his eyes, was not a little astonished to see by the glimmering of the fire, a large beast standing over him. He had presence of mind enough to snatch a brand from the fire, which was now very low, and thrust it at the nose of the animal, which thereupon made off. . . . In the morning we were not a little anxious to know how our companions had fared; and this anxiety was increased upon our tracing the footsteps of the

beast in the sand, in a direction towards the bell
tent. The impression was deep and plain, of a
large round foot well furnished with claws. Upon
acquainting the people in the tent with the circumstances of our story, we found that they had been
visited by the same unwelcome guest."

Mr. Andrew Murray, in his work on the Geographical Distribution of Mammals, gives the Straits
of Magellan as the extreme southern limit of the
puma's range, and in discussing the above passage
from Byron he writes: " This reference, however,
gives no support to the notion of the animal alluded
to having been a puma. . . . The description of the
footprints clearly shows that the animal could not
have been a puma. None of the cat tribe leave any
trace of a claw in their footprints. . . . The dogs,
on the other hand, leave a very well-defined claw-
mark. . . . Commodore Byron and his party had
therefore suffered a false alarm. The creature
which had disturbed them was, doubtless, one of the
harmless domestic dogs of the natives."

The assurance that the bold hardy adventurer
and his men suffered a false alarm, and were thrown
into a great state of excitement at the appearance of
one of the wretched domestic dogs of the Fuegians,
with which they were familiar, comes charmingly,
it must be said, from a closet naturalist, who
surveys the world of savage beasts from his London
study. He apparently forgets that Commodore
Byron lived in a time when the painful accuracy
and excessive minuteness we are accustomed to was
not expected from a writer, whenever he happened
to touch on any matters connected with zoology.

This kind of criticism, which seizes on a slight
inaccuracy in one passage, and totally ignores an
important statement in another—as, for instance,
that of the " great beast " seen in the woods—might
be extended to other portions of the book, and
Byron's entire narrative made to appear as purely
a work of the imagination as Peter Wilkin's adventures in those same antarctic seas.

Mr. J. W. Boddam Whetham, in his work *Across
Central America* (1877), gives an anecdote of the
puma, which he heard at Sacluk, in Guatemala, and
which strangely resembles some of the stories I
have heard on the pampas. He writes: " The
following event, most extraordinary if true, is said
to have occurred in this forest to a mahogany-cutter,
who had been out marking trees. As he was returning to his hut, he suddenly felt a soft body
pressing against him, and on looking down saw a
cougar, which, with tail erect, and purring like a
cat, twisted itself in and out of his legs, and glided
round him, turning up its fierce eyes as if with
laughter. Horror-stricken and with faltering steps
he kept on, and the terrible animal still circled
about, now rolling over, and now touching him with
a paw like a cat playing with a mouse. At last the
suspense became too great, and with a loud shout
he struck desperately at the creature with his axe.
It bounded on one side and crouched snarling and
showing its teeth. Just as it was about to spring,
the man's companion, who had heard his call,
appeared in the distance, and with a growl the beast
vanished into the thick bushes."

Now, after allowing for exaggeration, if there is

no foundation for stories of this character, it is really a very wonderful coincidence that they should be met with in countries so widely separated as Patagonia and Central America. Pumas, doubtless, are scarce in Guatemala; and, as in other places where they have met with nothing but persecution from man, they are shy of him; but had this adventure occurred on the pampas, where they are better known, the person concerned in it would not have said that the puma played with him as a cat with a mouse, but rather as a tame cat plays with a child; nor, probably, would he have been terrified into imagining that the animal, even after its caresses had met with so rough a return, was about to spring on him.

In Clavigero's *History of Lower California*, it is related that a very extraordinary state of things was discovered to exist in that country by the first missionaries who settled there at the end of the seventeenth century, and which was actually owing to the pumas. The author says that there were no bears or tigers (jaguars); these had most probably been driven out by their old enemies; but the pumas had increased to a prodigious extent, so that the whole peninsula was overrun by them; and this was owing to the superstitious regard in which they were held by the natives, who not only did not kill them, but never ventured to disturb them in any way. The Indians were actually to some extent dependent on the puma's success in hunting for their subsistence; they watched the movements of the vultures in order to discover the spot in which the remains of any animal it had captured had been left by the puma, and whenever the birds were seen circling about persistently over one place, they hastened to take possession of the carcass, discovered in this way. The domestic animals, imported by the missionaries, were quickly destroyed by the virtual masters of the country, and against these enemies the Jesuits preached a crusade in vain : for although the Indians readily embraced Christianity and were baptized, they were not to be shaken in their notions concerning the sacred *Chimbicá*, as the puma was called. The missions languished in consequence ; the priests existed in a state of semi-starvation, depending on provisions sent to them at long intervals from the distant Mexican settlements ; and for many years all their efforts to raise the savages from their miserable condition were thrown away. At length, in 1701, the mission of Loreto was taken charge of by one Padre Ugarte, described by Clavigero as a person of indomitable energy, and great physical strength and courage, a true muscular Christian, who occasionally varied his method of instruction by administering corporal chastisements to his hearers when they laughed at his doctrines, or at the mistakes he made in their language, while preaching to them. Ugarte, like his predecessors, could not move the Indians to hunt the puma, but he was a man of action, with a wholesome belief in the efficacy of example, and his opportunity came at last.

One day, while riding in the wood, he saw at a distance a puma walking deliberately towards him. Alighting from his mule, he took up a large stone and advanced to meet the animal, and when sufficiently near hurled the missile with such precision and force that he knocked it down senseless. After killing it, he found that the heaviest part of his task remained, as it was necessary for the success of his project to carry the beast, still warm and bleeding, to the Indian village; but now his mule steadfastly refused to approach it. Father Ugarte was not, however, to be defeated, and partly by stratagem, partly by force, he finally succeeded in getting the puma on to the mule's back, after which he rode in triumph to the settlement. The Indians at first thought it all a trick of their priest, who was so anxious to involve them in a conflict with the pumas, and standing at a distance they began jeering at him, and exclaiming that he had found the animal dead. But when they were induced to approach, and saw that it was still warm and bleeding, they were astonished beyond measure, and began to watch the priest narrowly, thinking that he would presently drop down and die in sight of them all. It was their belief that death would quickly overtake the slayer of a puma. As this did not happen, the priest gained a great influence over them, and in the end they were persuaded to turn their weapons against the Chimbicá.

Clavigero has nothing to say concerning the origin of this Californian superstition; but with some knowledge of the puma's character, it is not difficult to imagine what it may have been. No doubt these savages had been very well acquainted from ancient times with the animal's instinct of friendliness toward man, and its extreme hatred of

other carnivores, which prey on the human species;
and finding it ranged on their side, as it were, in the
hard struggle of life in the desert, they were induced
to spare it, and even to regard it as a friend ; and
such a feeling, among primitive men, might in the
course of time degenerate into such a superstition
as that of the Californians.

I shall, in conclusion, relate here the story of
Maldonada, which is not generally known, although
familiar to Buenos Ayreans as the story of Lady
Godiva's ride through Coventry is to the people of
that town. The case of Maldonada is circum-
stantially narrated by Rui Diaz de Guzman, in his
history of the colonization of the Plata : he was a
person high in authority in the young colonies, and
is regarded by students of South American history
as an accurate and sober-minded chronicler of the
events of his own times. He relates that in the
year 1536 the settlers at Buenos Ayres, having
exhausted their provisions, and being compelled by
hostile Indians to keep within their pallisades, were
reduced to the verge of starvation. The Governor
Mendoza went off to seek help from the other
colonies up the river, deputing his authority to one
Captain Ruiz, who, according to all accounts, displayed an excessively tyrannous and truculent
disposition while in power. The people were finally
reduced to a ration of six ounces of flour per day
for each person ; but as the flour was putrid and
only made them ill, they were forced to live on any
small animals they could capture, including snakes,
frogs and toads. Some horrible details are given
by Rui Diaz, and other writers ; one, Del Barco

Centenera, affirms that of two thousand persons in
the town eighteen hundred perished of hunger.
During this unhappy time, beasts of prey in large
numbers were attracted to the settlement by the
effluvium of the corpses, buried just outside the
pallisades; and this made the condition of the
survivors more miserable still, since they could
venture into the neighbouring woods only at the
risk of a violent death. Nevertheless, many did so
venture, and among these was the young woman
Maldonada, who, losing herself in the forest, strayed
to a distance, and was eventually found by a party
of Indians, and carried by them to their village.

Some months later, Captain Ruiz discovered
her whereabouts, and persuaded the savages to
bring her to the settlement; then, accusing her of
having gone to the Indian village in order to betray
the colony, he condemned her to be devoured by
wild beasts. She was taken to a wood at a distance of a league from the town, and left there, tied
to a tree, for the space of two nights and a day.
A party of soldiers then went to the spot, expecting
to find her bones picked clean by the beasts, but
were greatly astonished to find Maldonada still
alive, without hurt or scratch. She told them that
a puma had come to her aid, and had kept at her
side, defending her life against all the other beasts
that approached her. She was instantly released,
and taken back to the town, her deliverance through
the action of the puma probably being looked on as
a direct interposition of Providence to save her.

Rui Diaz concludes with the following paragraph,
in which he affirms that he knew the woman Mal-

donada, which may be taken as proof that she
was among the few that survived the first dis-
astrous settlement and lived on to more fortunate
times : his pious pun on her name would be lost
in a translation :—" De esta manera quedó libre la
que ofrecieron a las fieras : la cual mujer yo la
conocí, y la llamaban la Maldonada, que mas bien
se le podia llamar la BIENDONADA ; pues por este
suceso se ha de ver no haber merecído el castigo a
que la ofrecieron."

If such a thing were to happen now, in any
portion of southern South America, where the
puma's disposition is best known, it would not be
looked on as a miracle, as it was, and that unavoidably, in the case of Maldonada.

CHAPTER III.

FOR many years, while living in my own home on
the pampas, I kept a journal, in which all my daily
observations on the habits of animals and kindred
matters were carefully noted. Turning back to
1872-3, I find my jottings for that season contain a
history of one of those waves of life—for I can think
of no better name for the phenomenon in question
—that are of such frequent occurrence in thinly-
settled regions, though in countries like England,
seen very rarely, and on a very limited scale. An
exceptionally bounteous season, the accidental miti-
gation of a check, or other favourable circumstance,
often causes an increase so sudden and inordinate
of small prolific species, that when we actually
witness it we are no longer surprised at the notion
prevalent amongst the common people that mice,
frogs, crickets, &c., are occasionally rained down
from the clouds.

In the summer of 1872-3 we had plenty of sunshine, with frequent showers; so that the hot
months brought no dearth of wild flowers, as in
most years. The abundance of flowers resulted in
a wonderful increase of humble bees. I have never
known them so plentiful before; in and about the

plantation adjoining my house I found, during the season, no fewer than seventeen nests.

The season was also favourable for mice; that is, of course, favourable for the time being, unfavourable in the long run, since the short-lived, undue preponderance of a species is invariably followed by a long period of undue depression. These prolific little creatures were soon so abundant that the dogs subsisted almost exclusively on them; the fowls also, from incessantly pursuing and killing them, became quite rapacious in their manner; whilst the sulphur tyrant-birds (Pitangus) and the Guira cuckoos preyed on nothing but mice.

The domestic cats, as they invariably do in such plentiful seasons, absented themselves from the house, assuming all the habits of their wild congeners, and slinking from the sight of man—even of a former fireside companion—with a shy secrecy in their motions, an apparent affectation of fear, almost ludicrous to see. Foxes, weasels, and opossums fared sumptuously. Even for the common armadillo (Dasypus villosus) it was a season of affluence, for this creature is very adroit in capturing mice. This fact might seem surprising to anyone who marks the uncouth figure, toothless gums, and the motions —anything but light and graceful—of the armadillo; and perhaps fancying that, to be a dexterous mouser, an animal should bear some resemblance in habits and structure to the felidæ. But animals, like men, are compelled to adapt themselves to their surroundings; new habits are acquired, and the exact corelation between habit and structure is seldom maintained.

I kept an armadillo at this time, and good cheer and the sedentary life he led in captivity made him excessively fat ; but the mousing exploits of even this individual were most interesting. Occasionally I took him into the fields to give him a taste of liberty, though at such times I always took the precaution to keep hold of a cord fastened to one of his hind legs ; for as often as he came to a kennel of one of his wild fellows, he would attempt to escape into it. He invariably travelled with an ungainly trotting gait, carrying his nose, beagle-like, close to the ground. His sense of smell was exceedingly acute, and when near his prey he became agitated, and quickened his motions, pausing frequently to sniff the earth, till, discovering the exact spot where the mouse lurked, he would stop and creep cautiously to it; then, after slowly raising himself to a sitting posture, spring suddenly for-wards, throwing his body like a trap over the mouse, or nest of mice, concealed beneath the grass.

A curious instance of intelligence in a cat was brought to my notice at this time by one of my neighbours, a native. His children had made the discovery that some excitement and fun was to be had by placing a long hollow stalk of the giant thistle with a mouse in it—and every hollow stalk at this time had one for a tenant—before a cat, and then watching her movements. Smelling her prey, she would spring at one end of the stalk—the end to-wards which the mouse would be moving at the same time, but would catch nothing, for the mouse, instead of running out, would turn back to run to the other end ; whereupon the cat, all excitement,

would jump there to seize it; and so the contest
would continue for a long time, an exhibition of the
cleverness and the stupidity of instinct, both of the
pursuer and the pursued. There were several cats
at the house, and all acted in the same way except
one. When a stalk was placed before this cat,
instead of becoming excited like the others, it went
quickly to one end and smelt at the opening, then,
satisfied that its prey was inside, it deliberately bit
a long piece out of the stalk with its teeth, then
another strip, and so on progressively, until the
entire stick had been opened up to within six or
eight inches of the further end, when the mouse
came out and was caught. Every stalk placed
before this cat was demolished in the same business-
like way; but the other cats, though they were made
to look on while the stick was being broken up by
their fellow, could never learn the trick.

In the autumn of the year countless numbers of
storks (Ciconia maguari) and of short-eared owls
(Otus brachyotus) made their appearance. They
had also come to assist at the general feast.

Remembering the opinion of Mr. E. Newman,
quoted by Darwin, that two-thirds of the humble
bees in England are annually destroyed by mice, I
determined to continue observing these insects, in
order to ascertain whether the same thing occurred
on the pampas. I carefully revisited all the nests
I had found, and was amazed at the rapid disappearance of all the bees. I was quite convinced that
the mice had devoured or driven them out, for the
weather was still warm, and flowers and fruit on
which humble bees feed were very abundant.

After cold weather set in the storks went away, probably on account of the scarcity of water, for the owls remained. So numerous were they during the winter, that any evening after sunset I could count forty or fifty individuals hovering over the trees about my house. Unfortunately they did not confine their attentions to the mice, but became destructive to the birds as well. I frequently watched them at dusk, beating about the trees and bushes in a systematic manner, often a dozen or more of them wheeling together about one tree, like so many moths about a candle, and one occasionally dashing through the branches until a pigeon—usually the Zenaida maculata—or other bird was scared from its perch. The instant the bird left the tree they would all give chase, disappearing in the darkness. I could not endure to see the havoc they were making amongst the ovenbirds (Furnarius rufus—a species for which I have a regard and affection almost superstitious), so I began to shoot the marauders. Very soon, however, I found it was impossible to protect my little favourites. Night after night the owls mustered in their usual numbers, so rapidly were the gaps I made in their ranks refilled. I grew sick of the cruel war in which I had so hopelessly joined, and resolved, not without pain, to let things take their course. A singular circumstance was that the owls began to breed in the middle of winter. The field-labourers and boys found many nests with eggs and young birds in the neighbourhood. I saw one nest in July, our coldest month, with three half-grown young birds in it. They were excessively fat, and, though it was noon-day, had their crops full. There were three mice and two young cavies (Cavia australis) lying untouched in the nest.

The short-eared owl is of a wandering disposition, and performs long journeys at all seasons of the year in search of districts where food is abundant ; and perhaps these winter-breeders came from a region where scarcity of prey, or some such cause, had prevented them from nesting at their usual time in summer.

The gradual increase or decrease continually going on in many species about us is little remarked ; but the sudden infrequent appearance in vast numbers of large and comparatively rare species is regarded by most people as a very wonderful phenomenon, not easily explained. On the pampas, whenever grasshoppers, mice, frogs or crickets become excessively abundant we confidently look for the appearance of multitudes of the birds that prey on them. However obvious may be the cause of the first phenomenon—the sudden inordinate increase during a favourable year of a species always prolific—the attendant one always creates astonishment : For how, it is asked, do these large birds, seldom seen at other times, receive information in the distant regions they inhabit of an abundance of food in any particular locality ? Years have perhaps passed during which scarcely an individual of these kinds has been seen: all at once armies of the majestic white storks are seen conspicuously marching about the plain in all directions ; while the night air resounds with the

solemn hootings of innumerable owls. It is plain
that these birds have been drawn from over an
immense area to one spot ; and the question is
how have they been drawn ?

Many large birds possessing great powers of
flight are, when not occupied with the business of
propagation, incessantly wandering from place to
place in search of food. They are not, as a rule,
regular migrants, for their wanderings begin and
end irrespective of seasons, and where they find
abundance they remain the whole year. They fly
at a very great height, and traverse immense distances. When the favourite food of any one of
these species is plentiful in any particular region
all the individuals that discover it remain, and
attract to them all of their kind passing overhead.
This happens on the pampas with the stork, the
short-eared owl, the hooded gull and the dominican
or black-backed gull—the leading species among
the feathered nomads : a few first appear like
harbingers ; these are presently joined by new
comers in considerable numbers, and before long
they are in myriads. Inconceivable numbers of
birds are, doubtless, in these regions, continually
passing over us unseen. It was once a subject of
very great wonder to me that flocks of black-necked
swans should almost always appear flying by immediately after a shower of rain, even when none had
been visible for a long time before, and when they
must have come from a very great distance. When
the reason at length occurred to me, I felt very
much disgusted with myself for being puzzled over
so very simple a matter. After rain a flying swan

may be visible to the eye at a vastly greater distance than during fair weather; the sun shining on its intense white plumage against the dark background of a rain-cloud making it exceedingly conspicuous. The fact that swans are almost always seen after rain shows only that they are almost always passing.

Whenever we are visited by a dust-storm on the pampas myriads of hooded gulls—Larus maculipennis—appear flying before the dark dust-cloud, even when not a gull has been seen for months. Dust-storms are of rare occurrence, and come only after a long drought, and, the water-courses being all dry, the gulls cannot have been living in the region over which the storm passes. Yet in seasons of drought gulls must be continually passing by at a great height, seeing but not seen, except when driven together and forced towards the earth by the fury of the storm.

By August (1873) the owls had vanished, and they had, indeed, good cause for leaving. The winter had been one of continued drought; the dry grass and herbage of the preceding year had been consumed by the cattle and wild animals, or had turned to dust, and with the disappearance of their food and cover the mice had ceased to be. The famine-stricken cats sneaked back to the house. It was pitiful to see the little burrowing owls; for these birds, not having the powerful wings and prescient instincts of the vagrant Otus brachyotus, are compelled to face the poverty from which the others escape. Just as abundance had before made the domestic cats wild, scarcity now made the burrowing owls tame and fearless of man. They were so reduced as scarcely to be able to fly, and hung about the houses all day long on the look-out for some stray morsel of food. I have frequently seen one alight and advance within two or three yards of the door-step, probably attracted by the smell of roasted meat. The weather continued dry until late in spring, so reducing the sheep and cattle that incredible numbers perished during a month of cold and rainy weather that followed the drought.

How clearly we can see in all this that the tendency to multiply rapidly, so advantageous in normal seasons, becomes almost fatal to a species in seasons of exceptional abundance. Cover and food without limit enabled the mice to increase at such an amazing rate that the lesser checks interposed by predatory species were for a while inappreciable. But as the mice increased, so did their enemies. Insectivorous and other species acquired the habits of owls and weasels, preying exclusively on them ; while to this innumerable army of residents was shortly added multitudes of wandering birds coming from distant regions. No sooner had the herbage perished, depriving the little victims of cover and food, than the effects of the war became apparent. In autumn the earth so teemed with them that one could scarcely walk anywhere without treading on mice ; while out of every hollow weed-stalk lying on the ground dozens could be shaken ; but so rapidly had they been devoured by the trained army of persecutors, that in spring it was hard to find a survivor, even in the barns and houses. The fact that species tend to increase in a geometrical ratio makes these great and sudden changes frequent in many regions of the earth; but it is not often they present themselves so vividly as in the foregoing instance, for here, scene after scene in one of Nature's silent passionless tragedies opens before us, countless myriads of highly organized beings rising into existence only to perish almost immediately, scarcely a hard-pressed remnant remaining after the great reaction to continue the species.

CHAPTER IV.

STRICTLY speaking, the only weapons of vertebrates are teeth, claws, horns, and spurs. Horns belong only to the ruminants, and the spur is a rare weapon. There are also many animals in which teeth and claws are not suited to inflict injury, or in which the proper instincts and courage to use and develop them are wanted; and these would seem to be in a very defenceless condition. Defenceless they are in one sense, but as a fact they are no worse off than the well-armed species, having either a protective colouring or a greater swiftness or cunning to assist them in escaping from their enemies. And there are also many of these practically toothless and clawless species which have yet been provided with other organs and means of offence and defence out of Nature's curious armoury, and concerning a few of these species I propose to speak in this place.

Probably such distinctive weapons as horns, spurs, tusks and spines would be much more common in nature if the conditions of life always remained the same. But these things are long in fashioning; meanwhile, conditions are changing; climate, soil, vegetation vary; foes and rivals

diminish or increase; the old go, and others with
different weapons and a new strategy take their
place; and just as a skilful man "fighting the
wilderness" fashions a plough from a hunting-
knife, turns his implements into weapons of war,
and for everything he possesses discovers a use
never contemplated by its maker, so does Nature
—only with an ingenuity exceeding that of man—
use the means she has to meet all contingencies,
and enable her creatures, seemingly so ill-provided,
to maintain their fight for life. Natural selection,
like an angry man, can make a weapon of anything; and, using the word in this wide sense, the
mucous secretions the huanaco discharges into the
face of an adversary, and the pestilential drops
"distilled" by the skunk, are weapons, and may be
as effectual in defensive warfare as spines, fangs
and tushes.

I do not know of a more striking instance in the
animal kingdom of adaptation of structure to
habit than is afforded by the hairy armadillo—
Dasypus villosus. He appears to us, roughly
speaking, to resemble an ant-eater saddled with a
dish cover; yet this creature, with the cunning
which Nature has given it to supplement all de-
ficiencies, has discovered in its bony encumbrance a
highly efficient weapon of offence. Most other
edentates are diurnal and almost exclusively insectivorous, some feeding only on ants; they have
unchangeable habits, very limited intelligence, and
vanish before civilization. The hairy armadillo
alone has struck out a line for itself. Like its fast
disappearing congeners, it is an insect-eater still,

but does not like them seek its food on the surface
and in the ant-hill only; all kinds of insects are
preyed on, and by means of its keen scent it discovers worms and larvæ several inches beneath
the surface. Its method of taking worms and
grubs resembles that of probing birds, for it throws
up no earth, but forces its sharp snout and wedge-
shaped head down to the required depth; and probably while working it moves round in a circle, for
the hole is conical, though the head of the animal
is flat. Where it has found a rich hunting-ground,
the earth is seen pitted with hundreds of these neat
symmetrical bores. It is also an enemy to ground-
nesting birds, being fond of eggs and fledglings; and
when unable to capture prey it will feed on carrion
as readily as a wild dog or vulture, returning night
after night to the carcase of a horse or cow as long
as the flesh lasts. Failing animal food, it subsists
on vegetable diet; and I have frequently found
their stomachs stuffed with clover, and, stranger
still, with the large, hard grains of the maize,
swallowed entire.

It is not, therefore, strange that at all seasons,
and even when other animals are starving, the hairy
armadillo is always fat and vigorous. In the
desert it is diurnal; but where man appears it
becomes more and more nocturnal, and in populous
districts does not go abroad until long after dark.
Yet when a district becomes thickly settled it increases in numbers; so readily does it adapt itself
to new conditions. It is not to be wondered at
that the gauchos, keen observers of nature as they
are, should make this species the hero of many of

their fables of the "Uncle Remus" type, representing it as a versatile creature, exceedingly fertile
in expedients, and duping its sworn friend the fox
in various ways, just as " Brer Rabbit " serves the
fox in the North American fables.

The hairy armadillo will, doubtless, long survive
all the other armadillos, and on this account alone
it will have an ever-increasing interest for the
naturalist.   I have elsewhere described how it

Armadillo killing Snake.

captures mice ; when preying on snakes it proceeds
in another manner.   A friend of mine, a careful
observer, who was engaged in cattle-breeding
amongst the stony sierras near Cape Corrientes, described to me an encounter he witnessed between
an armadillo and a poisonous snake.   While seated
on the hillside one day he observed a snake, about
twenty inches in length, lying coiled up on a stone
five or six yards beneath him.   By-and-by, a hairy

armadillo appeared trotting directly towards it.
Apparently the snake perceived and feared its approach, for it quickly uncoiled itself and began
gliding away. Instantly the armadillo rushed on
to it, and, squatting close down, began swaying
its body backward and forward with a regular
sawing motion, thus lacerating its victim with the
sharp, deep-cut edges of its bony covering. The
snake struggled to free itself, biting savagely at its
aggressor, for its head and neck were disengaged.
Its bites made no impression, and very soon it
dropped its head, and when its enemy drew off, it
was dead and very much mangled. The armadillo
at once began its meal, taking the tail in its mouth
and slowly progressing towards the head; but when
about a third of the snake still remained it seemed
satisfied, and, leaving that portion, trotted away.

Altogether, in its rapacious and varied habits this
armadillo appears to have some points of resemblance with the hedgehog; and possibly, like the
little European mammal it resembles, it is not
harmed by the bite of venomous snakes.

I once had a cat that killed every snake it found,
purely for sport, since it never ate them. It would
jump nimbly round and across its victim, occasionally dealing it a blow with its cruel claws. The
enemies of the snake are legion. Burrowing owls
feed largely on them; so do herons and storks,
killing them with a blow of their javelin beaks,
and swallowing them entire. The sulphur tyrant-
bird picks up the young snake by the tail, and,
flying to a branch or stone, uses it like a flail till
its life is battered out. The bird is highly com-

mended in consequence, reminding one of very ancient words : " Happy shall he be that taketh thy little ones and dasheth them against the stones." In arraying such a variety of enemies against the snake, nature has made ample amends for having endowed it with deadly weapons. Besides, the power possessed by venomous snakes only seems to us disproportionate ; it is not really so, except in occasional individual encounters. Venomous snakes are always greatly outnumbered by non-venomous ones in the same district ; at any rate this is the case on the pampas. The greater activity of the latter counts for more in the result than the deadly weapons of the former.

The large teguexin lizard of the pampas, called iguana by the country people, is a notable snake-killer. Snakes have, in fact, no more formidable enemy, for he is quick to see, and swift to overtake them. He is practically invulnerable, and deals them sudden death with his powerful tail. The gauchos say that dogs attacking the iguana are sometimes known to have their legs broken, and I do not doubt it. A friend of mine was out riding one day after his cattle, and having attached one end of his lasso to the saddle, he let it trail on the ground. He noticed a large iguana lying apparently asleep in the sun, and though he rode by it very closely, it did not stir ; but no sooner had he passed it, than it raised its head, and fixed its attention on the forty feet of lasso slowly trailing by. Suddenly it rushed after the rope, and dealt it a succession of violent blows with its tail. When the whole of the lasso, several yards of which had been pounded in vain, had been dragged by, the lizard, with uplifted head, continued gazing after it with the greatest astonishment. Never had such a wonderful snake crossed its path before!

Molina, in his *Natural History of Chili*, says the vizcacha uses its tail as a weapon; but then Molina is not always reliable. I have observed vizcachas all my life, and never detected them making use of any weapon except their chisel teeth. The tail is certainly very curious, being straight at the base, then curving up outwardly, and slightly down again at the tip, resembling the spout of a china teapot. The under surface of the straight portion of the base is padded with a thick, naked, corneous skin; and, when the animal performs the curious sportive antics in which it occasionally indulges, it gives rapid loud-sounding blows on the ground with this part of the tail. The peculiar form of the tail also makes it a capital support, enabling the vizcacha to sit erect, with ease and security.

The frog is a most timid, inoffensive creature, saving itself, when pursued, by a series of saltatory feats unparalleled amongst vertebrates. Consequently, when I find a frog, I have no hesitation in placing my hands upon it, and the cold sensation it gives one is the worse result I fear. It came to pass, however, that I once encountered a frog that was not like other frogs, for it possessed an instinct and weapons of offence which greatly astonished me. I was out snipe shooting one day when, peering into an old disused burrow, two or three feet deep, I perceived a burly-looking frog sitting within it. It was larger and stouter-looking than

our common Rana, though like it in colour, and I
at once dropped on to my knees and set about its
capture.   Though it watched me attentively, the
frog remained perfectly motionless, and this greatly
surprised me.   Before I was sufficiently near to
make a grab, it sprang straight at my hand, and,
catching two of my fingers round with its fore legs,
administered a hug so sudden and violent as to
cause an acute sensation of pain ; then, at the very
instant I experienced this feeling, which made me
start back quickly, it released its hold and bounded
out and away.   I flew after it, and barely managed
to overtake it before it could gain the water.
Holding it firmly pressed behind the shoulders, it
was powerless to attack me, and I then noticed the
enormous development of the muscles of the fore
legs, usually small in frogs, bulging out in this
individual, like a second pair of thighs, and giving
it a strangely bold and formidable appearance.   On
holding my gun within its reach, it clasped the
barrel with such energy as to bruise the skin of its
breast and legs.   After allowing it to partially
exhaust itself in these fruitless huggings, I experi-
mented by letting it seize my hand again, and I
noticed that invariably after each squeeze it made a
quick, violent attempt to free itself.   Believing that
I had discovered a frog differing in structure from
all known species, and possessing a strange unique
instinct of self-preservation, I carried my captive
home, intending to show it to Dr. Burmeister, the
director of the National Museum at Buenos Ayres.
Unfortunately, after I had kept it some days, it
effected its escape by pushing up the glass cover of

its box, and I have never since met with another
individual like it. That this singular frog has it in
its power to seriously injure an opponent is, of
course, out of the question ; but its unexpected
attack must be of great advantage. The effect of
the sudden opening of an umbrella in the face of
an angry bull gives, I think, only a faint idea of

Wrestler Frog.

the astonishment and confusion it must cause an
adversary by its leap, quick as lightning, and the
violent hug it administers ; and in the confusion it
finds time to escape. I cannot for a moment believe
that an instinct so admirable, correlated as it is
with the structure of the fore legs, can be merely
an individual variation ; and I confidently expect

that all I have said about my lost frog will some
day be confirmed by others. Rana luctator would
be a good name for this species.

The toad is a slow-moving creature that puts
itself in the way of persecution ; yet, strange to say,
the acrid juice it exudes when irritated is a surer
protection to it than venomous fangs are to the
deadliest snake. Toads are, in fact, with a very
few exceptions, only attacked and devoured by
snakes, by lizards, and by their own venomous
relative, Ceratophrys ornata. Possibly the cold
sluggish natures of all these creatures protects them
against the toad's secretion, which would be poison
to most warm-blooded animals, but I am not so
sure that all fish enjoy a like immunity. I one day
noticed a good-sized fish (bagras) floating, belly
upmost, on the water. It had apparently just died,
and had such a glossy, well-nourished look about it,
and appeared so full, I was curious to know the
cause of its death. On opening it I found its
stomach quite filled with a very large toad it had
swallowed. The toad looked perfectly fresh, not
even a faint discoloration of the skin showing that
the gastric juices had begun to take effect ; the fish,
in fact, must have died immediately after swallowing
the toad. The country people in South America
believe that the milky secretion exuded by the toad
possesses wonderful curative properties; it is their
invariable specific for shingles—a painful, dangerous
malady common amongst them, and to cure it living
toads are applied to the inflamed part. I dare say
learned physicians would laugh at this cure, but
then, if I mistake not, the learned have in past

times laughed at other specifics used by the vulgar,
but which now have honourable places in the phar-
macopœia—pepsine, for example. More than two
centuries ago (very ancient times for South America)
the gauchos were accustomed to take the lining of
the rhea's stomach, dried and powdered, for ailments
caused by impaired digestion ; and the remedy is
popular still. Science has gone over to them, and
the ostrich-hunter now makes a double profit, one
from the feathers, and the other from the dried
stomachs which he supplies to the chemists of
Buenos Ayres. Yet he was formerly told that to
take the stomach of the ostrich to improve his digestion was as wild an idea as it would be to swallow
birds' feathers in order to fly.

I just now called Ceratophrys ornata venomous,
though its teeth are not formed to inject poison
into the veins, like serpents' teeth. It is a singular
creature, known as *escuerzo* in the vernacular, and
though beautiful in colour, is in form hideous beyond
description. The skin is of a rich brilliant green,
with chocolate-coloured patches, oval in form, and
symmetrically disposed. The lips are bright
yellow, the cavernous mouth pale flesh colour, the
throat and under-surface dull white. The body is
lumpy, and about the size of a large man's fist.
The eyes, placed on the summit of a disproportionately large head, are embedded in horn-like pro-
tuberances, capable of being elevated or depressed
at pleasure. When the creature is undisturbed, the
eyes, which are of a pale gold colour, look out as
from a couple of watch towers, but when touched
on the head or menaced, the prominences sink down

to a level with the head, closing the eyes completely, and giving the creature the appearance of being eyeless. The upper jaw is armed with minute teeth, and there are two teeth in the centre of the lower jaw, the remaining portions of the jaw being armed with two exceedingly sharp-edged bony plates. In place of a tongue, it has a round

Ceratophrys ornata.

muscular process with a rough flat disc the size of a halfpenny.

It is common all over the pampas, ranging as far south as the Rio Colorado in Patagonia. In the breeding season it congregates in pools, and one is then struck by their extraordinary vocal powers, which they exercise by night. The performance in no way resembles the series of percussive sounds uttered by most batrachians. The notes it utters

are long, as of a wind instrument, not unmelodious,
and so powerful as to make themselves heard distinctly a mile off on still evenings. After the
amorous period these toads retire to moist places
and sit inactive, buried just deep enough to leave
the broad green back on a level with the surface,
and it is then very difficult to detect them. In
this position they wait for their prey—frogs, toads,
birds, and small mammals. Often they capture and
attempt to swallow things too large for them, a
mistake often made by snakes. In very wet springs
they sometimes come about houses and lie in wait
for chickens and ducklings. In disposition they are
most truculent, savagely biting at anything that
comes near them; and when they bite they hang on
with the tenacity of a bulldog, poisoning the blood
with their glandular secretions. When teased, the
creature swells itself out to such an extent one
almost expects to see him burst; he follows his
tormentors about with slow awkward leaps, his
vast mouth wide open, and uttering an incessant
harsh croaking sound. A gaucho I knew was once
bitten by one. He sat down on the grass, and,
dropping his hand at his side, had it seized, and
only freed himself by using his hunting knife to
force the creature's mouth open. He washed and
bandaged the wound, and no bad result followed;
but when the toad cannot be shaken off, then the
result is different. One summer two horses were
found dead on the plain near my home. One, while
lying down, had been seized by a fold in the skin
near the belly; the other had been grasped by the
nose while cropping grass. In both instances the

vicious toad was found dead, with jaws tightly
closed, still hanging to the dead horse. Perhaps
they are sometimes incapable of letting go at will,
and, like honey bees, destroy themselves in these
savage attacks.

CHAPTER V.

FEAR IN BIRDS.

THE statement that birds instinctively fear man is
frequently met with in zoological works written
since the *Origin of Species* appeared ; but almost
the only reason—absolutely the only plausible
reason, all the rest being mere supposition—given
in support of such a notion is that birds in desert
islands show at first no fear of man, but afterwards,
finding him a dangerous neighbour, they become
wild ; and their young also grow up wild. It is
thus assumed that the habit acquired by the former
has become hereditary in the latter—or, at all
events, that in time it becomes hereditary. Instincts,
which are few in number in any species, and practically endure for ever, are not, presumably, acquired
with such extraordinary facility.

Birds become shy where persecuted, and the
young, even when not disturbed, learn a shy habit
from the parents, and from other adults they
associate with. I have found small birds shyer in
desert places, where the human form was altogether
strange to them, than in thickly-settled districts.
Large birds are actually shyer than the small ones,
although to the civilized or shooting man they seem
astonishingly tame where they have never been

fired at. I have frequently walked quite openly to
within twenty-five or thirty yards of a flock of
flamingoes without alarming them. This, however,
was when they were in the water, or on the opposite
side of a stream. Having no experience of guns,
they fancied themselves secure as long as a strip of
water separated them from the approaching object.
When standing on dry land they would not allow
so near an approach. Sparrows in England are
very much tamer than the sparrows I have observed
in desert places, where they seldom see a human
being. Nevertheless young sparrows in England
are very much tamer than old birds, as anyone may
see for himself. During the past summer, while
living near Kew Gardens, I watched the sparrows a
great deal, and fed forty or fifty of them every day
from a back window. The bread and seed was
thrown on to a low roof just outside the window, and
I noticed that the young birds when first able to fly
were always brought by the parents to this feeding
place, and that after two or three visits they would
begin to come of their own accord. At such times
they would venture quite close to me, showing as
little suspicion as young chickens. The adults,
however, although so much less shy than birds of
other species, were extremely suspicious, snatching
up the bread and flying away ; or, if they remained,
hopping about in a startled manner, craning their
necks to view me, and making so many gestures
and motions, and little chirps of alarm, that presently
the young would become infected with fear. The
lesson was taught them in a surprisingly short
time; their suspicion was seen to increase day by

day, and about a week later they were scarcely to
be distinguished in behaviour from the adults. It
is plain that, with these little birds, fear of man is
an associate feeling, and that, unless it had been
taught them, his presence would trouble them as
little as does that of horse, sheep, or cow. But
how about the larger species, used as food and
which have had a longer and sadder experience of
man's destructive power ?

The rhea, or South American ostrich, philosophers
tell us, is a very ancient bird on the earth; and
from its great size and inability to escape by flight,
and its excellence as food, especially to savages,
who prefer fat rank-flavoured flesh, it must have
been systematically persecuted by man as long as,
or longer than, any bird now existing on the globe.
If fear of man ever becomes hereditary in birds,
we ought certainly to find some trace of such an
instinct in this species. I have been unable to
detect any, though I have observed scores of young
rheas in captivity, taken before the parent bird had
taught them what to fear. I also once kept a brood
myself, captured just after they had hatched out.
With regard to food they were almost, or perhaps
quite, independent, spending most of the time
catching flies, grasshoppers, and other insects with
surprising dexterity; but of the dangers encom-
passing the young rhea they knew absolutely
nothing. They would follow me about as if they
took me for their parent; and, whenever I imitated
the loud snorting or rasping warning-call emitted
by the old bird in moments of danger, they would
rush to me in the greatest terror, though no animal

was in sight, and, squatting at my feet, endeavour
to conceal themselves by thrusting their heads and
long necks up my trousers. If I had caused a
person to dress in white or yellow clothes for several
consecutive days, and had then uttered the warning
cry each time he showed himself to the birds, I
have no doubt that they would soon have acquired a
habit of running in terror from him, even without
the warning cry, and that the fear of a person in
white or yellow would have continued all their lives.

Up to within about twenty years ago, rheas were
seldom or never shot in La Plata and Patagonia,
but were always hunted on horseback and caught
with the bolas. The sight of a mounted man would
set them off at once, while a person on foot could
walk quite openly to within easy shooting distance
of them ; yet their fear of a horseman dates only
two hundred years back—a very short time, when
we consider that, before the Indian borrowed the
horse from the invader, he must have systematically
pursued the rhea on foot for centuries. The rhea
changed its habits when the hunter changed his,
and now, if an *estanciero* puts down ostrich hunting
on his estate, in a very few years the birds, although
wild birds still, become as fearless and familiar
as domestic animals. I have known old and ill-
tempered males to become a perfect nuisance on
some estancias, running after and attacking every
person, whether on foot or on horseback, that
ventured near them. An old instinct of a whole
race could not be thus readily lost here and there
on isolated estates wherever a proprietor chose to
protect his birds for half a dozen years.

I suppose the Talegallus—the best-known brush-turkey—must be looked on as an exception to all other birds with regard to the point I am considering ; for this abnormal form buries its eggs in the huge mound made by the male, and troubles herself no more about them. When the young is fully developed it simply kicks the coffin to pieces in which its mother interred it, and, burrowing its way up to the sunshine, enters on the pleasures and pains of an independent existence from earliest infancy—that is, if a species born into the world in full possession of all the wisdom of the ancients, can be said ever to know infancy. At all events, from Mr. Bartlett's observations on the young hatched in the Zoological Gardens, it appears that they took no notice of the old birds, but lived quite independently from the moment they came out of the ground, even flying up into a tree and roosting separately at night. I am not sure, however, that these observations are quite conclusive; for it is certain that captivity plays strange pranks with the instincts of some species, and it is just possible that in a state of nature the old birds exercise at first some slight parental supervision, and, like all other species, have a peculiar cry to warn the young of the dangers to be avoided. If this is not so, then the young Talegallus must fly or hide with instinctive fear from every living thing that approaches it. I, at any rate, find it hard to believe that it has a knowledge, independent of experience, of the different habits of man and kangaroo, and discriminates at first sight between animals that are dangerous to it and those that are not. This interesting point will probably never be determined, as, most unhappily, the Australians are just now zealously engaged in exterminating their most wonderful bird for the sake of its miserable flesh; and with less excuse than the Maories could plead with regard to the moa, since they cannot deny that they have mutton and rabbit enough to satisfy hunger.

Whether birds fear or have instinctive knowledge of any of their enemies is a much larger question. Species that run freely on the ground from the time of quitting the shell know their proper food, and avoid whatever is injurious. Have all young birds a similarly discriminating instinct with regard to their enemies? Darwin says, "Fear of any particular enemy is certainly an instinctive quality, as may be seen in nestling birds." Here, even man seems to be included among the enemies feared instinctively; and in another passage he says, " Young chickens have lost, wholly from habit, that fear of the dog and cat which, no doubt, was originally instinctive in them." My own observations point to a contrary conclusion; and I may say that I have had unrivalled opportunities for studying the habits of young birds.

Animals of all classes, old and young, shrink with instinctive fear from any strange object approaching them. A piece of newspaper carried accidentally by the wind is as great an object of terror to an inexperienced young bird as a buzzard sweeping down with death in its talons. Among birds not yet able to fly there are, however, some curious exceptions; thus the young of most owls and pigeons are excited to anger rather than fear, and, puffing themselves up, snap and strike at an intruder with their beaks. Other fledglings simply shrink down in the nest or squat close on the ground, their fear, apparently, being in proportion to the suddenness with which the strange animal or object comes on them ; but, if the deadliest enemy approaches with slow caution, as snakes do—and snakes must be very ancient enemies to birds— there is no fear or suspicion shown, even when the enemy is in full view and about to strike. This, it will be understood, is when no warning-cry is uttered by the parent bird. This shrinking, and, in some cases, hiding from an object coming swiftly towards them, is the "wildness" of young birds, which, Darwin says again, is greater in wild than in·domestic species. Of the extreme tameness of the young rhea I have already spoken ; I have also observed young tinamous, plovers, coots, &c., hatched by fowls, and found them as incapable of distinguishing friend from foe as the young of domestic birds. The only difference between the young of wild and tame is that the former are, as a rule, much more sprightly and active. But there are many exceptions ; and if this greater alertness and activity is what is meant by "wildness," then the young of some wild birds—rhea, crested screamer, &c.—are actually much tamer than our newly-hatched chickens and ducklings.

To return to what may be seen in nestling birds. When very young, and before their education has well begun, if quietly approached and touched, they open their bills and take food as readily from a man

as from the parent bird. But if while being thus
fed the parent returns and emits the warning note,
they instantly cease their hunger-cries, close their
gaping mouths, and crouch down frightened in the
nest. This fear caused by the parent bird's warning note begins to manifest itself even before the
young are hatched—and my observations on this
point refer to several species in three widely
separated orders. When the little prisoner is
hammering at its shell, and uttering its feeble *peep*,
as if begging to be let out, if the warning note
is uttered, even at a considerable distance, the
strokes and complaining instantly cease, and the
chick will then remain quiescent in the shell for
a long time, or until the parent, by a changed note,
conveys to it an intimation that the danger is over.
Another proof that the nestling has absolutely no
instinctive knowledge of particular enemies, but is
taught to fear them by the parents, is to be found
in the striking contrast between the habits of parasitical and genuine young in the nest, and after they
have left it, while still unable to find their own
food. I have had no opportunities of observing the
habits of the young cuckoo in England with regard
to this point, and do not know whether other observers have paid any attention to the matter or
not, but I am very familiar with the manners of the
parasitical starling or cow-bird of South America.
The warning cries of the foster parent have no effect
on the young cow-bird at any time. Until they are
able to fly they will readily devour worms from the
hand of a man, even when the old birds are hovering close by and screaming their danger notes, and

while their own young, if the parasite has allowed any to survive in the nest, are crouching down in the greatest fear. After the cow-bird has left the nest it is still stupidly tame, and more than once I have seen one carried off from its elevated perch by a milvago hawk, when, if it had understood the warning cry of the foster parent, it would have dropped down into the bush or grass and escaped. But as soon as the young cow-birds are able to shift for themselves, and begin to associate with their own kind, their habits change, and they become suspicious and wild like other birds.

On this point—the later period at which the parasitical young bird acquires fear of man—and also bearing on the whole subject under discussion, I shall add here some observations I once made on a dove hatched and reared by a pigeon at my home on the pampas. A very large ombú tree grew not far from the dove-cote, and some of the pigeons used to make their nests on the lower horizontal branches. One summer a dove of the most common species, Zenaida maculata, in size a third less than the domestic pigeon, chanced to drop an egg in one of these nests, and a young dove was hatched and reared ; and, in due time, when able to fly, it was brought to the dove-cote. I watched it a great deal, and it was evident that this foster-young, though with the pigeons, was not nor ever would be of them, for it could not take kindly to their flippant flirty ways. Whenever a male approached it, and with guttural noises and strange gestures made a pompous declaration of amorous feelings, the dove would strike vigorously at its undesirable lover,

and drive him off, big as he was; and, as a
rule, it would sit apart, a foot or so, from the others.
The dove was also a male; but its male companions,
with instinct tainted by domestication, were ignorant alike of its sex and different species. Now, it
chanced that my pigeons, never being fed and
always finding their own living on the plain like
wild birds, were, although still domestic, not nearly
so tame as pigeons usually are in England. They
would not allow a person to approach within two
or three yards of them without flying, and if grain
was thrown to them they would come to it very
suspiciously, or not at all. And, of course, the
young pigeons always acquired the exact degree of
suspicion shown by the adults as soon as they were
able to fly and consort with the others. But the
foundling Zenaida did not know what their startled
gestures and notes of fear meant when a person
approached too near, and as he saw none of his own
kind, he did not acquire their suspicious habit. On
the contrary, he was perfectly tame, although by
parentage a wild bird, and showed no more fear of a
man than of a horse. Throughout the winter it
remained with the pigeons, going afield every day
with them, and returning to the dove-cote; but as
spring approached the slight tie which united him
to them began to be loosened; their company grew
less and less congenial, and he began to lead a
solitary life. But he did not go to the trees yet.
He came to the house, and his favourite perch was
on the low overhanging roof of a vine-covered porch,
just over the main entrance. Here he would pass
several hours every day, taking no notice of the

people passing in and out at all times; and when
the weather grew warm he would swell out his
breast and coo mournfully by the hour for our
pleasure.

We can, no doubt, learn best by observing the
behaviour of nestlings and young birds; nevertheless, I find much even in the confirmed habits of
adults to strengthen me in the belief that fear of
particular enemies is in nearly all cases—for I will
not say all—the result of experience and tradition.

Hawks are the most open, violent, and persistent
enemies birds have; and it is really wonderful to
see how well the persecuted kinds appear to know
the power for mischief possessed by different raptorial species, and how exactly the amount of alarm
exhibited is in proportion to the extent of the danger
to be apprehended. Some raptors never attack
birds, others only occasionally; still others prey only
on the young and feeble; and, speaking of La Plata
district, where I have observed hawks, from the
milvago chimango—chiefly a carrion-eater—to the
destructive peregrine falcon, there is a very great
variety of predatory habits, and all degrees of courage to be found; yet all these raptors are treated
differently by species liable to be preyed on, and
have just as much respect paid them as their
strength and daring entitles them to, and no more.
So much discrimination must seem almost incredible
to those who are not very familiar with the manners
of wild birds; I do not think it could exist if
the fear shown resulted from instinct or inherited
habit. There would be no end to the blunders of

such an instinct as that ; and in regions where hawks
are extremely abundant most of the birds would be
in a constant state of trepidation. On the pampas
the appearance of the comparatively harmless
chimango excites not the least alarm among small
birds, yet at a distance it closely resembles a hen-
harrier, and it also readily attacks young, sick, and
wounded birds ; all others know how little they
have to fear from it. When it appears unexpectedly,
sweeping over a hedge or grove with a rapid flight,
it is sometimes mistaken for a more dangerous
species ; there is then a little flutter of alarm, some
birds springing into the air, but in two or three
seconds of time they discover their mistake, and
settle down quietly again, taking no further notice
of the despised carrion-eater. On the other hand,
I have frequently mistaken a harrier (Circus cinereus,
in the brown state of plumage) for a chimango, and
have only discovered my mistake by seeing the commotion among the small birds. The harrier I have
mentioned, also the C. macropterus, feed partly on
small birds, which they flush from the ground and
strike down with their claws. When the harrier
appears moving along with a loitering flight near
the surface, it is everywhere attended by a little
whirlwind of alarm, small birds screaming or chirping excitedly and diving into the grass or bushes ;
but the alarm does not spread far, and subsides as
soon as the hawk has passed on its way. Buzzards
(Buteo and Urubitinga) are much more feared, and
create a more widespread alarm, and they are
certainly more destructive to birds than harriers.

Another curious instance is that of the sociable

hawk (Rostrhamus sociabilis). This bird spends the summer and breeds in marshes in La Plata, and birds pay no attention to it, for it feeds exclusively on water-snails (Ampullaria). But when it visits woods and plantations to roost, during migration, its appearance creates as much alarm as that of a true buzzard, which it closely resembles. Woodbirds, unaccustomed to see it, do not know its peculiar preying habits, and how little they need fear its presence. I may also mention that the birds of La Plata seem to fear the kite-like Elanus less than other hawks, and I believe that its singular resemblance to the common gull of the district in its size, snowy-white plumage and manner of flight, has a deceptive effect on most species, and makes them so little suspicious of it.

The wide-ranging peregrine falcon is a common species in La Plata, although, oddly enough, not included in any notice of the avifauna of that region before 1888. The consternation caused among birds by its appearance is vastly greater than that produced by any of the raptors I have mentioned ; and it is unquestionably very much more destructive to birds, since it preys exclusively on them, and, as a rule, merely picks the flesh from the head and neck, and leaves the untouched body to its jackal, the carrion-hawk. When the peregrine appears speeding through the air in a straight line at a great height, the feathered world, as far as one is able to see, is thrown into the greatest commotion, all birds, from the smallest up to species large as duck, ibis, and curlew, rushing about in the air as if distracted. When the falcon has disappeared in the sky, and the wave of terror attending its progress subsides behind it, the birds still continue wild and excited for some time, showing how deeply they have been moved ; for, as a rule, fear is exceedingly transitory in its effects on animals.

I must, before concluding this part of my subject, mention another raptor, also a true falcon, but differing from the peregrine in being exclusively a marsh-hawk. In size it is nearly a third less than the male peregrine, which it resembles in its sharp wings and manner of flight, but its flight is much more rapid. The whole plumage is uniformly of a dark grey colour. Unfortunately, though I have observed it not fewer than a hundred times, I have never been able to procure a specimen, nor do I find that it is like any American falcon already described ; so that for the present it must remain nameless. Judging solely from the effect produced by the appearance of this hawk, it must be even more daring and destructive than its larger relation, the peregrine. It flies at a great height, and sometimes descends vertically and with extraordinary velocity, the wings producing a sound like a deep-toned horn. The sound is doubtless produced at will, and is certainly less advantageous to the hawk than to the birds it pursues. No doubt it can afford to despise the wing-power of its quarry; and I have sometimes thought that it takes a tyrannous delight in witnessing the consternation caused by its hollow trumpeting sound. This may be only a fancy, but some hawks do certainly take pleasure in pursuing and striking birds when not seeking prey. The peregrine has been observed, Baird says, capturing birds, only to kill and drop them. Many of the Felidæ, we know, evince a similar habit; only these prolong their pleasure by practising a more refined and deliberate cruelty.

The sudden appearance overhead of this hawk produces an effect wonderful to witness. I have frequently seen all the inhabitants of a marsh struck with panic, acting as if demented, and suddenly grown careless to all other dangers; and on such occasions I have looked up confident of seeing the sharp-winged death suspended above them in the sky. All birds that happen to be on the wing drop down as if shot into the reeds or water; ducks away from the margin stretch out their necks horizontally and drag their bodies, as if wounded, into closer cover; not one bird is found bold enough to rise up and wheel about the marauder— a usual proceeding in the case of other hawks; while, at every sudden stoop the falcon makes, threatening to dash down on his prey, a low cry of terror rises from the birds beneath; a sound expressive of an emotion so contagious that it quickly runs like a murmur all over the marsh, as if a gust of wind had swept moaning through the rushes. As long as the falcon hangs overhead, always at a height of about forty yards, threatening at intervals to dash down, this murmuring sound, made up of many hundreds of individual cries, is heard swelling and dying away, and occasionally, when he drops lower than usual, rising to a sharp scream of terror.

Sometimes when I have been riding over marshy

ground, one of these hawks has placed himself
directly over my head, within fifteen or twenty
yards of me ; and it has perhaps acquired the habit
of following a horseman in this way in order to
strike at any birds driven up. On one occasion
my horse almost trod on a couple of snipe squatting
terrified in the short grass. The instant they rose
the hawk struck at one, the end of his wing violently
smiting my cheek as he stooped, and striking at
the snipe on a level with the knees of my horse.
The snipe escaped by diving under the bridle, and
immediately dropped down on the other side of me,
and the hawk, rising up, flew away.

To return. I think I am justified in believing that
fear of hawks, like fear of men, is, in very nearly
all cases, the result of experience and tradition.
Nevertheless, I think it probable that in some
species which have always lived in the open, continually exposed to attack, and which are preferred
as food by raptors, such as duck, snipe, and
plover, the fear of the falcon may be an inherited
habit. Among passerine birds I am also inclined
to think that swallows show inherited fear of hawks.
Swallows and humming-birds have least to fear
from raptors ; yet, while humming-birds readily
pursue and tease hawks, thinking as little of them
as of pigeons or herons, swallows everywhere manifest the greatest terror at the approach of a true
falcon ; and they also fear other birds of prey,
though in a much less degree. It has been said
that the European hobby occasionally catches swallows on the wing, but this seems a rare and exceptional habit, and in South America I have

never seen any bird of prey attempt the pursuit of a swallow. The question then arises, how did this unnecessary fear, so universal in swallows, originate? Can it be a survival of a far past—a time when some wide-ranging small falcon, aërial in habits as the swallow itself, preyed by preference on hirundines only?

[NOTE.—Herbert Spencer, who accepts Darwin's inference, explains how the fear of man, acquired by experience, becomes instinctive in birds, in the following passage : " It is well known that in newly-discovered lands not inhabited by man, birds are so devoid of fear as to allow themselves to be knocked over with sticks ; but that, in the course of generations, they acquire such a dread of man as to fly on his approach : and that this dread is manifested by young as well as by old. Now unless this change be ascribed to the killing-off of the least fearful, and the preservation and multiplication of the most fearful which, considering the comparatively small number killed by man, is an inadequate cause, it must be ascribed to accumulated experience ; and each experience must be held to have a share in producing it. We must conclude that in each bird that escapes with injuries inflicted by man, or is alarmed by the outcries of other members of the flock (gregarious creatures of any intelligence being necessarily more or less sympathetic), there is established an association of ideas between the human aspect and the pains, direct and indirect, suffered from human agency. And we must further conclude, that the state of consciousness which compels the bird to take flight, is at first nothing more than an ideal reproduction of those painful impressions which before followed man's approach ; that such ideal reproduction becomes more vivid and more massive as the painful experiences, direct or sympathetic, increase ; and that thus the emotion, in its incipient state, is nothing else than an aggregation of the revived pains before experience.

" As, in the course of generations, the young birds of this race begin to display a fear of man before yet they have been injured by him, it is an unavoidable inference that the nervous system of the race has been organically modified by these experiences, we have no choice but to conclude, that when a young bird is led to fly, it is because the impression produced in its senses by the approaching man entails, through an incipiently reflex action, a partial excitement of all those nerves which in its ancestors had been excited under the like conditions ; that this partial excitement has its accompanying painful consciousness, and that the vague painful consciousness thus arising constitutes emotion proper— *emotion undecomposable into specific experiences, and, therefore, seemingly homogeneous."*   (Essays, vol. i. p. 320.)

It is comforting to know that the " unavoidable inference " is, after all, erroneous, and that the nervous system in birds has not yet been organically altered as a result of man's persecution ; for in that case it would take long to undo the mischief, and we should be indeed far from that " better friendship " with the children of the air which many of us would like to see.

CHAPTER VI.

PARENTAL AND EARLY INSTINCTS.

UNDER this heading I have put together several notes from my journals on subjects which have no connection with each other, except that they relate chiefly to the parental instincts of some animals I have observed, and to the instincts of the young at a very early period of life.

While taking bats one day in December, I captured a female of our common Buenos Ayrean species (Molossus bonariensis), with her two young attached to her, so large that it seemed incredible she should be able to fly and take insects with such a weight to drag her down. The young were about a third less in size than the mother, so that she had to carry a weight greatly exceeding that of her own body. They were fastened to her breast and belly, one on each side, as when first born ; and, possibly, the young bat does not change its position, or move, like the young developed opossum, to other parts of the body, until mature enough to begin an independent life. On forcibly separating them from their parent, I found that they were not yet able to fly, but when set free fluttered feebly to the ground. This bat certainly appeared more burdened with its young

than any animal I had ever observed. I have seen
an old female opossum (Didelphys azaræ) with
eleven young, large as old rats—the mother being
less than a cat in size—all clinging to various
parts of her body; yet able to climb swiftly and
with the greatest agility in the higher branches of
a tree. The actual weight was in this case rela-

Didelphys azaræ and young.

tively much greater than in that of the female bat ;
but then the opossum never quitted its hold on
the tree, and it also supplemented its hand-like
feet, furnished with crooked claws, with its teeth
and long prehensile tail. The poor bat had to
seek its living in the empty air, pursuing its prey
with the swiftness of a swallow, and it seemed

wonderful to me that she should have been able to carry about that great burden with her one pair of wings, and withal to be active enough to supply herself and her young with food.

In the end I released her, and saw her fly away and disappear among the trees, after which I put back the two young bats in the place I had taken them from, among the thick-clustering foliage of a small acacia tree. When set free they began to work their way upwards through the leaves and slender twigs in the most adroit manner, catching a twig with their teeth, then embracing a whole cluster of leaves with their wings, just as a person would take up a quantity of loose clothes and hold them tight by pressing them against the chest. The body would then emerge above the clasped leaves, and a higher twig would be caught by the teeth; and so on successively, until they had got as high as they wished, when they proceeded to hook themselves to a twig and assume the inverted position side by side; after which, one drew in its head and went to sleep, while the other began licking the end of its wing, where my finger and thumb had pressed the delicate membrane. Later in the day I attempted to feed them with small insects, but they rejected my friendly attentions in the most unmistakable manner, snapping viciously at me every time I approached them. In the evening, I stationed myself close to the tree, and presently had the satisfaction of seeing the mother return, flying straight to the spot where I had taken her, and in a few moments she was away again and over the trees with her twins.

Assuming that these two young bats had, before
I found them, existed like parasites clinging to the
parent, their adroit actions when liberated, and
their angry demonstrations at my approach, were
very astonishing; for in all other mammals born
in a perfectly helpless state, like rodents, weasels,
edentates, and even marsupials, the instincts of
self-preservation are gradually developed after the
period of activity begins, when the mother leads
them out, and they play with her and with each
other. In the bat the instincts must ripen to perfection without exercise or training, and while the
animal exists as passively as a fruit on its stem.

I have observed that the helpless young of some
of the mammals I have just mentioned seem at first
to have no instinctive understanding of the language of alarm and fear in the parent, as all young
birds have, even before their eyes are open. Nor
is it necessary that they should have such an
instinct, since, in most cases, they are well concealed in kennels or other safe places; but when,
through some accident, they are exposed, the want
of such an instinct makes the task of protecting
them doubly hard for the parent. I once surprised
a weasel (Galictis barbara) in the act of removing
her young, or conducting them, rather; and when
she was forced to quit them, although still keeping
close by, and uttering the most piercing cries of
anger and solicitude, the young continued piteously
crying out in their shrill voices and moving about
in circles, without making the slightest attempt to
escape, or to conceal themselves, as young birds
do.

Some field mice breed on the surface of the ground in ill-constructed nests, and their young are certainly the most helpless things in nature. It is possible that where this dangerous habit exists, the parent has some admirable complex instincts to safeguard her young, in addition to the ordinary instincts of most animals of this kind. This idea was suggested to me by the action of a female mouse which I witnessed by chance. While walking in a field of stubble one day in autumn, near Buenos Ayres, I suddenly heard, issuing from near my feet, a chorus of shrill squealing voices—the familiar excessively sharp little needles of sound emitted by young, blind and naked mice, when they are disturbed or in pain. Looking down, I saw close to my foot a nest of them—there were nine in all, wriggling about and squealing ; for the parent, frightened at my step, had just sprung from them, overturning in her hurry to escape the slight loosely-felted dome of fine grass and thistle-down which had covered them. I saw her running away, but after going six or seven yards she stopped, and, turning partly round so as to watch me, waited in fear and trembling. I remained perfectly motionless—a sure way to allay fear and suspicion in any wild creature,—and in a few moments she returned, but with the utmost caution, frequently pausing to start and tremble, and masking her approach with corn stumps and little inequalities in the surface of the ground, until, reaching the nest, she took one of the young in her mouth, and ran rapidly away to a distance of eight or nine yards and concealed it in a tuft of dry grass.

Leaving it, she returned a second time, in the same cautious manner, and taking another, ran with it to the same spot, and concealed it along with the first. It was curious that the first young mouse had continued squealing after being hidden by the mother, for I could hear it distinctly, the air being very still, but when the second mouse had been placed with it, the squealing ceased. A third time the old mouse came, and then instead of going to the same spot, as I had expected, she ran off in an opposite direction and disappeared among the dry weeds; a fourth was carried to the same place as the third; and in this way they were all removed to a distance of some yards from the nest, and placed in couples, until the last and odd one remained. In due time she came for it, and ran away with it in a new direction, and was soon out of sight; and although I waited fully ten minutes, she did not return; nor could I afterwards find any of the young mice when I looked for them, or even hear them squeal.

I have frequently observed newly-born lambs on the pampas, and have never failed to be surprised at the extreme imbecility they display in their actions; although this may be due partly to inherited degeneracy caused by domestication. This imbecile condition continues for two, sometimes for three days, during which time the lamb apparently acts purely from instincts, which are far from perfect; but after that, experience and its dam teach it a better way. When born its first impulse is to struggle up on to its feet; its second to suck, but here it does not discriminate like the newly-hatched bird that picks up its proper food, for it does not know what to suck. It will take into its mouth whatever comes near, in most cases a tuft of wool on its dam's neck ; and at this it will continue sucking for an indefinite time. It is highly probable that the strong-smelling secretion of the sheep's udder attracts the lamb at length to that part ; and that without something of the kind to guide it, in many cases it would actually starve without finding the teats. I have often seen lambs many hours after birth still confining their attention to the most accessible locks of wool on the neck or fore legs of the dams, and believe that in such cases the long time it took them to find the source of nourishment arose from a defective sense of smell. Its next important instinct, which comes into play from the moment it can stand on its feet, impels it to follow after any object receding from it, and, on the other hand, to run from anything approaching it. If tho dam turns round and approaches it from even a very short distance, it will start back and run from her in fear, and will not understand her voice when she bleats to it : at the same time it will confidently follow after a man, dog, horse, or any other animal moving from it. A very common experience on the pampas, in the sheep-country, is to see a lamb start up from sleep and follow the rider, running along close to the heels of the horse. This is distressing to a merciful man, for he cannot shake the little simpleton off, and if he rides on, no matter how fast, it will keep up with him, or keep him in sight, for half a mile or a

mile, and never recover its dam. The gaucho, who
is not merciful, frequently saves himself all trouble
and delay by knocking it senseless with a blow of
his whip-handle, and without checking his horse.
I have seen a lamb, about two days old, start up
from sleep, and immediately start off in pursuit of
a puffball about as big as a man's head, carried
past it over the smooth turf by the wind, and
chase it for a distance of five hundred yards, until
the dry ball was brought to a stop by a tuft of
coarse grass. This blundering instinct is quickly
laid aside when the lamb has learned to distinguish
its dam from other objects, and its dam's voice from
other sounds. When four or five days old it will
start from sleep, but instead of rushing blindly away
after any receding object, it first looks about it, and
will then recognize and run to its dam.

I have often been struck with the superiority of
the pampa or creolla—the old native breed of sheep
—in the greater vigour of the young when born over
the improved European varieties. The pampa
descends to us from the first sheep introduced into
La Plata about three centuries ago, and is a tall,
gaunt bony animal, with lean dry flesh, like venison,
and long straight wool, like goats' hair. In their
struggle for existence in a country subject to sudden
great changes of temperature, to drought, and failure of grass, they have in a great measure lost the
qualities which make the sheep valuable to man as
a food and wool-producing animal; but on the
other hand they have to some extent recovered the
vigour of a wild animal, being hardy enough to
exist without any shelter, and requiring from their

master man only protection from the larger carnivores. They are keen-scented, swift of foot and
wonderfully active, and thrive where other breeds
would quickly starve. I have often seen a lamb
dropped on the frosty ground in bitterly cold windy
weather in midwinter, and in less than five seconds
struggle to its feet, and seem as vigorous as any
day-old lamb of other breeds. The dam, impatient

Pampa sheep.

at the short delay, and not waiting to give it suck,
has then started off at a brisk trot after the flock,
scattered and galloping before the wind like huanacos rather than sheep, with the lamb, scarcely a
minute in the world, running freely at her side.
Notwithstanding its great vigour it has been proved
that the pampa sheep has not so far outgrown the
domestic taint as to be able to maintain its own
existence when left entirely to itself. During the

first half of this century, when cattle-breeding began to be profitable, and wool was not worth the trouble of shearing, and the gaucho workman would not eat mutton when beef was to be had, some of the estancieros on the southern pampas determined to get rid of their sheep, which were of no value to them ; and many flocks were driven a distance out and lost in the wilds. Out of many thousands thus turned loose to shift for themselves, not one pair survived to propagate a new race of feral sheep ; in a short time pumas, wild dogs, and other beasts of prey, had destroyed them all. The sterling qualities of the pampa sheep had their value in other times; at present the improved kinds are alone considered worth having, and the original sheep of the country is now rapidly disappearing, though still found in remote and poor districts, especially in the province of Cordova ; and probably before long it will become extinct, together with the curious pug-nosed cow of the pampas.

I have had frequent opportunities of observing the young, from one to three days old, of the Cervus campestris—the common deer of the pampas, and the perfection of its instincts at that tender age seem very wonderful in a ruminant. When the doe with fawn is approached by a horseman, even when accompanied with dogs, she stands perfectly motionless, gazing fixedly at the enemy, the fawn motionless at her side ; and suddenly, as if at a preconcerted signal, the fawn rushes directly away from her at its utmost speed ; and going to a distance of six hundred to a thousand yards conceals itself in a hollow in the ground or among the long grass, lying down very close with neck stretched out horizontally, and will thus remain until sought by the dam. When very young if found in its hiding-place it will allow itself to be taken, making no further effort to escape. After the fawn has run away the doe still maintains her statuesque attitude, as if resolved to await the onset, and only when the dogs are close to her she also rushes away, but invariably in a direction as nearly opposite to that taken by the fawn as possible. At first she runs slowly, with a limping gait, and frequently pausing, as if to entice her enemies on, like a partridge, duck or plover when driven from its young ; but as they begin to press her more closely her speed increases, becoming greater the further she succeeds in leading them from the starting-point.

The alarm-cry of this deer is a peculiar whistling bark, a low but far-reaching sound ; but when approaching a doe with young I have never been able to hear it, nor have I seen any movement on the part of the doe. Yet it is clear that in some mysterious way she inspires the fawn with sudden violent fear ; while the fawn, on its side, instead of being affected like the young in other mammals, and sticking closer to its mother, acts in a contrary way, and runs from her.

Of the birds I am acquainted with, the beautiful jacana (Parra jacana) appears to come into the world with its faculties and powers in the most advanced state. It is, in fact, ready to begin active

life from the very moment of leaving the shell, as I
once accidentally observed.   I found a nest on a
small mound of earth in a shallow lagoon, containing four eggs, with the shells already chipped by
the birds in them.   Two yards from the small nest
mound there was a second mound covered with
coarse grass.   I got off my horse to examine the
nest, and the old birds, excited beyond measure,
fluttered round me close by pouring out their shrill
rapidly-reiterated cries in an unbroken stream,
sounding very much like a policeman's rattle.   While
I was looking closely at one of the eggs lying on
the palm of my hand, all at once the cracked shell
parted, and at the same moment the young bird
leaped from my hand and fell into the water.   I
am quite sure that the young bird's sudden escape
from the shell and my hand was the result of a
violent effort on its part to free itself; and it was
doubtless inspired to make the effort by the loud
persistent screaming of the parent birds, which it
heard while in the shell.   Stooping to pick it up to
save it from perishing, I soon saw that my assistance
was not required, for immediately on dropping into
the water, it put out its neck, and with the body
nearly submerged, like a wounded duck trying to
escape observation, it swam rapidly to the second
small mound I have mentioned, and, escaping from
the water, concealed itself in the grass, lying close
and perfectly motionless like a young plover.

In the case of the pampa or creolla sheep, I have
shown that during its long, rough life in La Plata,
this variety has in some measure recovered the
natural vigour and ability to maintain existence in

adverse circumstances of its wild ancestors. As much can be said of the creolla fowl of the pampas ; and some observations of mine on the habits of this variety will perhaps serve to throw light on a vexed question of Natural History—namely, the cackling of the hen after laying, an instinct which has been described as " useless " and " disadvantageous." In fowls that live unconfined, and which are allowed to lay where they like, the instinct, as we know it, is certainly detrimental, since egg-eating dogs and pigs soon learn the cause of the outcry, and acquire a habit of rushing off to find the egg when they hear it. The question then arises : Does the wild jungle fowl possess the same pernicious instinct ?

The creolla is no doubt the descendant of the fowl originally introduced about three centuries ago by the first colonists in La Plata, and has probably not only been uncrossed with any other improved variety, such as are now fast taking its place, and has lived a much freer life than is usual with the fowl in Europe. It is a rather small, lean, extremely active bird, lays about a dozen eggs, and hatches them all, and is of a yellowish red colour—a hue which is common, I believe, in the old barn-door fowl of England. The creolla fowl is strong on the wing, and much more carnivorous and rapacious in habits than other breeds ; mice, frogs, and small snakes are eagerly hunted and devoured by it. At my home on the pampas a number of these fowls were kept, and were allowed to range freely about the plantation, which was large, and the adjacent grounds, where there were thickets of giant cardoon thistle, red-weed, thorn apple, &c. They always nested at a distance from the house, and it was almost impossible ever to find their eggs, on account of the extreme circumspection they observed in going to and from their nests; and when they succeeded in escaping foxes, skunks, weasels, and opossums, which, strange to say, they often did, they would rear their chickens away out of sight and hearing of the house, and only bring them home when winter deprived them of their leafy covering and made food scarce. During the summer, in my rambles about the plantation, I would occasionally surprise one of these half-wild hens with her brood; her distracted screams and motions would then cause her chicks to scatter and vanish in all directions, and, until the supposed danger was past, they would lie as close and well-concealed as young partridges. These fowls in summer always lived in small parties, each party composed of one cock and as many hens as he could collect—usually three or four. Each family occupied its own feeding ground, where it would pass a greater portion of each day. The hen would nest at a considerable distance from the feeding ground, sometimes as far as four or five hundred yards away. After laying an egg she would quit the nest, not walking from it as other fowls do, but flying, the flight extending to a distance of from fifteen to about fifty yards; after which, still keeping silence, she would walk or run, until, arrived at the feeding ground, she would begin to cackle. At once the cock, if within hearing, would utter a responsive cackle, whereupon she would run to him and cackle no more. Frequently the cackling call-note would not be uttered more than two or three times, sometimes only once, and in a much lower tone than in fowls of other breeds.

If we may assume that these fowls, in their long, semi-independent existence in La Plata, have reverted to the original instincts of the wild Gallus bankiva, we can see here how advantageous the cackling instinct must be in enabling the hen in dense tropical jungles to rejoin the flock after laying an egg. If there are egg-eating animals in the jungle intelligent enough to discover the meaning of such a short, subdued cackling call, they would still be unable to find the nest by going back on the bird's scent, since she flies from the nest in the first place; and the wild bird probably flies further than the creolla hen of La Plata. The clamorous cackling of our fowls would appear then to be nothing more than a perversion of a very useful instinct.

CHAPTER VII.

THE MEPHITIC SKUNK.

It might possibly give the reader some faint conception of the odious character of this creature (for adjectives are weak to describe it) when I say that, in talking to strangers from abroad, I have never thought it necessary to speak of sunstroke, jaguars, or the assassin's knife, but have never omitted to warn them of the skunk, minutely describing its habits and personal appearance.

I knew an Englishman who, on taking a first gallop across the pampas, saw one, and, quickly dismounting, hurled himself bodily on to it to effect its capture. Poor man! he did not know that the little animal is never unwilling to be caught. Men have been blinded for ever by a discharge of the fiery liquid full in their faces. On a mucous membrane it burns like sulphuric acid, say the unfortunates who have had the experience. How does nature protect the skunk itself from the injurious effects of its potent fluid ? I have not unfrequently found individuals stone-blind, sometimes moving so briskly about that the blindness must have been of long standing—very possibly in some cases an accidental drop discharged by the animal itself has caused the loss of sight. When coming to close

quarters with a skunk, by covering up the face,
one's clothes only are ruined. But this is not all one
has to fear from an encounter ; the worst is that
effluvium, after which crushed garlic is lavender,
which tortures the olfactory nerves, and appears to
pervade the whole system like a pestilent ether,
nauseating one until sea-sickness seems almost a
pleasant sensation in comparison.

To those who know the skunk only from reputation, my words might seem too strong ; many,
however, who have come to close quarters with the
little animal will think them ridiculously weak.
And consider what must the feelings be of one who
has had the following experience—not an uncommon
experience on the pampas. There is to be a dance
at a neighbouring house a few miles away ; he
has been looking forward to it, and, dressing himself
with due care, mounts his horse and sets out full of
joyous anticipations. It is a dark windy evening,
but there is a convenient bridle-path through the
dense thicket of giant thistles, and striking it he puts
his horse into a swinging gallop. Unhappily the
path is already occupied by a skunk, invisible in the
darkness, that, in obedience to the promptings of
its insane instinct, refuses to get out of it, until the
flying hoofs hit it and send it like a well-kicked
football into the thistles. But the forefoot of the
horse, up as high as his knees perhaps, have been
sprinkled, and the rider, after coming out into the
open, dismounts and walks away twenty yards from
his animal, and literally *smells* himself all over, and
with a feeling of profound relief pronounces himself
clean. Not the minutest drop of the diabolical spray

has touched his dancing shoes ! Springing into the
saddle he proceeds to his journey's end, is warmly
welcomed by his host, and speedily forgetting his
slight misadventure, mingles with a happy crowd of
friends. In a little while people begin exchanging
whispers and significant glances ; men are seen
smiling at nothing in particular ; the hostess wears
a clouded face; the ladies cough and put their
scented handkerchiefs to their noses, and presently
they begin to feel faint and retire from the room.
Our hero begins to notice that there is something
wrong, and presently discovers its cause; he, unhappily, has been the last person in the room to
remark that familiar but most abominable odour,
rising like a deadly exhalation from the floor, conquering all other odours, and every moment becoming more powerful. A drop *has* touched his shoe
after all; and fearing to be found out, and edging
towards the door, he makes his escape, and is
speedily riding home again ; knowing full well that
his sudden and early departure from the scene will
be quickly discovered and set down to the right
cause.

In that not always trustworthy book *The Natural
History of Chili*, Molina tells us how they deal with
the animal in the trans-Andine regions. " When
one appears," he says, " some of the company begin
by caressing it, until an opportunity offers for one
of them to seize it by the tail. In this position the
muscles become contracted, the animal is unable to
eject its fluid, and is quickly despatched." One
might just as well talk of caressing a cobra de
capello ; yet this laughable fiction finds believers

all over South and North America. Professor
Baird gravely introduces it into his great work on
the mammalia. I was once talking about animals
in a rancho, when a person present (an Argentine
officer) told that, while visiting an Indian encamp-
ment, he had asked the savages how they contrived
to kill skunks without making even a life in the
desert intolerable. A grave old Cacique informed
him that the secret was to go boldly up to the
animal, take it by the tail, and despatch it ; for, he
said, when you fear it not at all, then it respects
your courage and dies like a lamb—sweetly. The
officer, continuing his story, said that on quitting
the Indian camp he started a skunk, and, glad of an
opportunity to test the truth of what he had heard,
dismounted and proceeded to put the Indian plan
in practice. Here the story abruptly ended, and
when I eagerly demanded to hear the sequel, the
amateur hunter of furs lit a cigarette and vacantly
watched the ascending smoke. The Indians are
grave jokers, they seldom smile ; and this old traditional skunk-joke, which has run the length of a
continent, finding its way into many wise books, is
their revenge on a superior race.

I have shot a great many eagles, and occasionally
a carancho (Polyborus tharus), with the plumage
smelling strongly of skunk, which shows that these
birds, pressed by hunger, often commit the fearful
mistake of attacking the animal. My friend Mr.
Ernest Gibson, of Buenos Ayres, in a communication to the *Ibis,* describes an encounter he actually
witnessed between a carancho and a skunk. Riding
home one afternoon, he spied a skunk " shuffling

along in the erratic manner usual to that odorifer-
ous quadruped;" following it at a very short
distance was an eagle-vulture, evidently bent on mischief. Every time the bird came near the bushy
tail rose menacingly; then the carancho would fall
behind, and, after a few moments' hesitation, follow
on again. At length, growing bolder, it sprung
forward, seizing the threatening tail with its claw,
but immediately after "began staggering about with
dishevelled plumage, tearful eyes, and a profoundly
woe-begone expression on its vulture face. The
skunk, after turning and regarding its victim with
an I-told-you-so look for a few moments, trotted
unconcernedly off."

I was told in Patagonia by a man named Molinos,
who was frequently employed by the Government as
guide to expeditions in the desert, that everywhere
throughout that country the skunk is abundant.
Some years ago he was sent with two other men to
find and treat with an Indian chief whose whereabouts were not known. Far in the interior Molinos
was overtaken by a severe winter, his horses died of
thirst and fatigue, and during the three bitterest
months of the year he kept himself and his followers
alive by eating the flesh of skunks, the only wild
animal that never failed them. No doubt, on those
vast sterile plains where the skunk abounds, and
goes about by day and by night careless of enemies,
the terrible nature of its defensive weapon is the
first lesson experience teaches to every young eagle,
fox, wild cat, and puma.

Dogs kill skunks when made to do so, but it is
not a sport they delight in. One moonlight night,

at home, I went out to where the dogs, twelve in
number, were sleeping : while I stood there a
skunk appeared and deliberately came towards
me, passing through the dogs where they lay,
and one by one as he passed them they rose
up, and, with their tails between their legs,
skulked off. When made to kill skunks often
they become seasoned ; but always perform the
loathsome task expeditiously, then rush away with
frothing mouths to rub their faces in the wet
clay and rid themselves of the fiery sensation. At
one time I possessed only one dog that could be
made to face a skunk, and as the little robbers were
very plentiful, and continually coming about the
house in their usual open, bold way, it was rather
hard for the poor brute. This dog detested them
quite as strongly as the others, only he was more
obedient, faithful, and brave. Whenever I bade
him attack one of them he would come close up to
me and look up into my face with piteous pleading
eyes, then, finding that he was not to be let off from
the repulsive task, he would charge upon the doomed
animal with a blind fury wonderful to see. Seizing
it between his teeth, he would shake it madly,
crushing its bones, then hurl it several feet from
him, only to rush again and again upon it to repeat
the operation, doubtless with a Caligula-like wish in
his frantic breast that all the skunks on the globe
had but one backbone.

I was once on a visit to a sheep-farming brother,
far away on the southern frontier of Buenos Ayres,
and amongst the dogs I found there was one most
interesting creature. He was a great, lumbering,

stupid, good-tempered brute, so greedy that when
you offered him a piece of meat he would swallow
half your arm, and so obedient that at a word he
would dash himself against the horns of a bull, and
face death and danger in any shape. But, my
brother told me, he would not face a skunk—he
would die first. One day I took him out and found a
skunk, and for upwards of half an hour I sat on my
horse vainly cheering on my cowardly follower, and
urging him to battle. The very sight of the enemy
gave him a fit of the shivers ; and when the irascible
little enemy began to advance against us, going
through the performance by means of which he
generally puts his foes to flight without resorting to
malodorous measures—stamping his little feet in
rage, jumping up, spluttering and hissing and
flourishing his brush like a warlike banner above his
head—then hardly could I restrain my dog from
turning tail and flying home in abject terror. My
cruel persistence was rewarded at last. Continued
shouts, cheers, and hand-clappings began to stir the
brute to a kind of frenzy. Torn by conflicting
emotions, he began to revolve about the skunk at a
lumbering gallop, barking, howling, and bristling
up his hair ; and at last, shutting his eyes, and with
a yell of desperation, he charged. I fully expected
to see the enemy torn to pieces in a few seconds,
but when the dog was still four or five feet from
him the fatal discharge came, and he dropped down
as if shot dead. For some time he lay on the earth
perfectly motionless, watched and gently bedewed
by the victorious skunk ; then he got up and crept
whining away. Gradually he quickened his pace,

finally breaking into a frantic run. In vain I followed him, shouting at the top of my lungs; he stayed not to listen, and very speedily vanished from sight—a white speck on the vast level plain. At noon on the following day he made his appearance, gaunt and befouled with mud, staggering forward like a galvanized skeleton. Too worn out

Skunk and dog.

even to eat, he flung himself down, and for hours lay like a dead thing, sleeping off the effects of those few drops of perfume.

Dogs, I concluded, like men, have their idiosyncrasies; but I had gained my point, and proved once more—if any proof were needed—the truth of that noble panegyric of Bacon's on our faithful servant and companion.

CHAPTER VIII.

MIMICRY AND WARNING COLOURS IN GRASSHOPPERS.

THERE is in La Plata a large handsome grasshopper
(Zoniopoda tarsata), the habits of which in its larva
and imago stages are in strange contrast, like those
in certain lepidoptera, in which the caterpillars form
societies and act in concert. The adult has a
greenish protective colouring, brown and green
banded thighs, bright red hind wings, seen only
during flight. It is solitary and excessively shy in
its habits, living always in concealment among the
dense foliage near the surface of the ground. The
young are intensely black, like grasshoppers cut
out of jet or ebony, and gregarious in habit, living
in bands of forty or fifty to three or four hundred ;
and so little shy, that they may sometimes be taken
up by handfuls before they begin to scatter in
alarm. Their gregarious habits and blackness—of
all hues in nature the most obvious to the sight—
would alone be enough to make them the most
conspicuous of insects ; but they have still other
habits which appear as if specially designed to
bring them more prominently into notice. Thus,
they all keep so close together at all times as to
have their bodies actually touching, and when

travelling, move so slowly that the laziest snail might easily overtake and pass one of their bands, and even disappear beyond their limited horizon in a very short time.

They often select an exposed weed to feed on, clustering together on its summit above the surrounding verdure, an exceedingly conspicuous object to every eye in the neighbourhood. They also frequently change their feeding-ground; at such times they deliberately cross wide roads and other open spaces, barren of grass, where, moving so slowly that they scarcely seem to move at all, they look at a distance like a piece of black velvet lying on the ground. Thus in every imaginable way they expose themselves and invite attack; yet, in spite of it all, I have never detected birds preying on them, and I have sometimes kept one of these black societies under observation near my house for several days, watching them at intervals, in places where the trees overhead were the resort of Icterine and tyrant birds, Guira cuckoos, and other species, all great hunters after grasshoppers. A young grasshopper is, moreover, a morsel that seldom comes amiss to any bird, whether insect or seed eater; and, as a rule, it is extremely shy, nimble, and inconspicuous. It seems clear that, although the young Zoniopoda does not mimic in its form any black protected insect, it nevertheless owes its safety to its blackness, together with the habit it possesses of exposing itself in so open and bold a manner. Blackness is so common in large protected insects, as, for instance, in the unpalatable leaf-cutting ants, scorpions, mygale spiders, wasps, and other dangerous kinds, that it is manifestly a "warning colour," the most universal and best known in nature; and the grasshopper, I believe, furthermore mimics the fearless demeanour of the protected or venomous species, which birds and other insect-eaters know and respect. It might be supposed that the young Zoniopoda is itself unpalatable; but this is scarcely probable, for when the deceptive black mask is once dropped, the excessive shyness, love of concealment, and protective colouring of the insect show that it is much sought after by birds.

While setting this down as an undoubted case of "mimicry," although it differs in some respects from all other cases I have seen reported, I cannot help remarking that this most useful word appears to be in some danger of losing the meaning originally attached to it in zoology. There are now very few cases of an accidental resemblance found between two species in nature which are not set down by someone to "mimicry," some in which even the wildest imagination might well fail to see any possible benefit to the supposed mimic. In cases where the outward resemblance of some feeble animal to a widely different and well-protected species, or to some object like a leaf or stick, and where such resemblance is manifestly advantageous and has reacted on and modified the life habits, it is conceivable that slight spontaneous variations in the structure and colouring of the unprotected species have been taken advantage of by the principle of natural selection, and a case of "mimicry" set up, to become more and more perfect in time, as successive casual variations in the same direction increased the resemblance.

The stick-insect is perhaps the most perfect example where resemblance to an inanimate object has been the result aimed at, so to speak, by nature ; the resemblance of the volucella fly to the humble-bee, on which it is parasitical, is the most familiar example of one species growing like another to its own advantage, since only by means of its deceptive likeness to the humble-bee is it able to penetrate into the nest with impunity. These two cases, with others of a similar character, were first called cases of " mimicry " by Kirby and Spence, in their ever-delightful *Introduction to Entomology*—an old book, but, curiously enough in these days of popular treatises on all matters of the kind, still the only general work on insects in the English language which one who is not an entomologist can read with pleasure.

A second case of mimicry not yet noticed by any naturalist is seen in another grasshopper, also common in La Plata (Rhomalea speciosa of Thunberg). This is an extremely elegant insect; the head and thorax chocolate, with cream-coloured markings ; the abdomen steel-blue or purple, a colour I have not seen in any other insects of this family. The fore wings have a protective colouring ; the hind wings are bright red. When at rest, with the red and purple tints concealed, it is only a very pretty grasshopper, but the instant it takes wing it becomes the fac-simile of a very common wasp of the genus Pepris. These wasps vary greatly in size, some being as large as the hornet ;

they are solitary, and feed on the honey of flowers
and on fruit, and, besides being furnished with
stings like other wasps—though their sting is not
so venomous as in other genera—they also, when
angry, emit a most abominable odour, and are thus
doubly protected against their enemies. Their excessive tameness, slow flight, and indolent motions
serve to show that they are not accustomed to be
interfered with. All these strong-smelling wasps
have steel-blue or purple bodies, and bright red
wings. So exactly does the Rhomalea grasshopper
mimic the Pepris when flying, that I have been
deceived scores of times. I have even seen it on
the leaves, and, after it has flown and settled once
more, I have gone to look at it again, to make sure
that my eyes had not deceived me. It is curious
to see how this resemblance has reacted on and
modified the habits of the grasshopper. It is a
great flyer, and far more aërial in its habits than
any other insect I am acquainted with in this
family, living always in trees, instead of on or near
the surface of the ground. It is abundant in
orchards and plantations round Buenos Ayres,
where its long and peculiarly soft, breezy note may
be heard all summer. If the ancient Athenians
possessed so charming an insect as this, their great
regard for the grasshopper was not strange : I
only wish that the " Athenians of South America,"
as my fellow-townsmen sometimes call themselves
in moments of exaltation, had a feeling of the same
kind—the regard which does *not* impale its object
on a pin—for the pretty light-hearted songster of
their groves and gardens.

When taken in the hand, it has the habit, common to most grasshoppers, of pouring out an inky fluid from its mouth ; only the discharge is unusually copious in this species. It has another habit in defending itself which is very curious. When captured it instantly curls its body round, as a wasp does to sting. The suddenness of this action has more than once caused me to drop an insect I had taken, actually thinking for the moment that I had taken hold of a wasp. Whether birds would be deceived and made to drop it or not is a question it would not be easy to settle ; but the instinct certainly looks like one of a series of small adaptations, all tending to make the resemblance to a wasp more complete and effective.

CHAPTER IX.

DRAGON-FLY STORMS.

ONE of the most curious things I have encountered in my observations on animal life relates to a habit of the larger species of dragon-flies inhabiting the Pampas and Patagonia. Dragon-flies are abundant throughout the country wherever there is water. There are several species, all more or less brilliantly coloured. The kinds that excited my wonder, from their habits, are twice as large as the common widely distributed insects, being three inches to four inches in length, and as a rule they are sober-coloured, although there is one species—the largest among them—entirely of a brilliant scarlet. This kind is, however, exceedingly rare. All the different kinds (of the large dragon-flies) when travelling associate together, and occasionally, in a flight composed of countless thousands, one of these brilliant-hued individuals will catch the eye, appearing as conspicuous among the others as a poppy or scarlet geranium growing alone in an otherwise flowerless field. The most common species—and in some cases the entire flight seems to be composed of this kind only—is the Æschna bonariensis Raml, the prevailing colour of which is pale blue. But the really wonderful thing about them all alike is, that they appear only when flying before the south-west wind, called *pampero*—the wind that blows from the interior of the pampas. The pampero is a dry, cold wind, exceedingly violent. It bursts on the plains very suddenly, and usually lasts only a short time, sometimes not more than ten minutes; it comes irregularly, and at all seasons of the year, but is most frequent in the hot season, and after exceptionally sultry weather. It is in summer and autumn that the large dragon-flies appear ; not *with* the wind, but—and this is the most curious part of the matter—in advance of it ; and inasmuch as these insects are not seen in the country at other times, and frequently appear in seasons of pro-longed drought, when all the marshes and water-courses for many hundreds of miles are dry, they must of course traverse immense distances, flying before the wind at a speed of seventy or eighty miles an hour. On some occasions they appear almost simultaneously with the wind, going by like a flash, and instantly disappearing from sight. You have scarcely time to see them before the wind strikes you. As a rule, however, they make their appear-ance from five to fifteen minutes before the wind strikes ; and when they are in great numbers the air, to a height of ten or twelve feet above the surface of the ground, is all at once seen to be full of them, rushing past with extraordinary velocity in a north-easterly direction. In very oppressive weather, and when the swiftly advancing pampero brings no moving mountains of mingled cloud and dust, and is consequently not expected, the sudden apparition of the dragon-fly is a most welcome one, for then an immediate burst of cold wind is confidently looked for. In the expressive vernacular of the gauchos the large dragon-fly is called *hijo del pampero*—son of the south-west wind.

It is clear that these great and frequent dragon-fly movements are not explicable on any current hypothesis regarding the annual migrations of birds, the occasional migrations of butterflies, or the migrations of some mammals, like the reindeer and buffalo of Arctic America, which, according to Rae and other observers, perform long journeys north and south at regular seasons, "from a sense of polarity." Neither this hypothetical sense in animals, nor "historical memory" will account for the dragon-fly storms, as the phenomenon of the pampas might be called, since the insects do not pass and repass between "breeding and subsistence areas," but all journey in a north-easterly direction; and of the countless millions flying like thistle-down before the great pampero wind, not one solitary traveller ever returns.

The cause of the flight is probably dynamical, affecting the insects with a sudden panic, and compelling them to rush away before the approaching tempest. The mystery is that they should fly from the wind before it reaches them, and yet travel in the same direction with it. When they pass over the level, treeless country, not one insect lags behind, or permits the wind to overtake it; but, on arriving at a wood or large plantation they swarm into it, as if seeking shelter from some swift-pursuing enemy, and on such occasions they sometimes remain clinging to the trees while the

STORM OF DRAGON FLIES.

[Page 132.

wind spends its force. This is particularly the case when the wind blows up at a late hour of the day; then, on the following morning, the dragon-flies are seen clustering to the foliage in such numbers that many trees are covered with them, a large tree often appearing as if hung with curtains of some brown glistening material, too thick to show the green leaves beneath.

In Patagonia, where the phenomenon of dragon-fly storms is also known, an Englishman residing at the Rio Negro related to me the following occurrence which he witnessed there. A race meeting was being held near the town of El Carmen, on a high exposed piece of ground, when, shortly before sunset, a violent pampero wind came up, laden with dense dust-clouds. A few moments before the storm broke, the air all at once became obscured with a prodigious cloud of dragon-flies. About a hundred men, most of them on horseback, were congregated on the course at the time, and the insects, instead of rushing by in their usual way, settled on the people in such quantities that men and horses were quickly covered with clinging masses of them. My informant said—and this agrees with my own observation—that he was greatly impressed by the appearance of terror shown by the insects; they clung to him as if for dear life, so that he had the greatest difficulty in ridding himself of them.

Weissenborn, in Loudon's *Magazine of Natural History* (N. S. vol. iii.) describes a great migration of dragon-flies which he witnessed in Germany in 1839, and also mentions a similar phenomenon occurring in 1816, and extending over a large portion of Europe. But in these cases the movement took place at the end of May, and the insects travelled due south ; their migrations were therefore similar to those of birds and butterflies, and were probably due to the same cause. I have been unable to find any mention of a phenomenon resembling the one with which we are so familiar on the pampas, and which, strangely enough, has not been recorded by any European naturalists who have travelled there.

CHAPTER X.

THERE cannot be a doubt that some animals possess an instinctive knowledge of their enemies —or, at all events, of some of their enemies— though I do not believe that this faculty is so common as many naturalists imagine. The most striking example I am acquainted with is seen in gnats or mosquitoes, and in the minute South American sandflies (Simulia), when a dragon-fly appears in a place where they are holding their aërial pastimes. The sudden appearance of a ghost among human revellers could not produce a greater panic. I have spoken in the last chapter of periodical storms or waves of dragon-flies in the Plata region, and mentioned incidentally that the appearance of these insects is most welcome in oppressively hot weather, since they are known to come just in advance of a rush of cool wind. In La Plata we also look for the dragon-fly, and rejoice at its coming, for another reason. We know that the presence of this noble insect will cause the clouds of stinging gnats and flies, which make life a burden, to vanish like smoke

When a flight of dragon-flies passes over the country many remain along the route, as I have said, sheltering themselves wherever trees occur; and, after the storm blows over, these strangers and stragglers remain for some days hawking for prey in the neighbourhood. It is curious to note that they do not show any disposition to seek for watercourses. It may be that they feel lost in a strange region, or that the panic they have suffered, in their long flight before the wind, has unsettled their instincts; for it is certain that they do not, like the dragon-fly in Mrs. Browning's poem, " return to dream upon the river." They lead instead a kind of vagabond existence, hanging about the plantations, and roaming over the surrounding plains. It is then remarked that gnats and sand-flies apparently cease to exist, even in places where they have been most abundant. They have not been devoured by the dragon-flies, which are perhaps very few in number; they have simply got out of the way, and will remain in close concealment until their enemies take their departure, or have all been devoured by martins, tyrant birds, and the big robber-flies or devil's dykes—no name is bad enough for them—of the family Asilidæ. During these peaceful gnatless days, if a person thrusts himself into the bushes or herbage in some dark sheltered place, he will soon begin to hear the thin familiar sounds, as of " horns of elf-land faintly blowing "; and presently, from the ground and the under surface of every leaf, the ghost-like withered little starvelings will appear in scores and in hundreds to settle on him, fear not having blunted their keen appetites.

When riding over the pampas on a hot still day,

with a pertinacious cloud of gnats or sandflies
hovering just above my head and keeping me
company for miles, I have always devoutly wished
for a stray dragon-fly to show himself. Frequently
the wish has been fulfilled, the dragon-fly, apparently " sagacious of his quarry from afar," sweeping
straight at his prey, and instantly, as if by miracle,
the stinging rain has ceased and the noxious cloud
vanished from overhead, to be re-formed no more.
This has always seemed very extraordinary to me;
for in other matters gnats do not appear to possess
even that proverbial small dose of intellect for which
we give most insects credit. Before the advent of
the dragon-fly it has perhaps happened that I have
been vigorously striking at them, making it very
unpleasant for them, and also killing and disabling
many hundreds—a larger number than the most
voracious dragon-fly could devour in the course of
a whole day ; and yet, after brushing and beating
them off until my arms have ached with the exertion, they have continued to rush blindly on their
fate, exhibiting not the faintest symptom of fear.
I suppose that for centuries mosquitoes have, in this
way, been brushed and beaten away with hands and
with tails, without learning caution. It is not in
their knowledge that there are hands and tails. A
large animal is simply a field on which they confidently settle to feed, sounding shrill flourishes on
their little trumpets to show how fearless they are.
But the dragon-fly is very ancient on the earth, and
if, during the Devonian epoch, when it existed, it
preyed on some blood-sucking insect from which
our Culicidæ have come, then these stupid little

insects have certainly had ample time in which to learn well at least one lesson.

There is not in all organic nature, to my mind, any instance of wasted energy comparable in magnitude with the mosquito's thirst for blood, and the instincts and elaborate blood-pumping apparatus with which it is related. The amount of pollen given off by some wind-fertilized trees—so great in some places that it covers hundreds of square miles of earth and water with a film of yellow dust— strikes us as an amazing waste of material on the part of nature; but in these cases we readily see that this excessive prodigality is necessary to con- tinue the species, and that a sufficient number of flowers would not be impregnated unless the entire trees were bathed for days in the fertilizing cloud, in which only one out of many millions of floating particles can ever hit the mark. The mosquito is able to procreate without ever satisfying its ravenous appetite for blood. To swell its grey thread-like abdomen to a coral bead is a delight to the insect, but not necessary to its existence, like food and water to ours; it is the great prize in the lottery of life, which few can ever succeed in drawing. In a hot summer, when one has ridden perhaps for half a day over a low-lying or wet district, through an atmosphere literally obscured with a fog of mosquitoes, this fact strikes the mind very forcibly, for in such places it frequently is the case that mammals do not exist, or are exceedingly rare. In Europe it is different. There, as Réaumur said, possibly one gnat in every hundred may be able to gratify its appetite for blood ; but of the gnats in many districts in South America it would be nearer the mark to say that only one in a hundred millions can ever do so.

Curtis discovered that only the female mosquito bites or sucks blood, the male being without tongue or mandibles; and he asks, What, then, does the male feed on? He conjectures that it feeds on flowers ; but, had he visited some swampy places in hot countries, where flowers are few and the insects more numerous than the sands on the sea-shore, he would most probably have said that the males subsist on decaying vegetable matter and moisture of slime. It is, however, more important to know what the female subsists on. We know that she thirsts for warm mammalian blood, that she seeks it with avidity, and is provided with an admirable organ for its extraction—only, unfortunately for her, she does not get it, or, at all events, the few happy individuals that do get it are swamped in the infinite multitude of those that are doomed by nature to total abstinence.

I should like to know whether this belief of Curtis, shared by Westwood and other distinguished entomologists, but originally put forward merely as a conjecture, has ever been tested by careful observation and experiment. If not, then it is strange that it should have crept into many important works, where it is stated not as a mere guess, but as an established fact. Thus, Van Beneden, in his work on parasites, while classing female mosquitoes with his "miserable wretches," yet says, " If blood fails them, they live, like the males, on the juices of flowers." If this be so, it is quite certain that the juices fail to satisfy them ; and that, like Dr. Tanner, who was ravenously hungry during his forty days' fast, in spite of his frequent sips of water, the mosquito still craves for something better than a cool vegetarian diet. I cannot help thinking, though the idea may seem fanciful, that mosquitoes feed on nothing. We know that the ephemeræ take no refreshment in the imago state, the mouth being aborted or atrophied in these short-lived creatures ; but we also know that they belong to an exceedingly ancient tribe, and possibly, after the earth had ceased to produce their proper nourishment there came in their history a long hungry period, which did not kill them, but lasted until their feeding instincts became obsolete, the mouth lost its use, and their life in its perfect state dwindled to its present length.

In any case, how unsatisfactory is the mosquitoes' existence, and what a curious position they occupy in nature ! Let us suppose that, owing to some great change in the conditions of the earth, rapacious birds were no longer able to capture prey, and that, by a corresponding change in their organizations, they were able to subsist on the air they breathed, with perhaps an occasional green leaf and a sip of water, and yet retained the old craving for solid food, and the old predatory instincts and powers undiminished ; they would be in the position of mosquitoes in the imago state. And if then fifty or a hundred individuals were to succeed every year in capturing something and making one hearty meal, these few fortunate diners would bear about

the same proportion to all the raptors on the globe
as the mosquitoes that succeed in sucking blood to
their unsuccessful fellows. In the case of the hawks,
the effect of the few meals on the entire rapacious
family or order would certainly be *nil;* and it is
impossible to believe for a moment that the comparatively infinitesimal amount of blood sucked by
mosquitoes can serve to invigorate the species.
The wonder is that the machinery, which accom-
plishes nothing, should continue in such perfect
working order.

When we consider the insect's delicate organ, so
admirably fitted for the purpose to which it is applied, it becomes difficult to believe that it could
have been so perfected except in a condition of
things utterly unlike the present. There must have
been a time when mosquitoes found their proper
nourishment, and when warm mammalian blood
was as necessary to their existence as honey is to
that of the bee, or insect food to the dragon-fly.

This applies to many blood-sucking insects besides
mosquitoes, and with special force to the tick tribes
(Ixodes), which swarm throughout Central and South
America; for in these degraded spiders the whole
body has been manifestly modified to fit it for a
parasitical life ; while the habits of the insect during
its blind, helpless, waiting existence on trees, and
its sudden great development when it succeeds in
attaching itself to an animal body, also point irre-
sistibly to the same conclusion. In the sunny uplands they act (writes Captain Burton) like the
mosquitoes of the hot, humid Beiramar. "The
nuisance is general; it seems to be in the air; every

blade of grass has its colony ; clusters of hundreds
adhere to the twigs ; myriads are found in the bush
clumps.   Lean and flat when growing to the leaves,
the tick catches man or beast brushing by, fattens
rapidly, and, at the end of a week's good living,
drops off, *plena cruoris."*   When on trees, Belt says,
they instinctively place themselves on the extreme
tips of leaves and shoots, with their hind legs stretching out, each foot armed with two hooks or claws,
with which to lay hold of any animal brushing by.

During this wretched, incomplete existence (from which, in
most cases, it is never destined
to emerge), its greatest length
is about one-fourth of an inch ;
but where it fastens itself to an
animal the abdomen increases to
a globe as big as a medium-sized

Ixodes; before and after
a blood diet.

Barcelona nut.   Being silvery-grey or white in
colour, it becomes, when thus distended, very conspicuous on any dark surface.   I have frequently
seen black, smooth-haired dogs with their coats
turned into a perfect garden of these white spider-
flowers or mushrooms.   The white globe is leathery,
and nothing can injure it ; and the poor beast
cannot rub, bite, or scratch it off, as it is anchored
to his flesh by eight sets of hooks and a triangle
of teeth.

The ticks inhabiting regions rich in bird and
insect life, but with few mammals, are in the same
condition as mosquitoes, as far as the supply of
blood goes ; and, like the mosquitoes, they are compelled and able to exist without the nourishment

best suited to them. They are nature's miserable
castaways, parasitical tribes lost in a great dry
wilderness where no blood is ; and every marsh-
born mosquito, piping of the hunger gnawing its
vitals, and every forest tick, blindly feeling with its
grappling-irons for the beast that never brushes by,
seems to tell us of a world peopled with gigantic
forms, mammalian and reptilian, which once afforded
abundant pasture to the parasite, and which the
parasite perhaps assisted to overthrow.

It is almost necessary to transport oneself to the
vast tick-infested wilderness of the New World to
appreciate the full significance of a passage in Belt's
Naturalist in Nicaragua, in which it is suggested that
man's hairless condition was perhaps brought about
by natural selection in tropical regions, where he was
greatly troubled with parasites of this kind. It is
certain that if in such a country as Brazil he possessed a hairy coat, affording cover to the tick and
enabling it to get a footing on the body, his condition would be a very sad one. Savages abhor hairs
on the body, and even pluck them off their faces.
This seems like a survival of an ancient habit acquired when the whole body was clothed with hair;
and if primitive man ever possessed such a habit,
nature only followed his lead in giving him a hairless offspring.

Is it not also probable that the small amount of
mammalian life in South America, and the aquatic
habits of nearly all the large animals in the warmer
districts, is due to the persecutions of the tick ?
The only way in which a large animal can rid itself
of the pest is by going into the water or wallowing

in the mud; and this perhaps accounts for the more
or less aquatic habits of the jaguar, aguará-guazú,
the large Cervus paludosus, tapir, capybara, and
peccary. Monkeys, which are most abundant, are
a notable exception; but these animals have the
habit of attending to each other's skins, and spend
a great deal of their time in picking off the parasites.

But how do birds escape the ticks, since these
parasites do not confine their attacks to any one
class of animals, but attach themselves impartially
to any living thing coming within reach of their
hooks, from snake to man? My own observations
bearing on this point refer less to the Ixodes than
to the minute bête-rouge, which is excessively
abundant in the Plata district, where it is known as
bicho colorado, and in size and habits resembles the
English Leptus autumnalis. It is so small that,
notwithstanding its bright scarlet colour, it can only
be discerned by bringing the eye close to it; and
being, moreover, exceedingly active and abundant
in all shady places in summer—making life a misery
to careless human beings—it must be very much
more dangerous to birds than the larger sedentary
Ixodes. The bête-rouge invariably lodges beneath
the wings of birds, where the loose scanty plumage
affords easy access to the skin. Domestic birds
suffer a great deal from its persecutions, and their
young, if allowed to run about in shady places, die
of the irritation. Wild birds, however, seem to be
very little troubled, and most of those I have examined have been almost entirely free from parasites.
Probably they are much more sensitive than the
domestic birds, and able to feel and pick off the

insects with their beaks before they have penetrated into the skin. I believe they are also able to protect themselves in another way, namely, by preventing the parasites from reaching their bodies at all. I was out under the trees one day with a pet ovenbird (Furnarius rufus), which had full liberty to range about at will, and noticed that at short intervals it went through the motions of picking something from its toes or legs, though I could see nothing on them. At length I approached my eyes to within a few inches of the bird's feet, and discovered that the large dry branch on which it stood was covered with a multitude of parasites, all running rapidly about like foraging ants, and whenever one came to the bird's feet it at once ran up the leg. Every time this happened, so far as I could see, the bird felt it, and quickly and deftly picked it off with the point of its bill. It seemed very astonishing that the horny covering of the toes and legs should be so exquisitely sensitive, for the insects are so small and light that they cannot be felt on the hand, even when a score of them are running over it; but the fact is as I have stated, and it is highly probable, I think, that most wild birds keep themselves free from these little torments in the same way.

Some observations of mine on a species of Ornithomyia—a fly parasitical on birds—might possibly be of use in considering the question of the anomalous position in nature of insects possessing the instincts and aptitudes of parasites, and organs manifestly modified to suit a parasitical mode of life, yet compelled and able to exist free, feeding, perhaps, on

vegetable juices, or, like the ephemeræ, on nothing
at all. For it must be borne in mind that I do not
assert that these "occasional" or "accidental"
parasites, as some one calls them, explaining nothing, do not feed on such juices. I do not know
what they feed on. I only know that the joyful
alacrity with which gnats and stinging flies of all
kinds abandon the leaves, supposed to afford them
pasture, to attack a warm-blooded animal, serves to
show how strong the impulse is, and how ineradicable
the instinct, which must have had an origin. Perhaps the habits of the bird-fly I have mentioned
will serve to show how, in some cases, the free life
of some blood-sucking flies and other insects might
have originated.

Kirby and Spence, in their *Introduction,* mention
that one or two species of Ornithomyia have been
observed flying about and alighting on men; and in
one case the fly extracted blood and was caught, the
species being thus placed beyond doubt. This circumstance led the authors to believe that the insect,
when the bird it is parasitical on dies, takes to
flight and migrates from body to body, occasionally
tasting blood until, coming to the right body—to
wit, that of a bird, or of a particular species of bird
—it once more establishes itself permanently in the
plumage. I fancy that the insect sometimes leads
a freer life and ranges much more than the authors
imagined; and I refer to Kirby and Spence, with
apologies to those who regard the *Introduction* as
out of date, only because I am not aware that we
have any later observations on the subject.

There is in La Plata a small very common

Dendrocolaptine bird—Anumbius acuticaudatus—
much infested by an Ornithomyia, a pretty, pale
insect, half the size of a house-fly, and elegantly
striped with green. It is a very large parasite for
so small a bird, yet so cunning and alert is it, and

Firewood-gatherer and Bird-fly.

so swiftly is it able to swim through the plumage,
that the bird is unable to rid itself of so undesirable a companion. The bird lives with its
mate all the year round, much of the time with its
grown-up young, in its nest—a large structure, in

which so much building-material is used that the
bird is called in the vernacular Leñatero, or Firewood-gatherer.   On warm bright days without
wind, during the absence of the birds, I have
frequently seen a company of from half a dozen to
a dozen or fifteen of the parasitical fly wheeling
about in the air above the nest, hovering and
gambolling together, just like house-flies in a room
in summer; but always on the appearance of the
birds, returning from their feeding-ground, they
would instantly drop down and disappear into the
nest.   How curious this instinct seems!   The fly
regards the bird, which affords it the warmth and
food essential to life, as its only deadly enemy;
and with an inherited wisdom, like that of the
mosquito with regard to the dragon-fly, or of the
horse-fly with regard to the Monedula wasp,
vanishes like smoke from its presence, and only
approaches the bird secretly from a place of concealment.

The parasitical habit tends inevitably to degrade
the species acquiring it, dulling its senses and
faculties, especially those of sight and locomotion;
but the Ornithomyia seems an exception, its
dependent life having had a contrary effect; the
extreme sensitiveness, keenness of sight, and quick-
ness of the bird having reacted on the insect,
giving it a subtlety in its habits and motions almost
without a parallel even among free insects.   A
man with a blood-sucking flat-bodied flying squirrel,
concealing itself among his clothing and gliding and
dodging all over his body with so much artifice
and rapidity as to defeat all efforts made to capture

it or knock it off, would be a case parallel to that of the bird-fly on the small bird. It might be supposed that the Firewood-gatherer, like some ants that keep domestic pets, makes a pet of the fly; for it is a very pretty insect, barred with green, and with rainbow reflections on its wings— and birds are believed by some theorists to possess æsthetic tastes; but the discomfort of having such a vampire on the body would, I imagine, be too great to allow a kindly instinct of that nature to grow up. Moreover, I have on several occasions seen the bird making frantic efforts to capture one of the flies, which had incautiously flown up from the nest at the wrong moment. Bird and fly seem to know each other wonderfully well.

Here, then, we have a parasitical insect specialized in the highest degree, yet retaining all its pristine faculties unimpaired, its love of liberty, and of associating in numbers together for sportive exercises, and well able to take care of itself during its free intervals. And probably when thrown on the world, as when nests are blown down, or the birds get killed, or change their quarters, as they often do, it is able to exist for some time without avian blood. Let us then imagine some of these orphaned colonies, unable to find birds, but through a slight change in habits or organization able to exist in the imago state without sucking blood until they laid their eggs; and succeeding generations, still better able to stand the altered conditions of life until they become practically independent (like gnats), multiplying greatly, and disporting themselves in clouds over birdless forests. yet still retaining the old hunger for blood and the power to draw it, and ready at any moment to return to the ancestral habit. It might be said that if such a result were possible it would have occurred, but that we find no insect like the Ornithomyia existing independently. With the bird-fly it has not occurred, as far as we know ; but in the past history of some independent parasites it is possible that something similar to the imaginary case I have sketched may have taken place. The bush-tick is a more highly specialized, certainly a more degraded, creature than the bird-fly, and the very fact of its existence seems to show that it is possible for even the lowest of the fallen race of parasites to start afresh in life under new conditions, and to reascend in the scale of being, although still bearing about it the marks of former degeneracy.

The connection between the flea and the mammal it feeds on is even less close than that which exists between the Ornithomyia and bird. The fact that fleas are so common and universal—for in all lands we have them, like the poor, always with us ; and that they are found on all mammals, from the king of beasts to the small modest mouse—seems to show a great amount of variability and adaptiveness, as well as a very high antiquity. It has often been reported that fleas have been found hopping on the ground in desert places, where they could not have been dropped by man or beast; and it has been assumed that these " independent " fleas must, like gnats and ticks, subsist on vegetable juices. There is no doubt that they are able to exist and propagate

for one or two years after being deprived of their
proper aliment; houses shut up for a year or
longer are sometimes found infested with them;
possibly in the absence of " vegetable juices " they
flourish on dust. I have never detected them
hopping on the ground in uninhabited places,
although I once found them in Patagonia, in a
hamlet which had been attacked and depopulated
by the Indians about twenty months before my
visit. On entering one of the deserted huts I found
the floor literally swarming with fleas, and in less
than ten seconds my legs, to the height of my knees,
were almost black with their numbers. This proves
that they are able to increase greatly for a period without blood ; but I doubt that they can go on existing
and increasing for an indefinite time; perhaps their
true position, with regard to the parasitical habit, is
midway between that of the strict parasite which
never leaves the body, and that of independent
parasites like the Culex and the Ixodes, and all
those which are able to exist free for ever, and are
parasitical only when the opportunity offers.

Entomologists regard the flea as a degraded fly.
Certainly it is very much more degraded than the
bird-borne Ornithomyia, with its subtle motions
and instinct, its power of flight and social pastimes.
The poor pulex has lost every trace of wings ;
nevertheless, in its fallen condition it has developed
some remarkable qualities and saltatory powers,
which give it a lower kind of glory ; and, compared
with another parasite with which it shares the
human species, it is almost a noble insect. Darwin
has some remarks about the smallness of the brain

of an ant, assuming that this insect possesses a very
high intelligence, but I doubt very much that the ant,
which moves in a groove, is mentally the superior
of the unsocial flea.   The last is certainly the most
teachable; and if fleas were generally domesticated
and made pets of, probably there would be as many
stories about their marvellous intelligence and
fidelity to man as we now hear about our over-
praised "friend" the dog

With regard to size, the flea probably started on
its downward course as a comparatively large insect,
probably larger than the Ornithomyia.   That insect
has been able to maintain its existence, without
dwindling like the Leptus into a mere speck, through
the great modification in organs and instinct, which
adapt it so beautifully to the feathery element in
which it moves.   The bush-tick, wingless from the
beginning, and diverging in another direction, has
probably been greatly increased in size by its parasitical habit; this seems proven by the fact, that as
long as it is parasitical on nothing it remains small,
but when able to fasten itself to an animal it rapidly
developes to a great size.   Again, the big globe of
its abdomen is coriaceous and elastic, and is probably as devoid of sensation as a ball of india-rubber.
The insect, being made fast by hooks and teeth to its
victim, all efforts to remove it only increase the
pain it causes; and animals that know it well do
not attempt to rub, scratch, or bite it off, therefore the great size and the conspicuous colour of
the tick are positive advantages to it.   The flea,
without the subtlety and highly-specialized organs
of the Ornithomyia, or the stick-fast powers and

leathery body of the Ixodes, can only escape its vigilant enemies by making itself invisible; hence every variation, i.e. increase in jumping-power and diminished bulk, tending towards this result, has been taken advantage of by natural selection.

CHAPTER XI

Two humble-bees, Bombus thoracicus and B. violaceus, are found on the pampas; the first, with a primrose yellow thorax, and the extremity of the abdomen bright rufous, slightly resembles the English B. terrestris; the rarer species, which is a trifle smaller than the first, is of a uniform intense black, the body having the appearance of velvet, the wings being of a deep violaceous blue.

A census of the humble-bees in any garden or field always shows that the yellow bees outnumber the black in the proportion of about seven to one; and I have also found their nests for many years in the same proportion; about seven nests of the yellow to one nest of the black species. In habits they are almost identical, and when two species so closely allied are found inhabiting the same locality, it is only reasonable to infer that one possesses some advantage over the other, and that the least favoured species will eventually disappear. In this case, where one so greatly outnumbers the other, it might be thought that the rarer species is dying out, or that, on the contrary, it is a new-comer destined to supplant the older more numerous species. Yet, during the twenty years I have ob-

served them, there has occurred no change in their
relative positions; though both have greatly increased in numbers during that time, owing to the
spread of cultivation. And yet it would scarcely
be too much to expect some marked change in a
period so long as that, even through the slow-
working agency of natural selection; for it is not
as if there had been an exact balance of power between them. In the same period of time I have
seen several species, once common, almost or quite
disappear, while others, very low down as to
numbers, have been exalted to the first rank. In
insect life especially, these changes have been
numerous, rapid, and widespread.

In the district where, as a boy, I chased and
caught tinamous, and also chased ostriches, but
failed to catch them, the continued presence of
our two humble-bees, sucking the same flowers
and making their nests in the same situations, has
remained a puzzle to my mind.

The site of the nest is usually a slight depression
in the soil in the shelter of a cardoon bush. The
bees deepen the hollow by burrowing in the earth;
and when the spring foliage sheltering it withers
up, they construct a dome-shaped covering of small
sticks, thorns, and leaves bitten into extremely
minute pieces. They sometimes take possession of
a small hole or cavity in the ground, and save
themselves the labour of excavation.

Their architecture closely resembles that of B.
terrestris. They make rudely-shaped oval honey-
cells, varying from half an inch to an inch and a
half in length, the smaller ones being the first

made ; later in the season the old cocoons are utilized for storing honey. The wax is chocolate-coloured, and almost the only difference I can find in the economy of the two species is that the black bee uses a large quantity of wax in plastering the interior of its nest. The egg-cell of the yellow bee always contains from twelve to sixteen eggs ; that of the black bee from ten to fourteen; and the eggs of this species are the largest though the bee is smallest. At the entrance on the edge of the mound one bee is usually stationed, and, when approached, it hums a shrill challenge, and throws itself into a menacing attitude. The sting is exceedingly painful.

One summer I was so fortunate as to discover two nests of the two kinds within twelve yards of each other, and I resolved to watch them very carefully, in order to see whether the two species ever came into collision, as sometimes happens with ants of different species living close together. Several times I saw a yellow bee leave its own nest and hover round or settle on the neighbouring one, upon which the sentinel black bee would attack and drive it off. One day, while watching, I was delighted to see a yellow bee actually enter its neighbour's nest, the sentinel being off duty. In about five minutes' time it came out again and flew away unmolested. I concluded from this that humble-bees, like their relations of the hive, occasionally plunder each other's sweets. On another occasion I found a black bee dead at the entrance of the yellow bees' nest ; doubtless this individual had been caught in the act of stealing honey, and, after

it had been stung to death, it had been dragged
out and left there as a warning to others with like
felonious intentions.

There is one striking difference between the two
species. The yellow bee is inodorous ; the black
bee, when angry and attacking, emits an exceedingly powerful odour : curiously enough, this smell
is identical in character with that made when angry
by all the wasps of the South American genus
Pepris—dark blue wasps with red wings. This
odour at first produces a stinging sensation on the
nerve of smell, but when inhaled in large measure
becomes very nauseating. On one occasion, while
I was opening a nest, several of the bees buzzing
round my head and thrusting their stings through
the veil I wore for protection, gave out so pungent
a smell that I found it unendurable, and was compelled to retreat.

It seems strange that a species armed with a
venomous sting and possessing the fierce courage
of the humble-bee should also have this repulsive
odour for a protection. It is, in fact, as incongruous
as it would be were our soldiers provided with
guns and swords first, and after with phials of
assafœtida to be uncorked in the face of an enemy.

Why, or how, animals came to be possessed of the
power of emitting pestiferous odours is a mystery ;
we only see that natural selection has, in some
instances, chiefly among insects, taken advantage
of it to furnish some of the weaker, more unprotected species with a means of escape from their
enemies. The most striking example I know is that

of a large hairy caterpillar I have found on dry wood in Patagonia, and which, when touched, emits an intensely nauseous effluvium. Happily it is very volatile, but while it lasts it is even more detestable than that of the skunk.

The skunk itself offers perhaps the one instance amongst the higher vertebrates of an animal in which all the original instincts of self-preservation have died out, giving place to this lower kind of protection. All the other members of the family it belongs to are cunning, swift of foot, and, when overtaken, fierce-tempered and well able to defend themselves with their powerful well-armed jaws.

For some occult reason they are provided with a gland charged with a malodorous secretion ; and out of this mysterious liquor Nature has elaborated the skunk's inglorious weapon. The skunk alone when attacked makes no attempt to escape or to defend itself by biting ; but, thrown by its agitation into a violent convulsion, involuntarily discharges its foetid liquor into the face of an opponent. When this animal had once ceased to use so good a weapon as its teeth in defending itself, degenerating at the same time into a slow-moving creature, without fear and without cunning, the strength and vileness of its odour would be continually increased by the cumulative process of natural selection : and how effective the protection has become is shown by the abundance of the species throughout the whole American continent. It is lucky for mankind— especially for naturalists and sportsmen—that other species have not been improved in the same direction.

But what can we say of the common deer of the
pampas (Cervus campestris), the male of which gives
out an effluvium quite as far-reaching although not
so abominable in character as that of the Mephitis?
It comes in disagreeable whiffs to the human
nostril when the perfumer of the wilderness is not
even in sight. Yet it is not a protection; on the
contrary, it is the reverse, and, like the dazzling
white plumage so attractive to birds of prey, a
direct disadvantage, informing all enemies for
leagues around of its whereabouts. It is not, therefore, strange that wherever pumas are found, deer
are never very abundant; the only wonder is that,
like the ancient horse of America, they have not
become extinct.

The gauchos of the pampas, however, give *a
reason* for the powerful smell of the male deer;
and, after some hesitation, I have determined to
set it down here, for the reader to accept or reject,
as he thinks proper. I neither believe nor disbelieve it; for although I do not put great faith
in gaucho natural history, my own observations
have not infrequently confirmed statements of
theirs, which a sceptical person would have regarded
as wild indeed. To give one instance: I heard a
gaucho relate that while out riding he had been
pursued for a considerable distance by a large
spider; his hearers laughed at him for a romancer;
but as I myself had been attacked and pursued,
both when on foot and on horseback, by a large
wolf-spider, common on the pampas, I did not join
in the laugh. They say that the effluvium of C.
campestris is abhorrent to snakes of all kinds, just

as pyrethrum powder is to most insects, and even
go so far as to describe its effect as fatal to them;
according to this, the smell is therefore a protection to the deer.   In places where venomous
snakes are extremely abundant, as in the Sierra
district on the southern pampas of Buenos Ayres,
the gaucho frequently ties a strip of the male
deer's skin, which retains its powerful odour for an
indefinite time, round the neck of a valuable horse
as a protection.   It is certain that domestic animals
are frequently lost here through snake-bites.   The
most common poisonous species—the Craspedo-
cephalus alternatus, called *Vivora de la Cruz* in the
vernacular—has neither bright colour nor warning
rattle to keep off heavy hoofs, and is moreover of
so sluggish a temperament that it will allow itself
to be trodden on before stirring, with the result
that its fangs are not infrequently struck into the
nose or foot of browsing beast.   Considering, then,
the conditions in which C. campestris is placed—
and it might also be supposed that venomous snakes
have in past times been much more numerous than
they are now—it is not impossible to believe that
the powerful smell it emits has been made protective, especially when we see in other species how
repulsive odours have been turned to account by
the principle of natural selection.

   After all, perhaps the wild naturalist of the
pampas knows what he is about when he ties a
strip of deer-skin to the neck of his steed and
turns him loose to graze among the snakes.

   The gaucho also affirms that the deer cherishes
a wonderful animosity against snakes ; that it be-

comes greatly excited when it sees one, and proceeds at once to destroy it ; *they say*, by running round and round it in a circle, emitting its violent smell in larger measure, until the snake dies of suffocation. It is hard to believe that the effect can be so great ; but that the deer is a snake hater and killer is certainly true : in North America, Ceylon, and other districts deer have been observed excitedly leaping on serpents, and killing them with their sharp cutting hoofs.

CHAPTER XII.

A NOBLE WASP.

(*Monedula punctata.*)

NATURALISTS, like kings and emperors, have their favourites, and as my zoological sympathies, which are wider than my knowledge, embrace all classes of beings, there are of course several insects for which I have a special regard; a few in each of the principal orders. My chief favourite among the hymenopteras is the one representative of the curious genus Monedula known in La Plata. It is handsome and has original habits, but it is specially interesting to me for another reason : I can remember the time when it was extremely rare on the pampas, so rare that in boyhood the sight of one used to be a great event to me; and I have watched its rapid increase year by year till it has come to be one of our commonest species. Its singular habits and intelligence give it a still better claim to notice. It is a big, showy, loud-buzzing insect, with pink head and legs, wings with brown reflections, and body encircled with alternate bands of black and pale gold, and has a preference for large composite flowers, on the honey of which it feeds. Its young is, however, an insect-eater ; but the Monedula does not, like other burrowing or sand wasps, put away a store of insects or spiders, partially paralyzed, as a provision for the grub till it reaches the pupa state; it actually supplies the grub with fresh-caught insects as long as food is required, killing the prey it captures outright, and bringing it in to its young; so that its habits, in this particular, are more bird- than wasp-like.

The wasp lays its solitary egg at the extremity of a hole it excavates for itself on a bare hard piece of ground, and many holes are usually found close together. When the grub—for I have never been able to find more than one in a hole—has come out from the egg, the parent begins to bring in insects, carefully filling up the mouth of the hole with loose earth after every visit. Without this precaution, which entails a vast amount of labour, I do not believe one grub out of every fifty would survive, so overrun are these barren spots of ground used as breeding-places with hunting spiders, ants, and tiger-beetles. The grub is a voracious eater, but the diligent mother brings in as much as it can devour. I have often found as many as six or seven insects, apparently fresh killed, and not yet touched by the pampered little glutton, coiled up in the midst of them waiting for an appetite.

The Monedula is an adroit fly-catcher, for though it kills numbers of fire-flies and other insects, flies are always preferred, possibly because they are so little encumbered with wings, and are also more easily devoured. It occasionally captures insects on the wing, but the more usual method is to pounce down on its prey when it is at rest. At one time, before I had learnt their habits, I used

frequently to be startled by two or three or more
of these wasps rushing towards my face, and continuing hovering before it, loudly buzzing, attending
me in my walks about the fields. The reason of
this curious proceeding is that the Monedula preys
largely on stinging flies, having learnt from experience that the stinging fly will generally neglect
its own safety when it has once fastened on a good
spot to draw blood from. When a man or horse
stands perfectly motionless the wasps take no
notice, but the moment any movement is made of
hand, tail, or stamping hoof, they rush to the
rescue, expecting to find a stinging fly. On the
other hand, the horse has learnt to know and value
this fly-scourge, and will stand very quietly with
half a dozen loud wasps hovering in an alarming
manner close to his head, well knowing that every
fly that settles on him will be instantly snatched
away, and that the boisterous Monedula is a better
protection even than the tail—which, by the way,
the horse wears very long in Buenos Ayres.

I have, in conclusion, to relate an incident I once
witnessed, and which does not show the Monedula
in a very amiable light. I was leaning over a gate
watching one of these wasps feeding on a sunflower. A small leaf-cutting bee was hurrying
about with its shrill busy hum in the vicinity, and
in due time came to the sunflower and settled on
it. The Monedula became irritated, possibly at the
shrill voice and bustling manner of its neighbour,
and, after watching it for a few moments on the
flower, deliberately rushed at and drove it off.
The leaf-cutter quickly returned, however—for bees

are always extremely averse to leaving a flower
unexplored—but was again driven away with threats
and demonstrations on the part of the Monedula.
The little thing went off and sunned itself on a leaf
for a time, then returned to the flower, only to be
instantly ejected again. Other attempts were made,

A Bee's Revenge.

but the big wasp now kept a jealous watch on its
neighbour's movements, and would not allow it to
come within several inches of the flower without
throwing itself into a threatening attitude. The
defeated bee retired to sun itself once more, apparently determined to wait for the big tyrant to go
away; but the other seemed to know what was

wanted, and spitefully made up its mind to stay where it was. The leaf-cutter then gave up the contest. Suddenly rising up into the air, it hovered, hawk-like, above the Monedula for a moment, then pounced down on its back, and clung there, furiously biting, until its animosity was thoroughly appeased; then it flew off, leaving the other master of the field certainly, but greatly discomposed, and perhaps seriously injured about the base of the wings. I was rather surprised that they were not cut quite off, for a leaf-cutting bee can use its teeth as deftly as a tailor can his shears.

Doubtless to bees, as to men, revenge is sweeter than honey. But, in the face of mental science, can a creature as low down in the scale of organization as a leaf-cutting bee be credited with anything so intelligent and emotional as deliberate anger and revenge, " which implies the need of retaliation to satisfy the feelings of the person (or bee) offended?" According to Bain (*Mental and Moral Science*) only the highest animals—stags and bulls he mentions— can be credited with the developed form of anger, which he describes as an excitement caused by pain, reaching the centres of activity, and containing an impulse knowingly to inflict suffering on another sentient being. Here, if man only is meant, the spark is perhaps accounted for, but not the barrel of gunpowder. The explosive material is, however, found in the breast of nearly every living creature. The bull—ranking high according to Bain, though I myself should place him nearly on a level mentally

with the majority of the lower animals, both vertebrate and insect—is capable of a wrath exceeding
that of Achilles; and yet the fact that a red rag
can manifestly have no associations, personal or
political, for the bull, shows how unintellectual
his anger must be. Another instance of mis-
directed anger in nature, not quite so familiar as
that of the bull and red rag, is used as an
illustration by one of the prophets : " My heritage
is unto me as a speckled bird; the birds round
about are against it." I have frequently seen the
birds of a thicket gather round some singularly
marked accidental visitor, and finally drive him
with great anger from the neighbourhood. Possibly
association comes in a little here, since any bird,
even a small one, strikingly coloured or marked,
might be looked on as a bird of prey.

The flesh-fly laying its eggs on the carrion-
flower is only a striking instance of the mistakes
all instincts are liable to, never more markedly
than in the inherited tendency to fits of frenzied
excitement : the feeling is frequently excited by
the wrong object, and explodes at inopportune
moments.

CHAPTER XIII.

NATURE'S NIGHT LIGHTS.

(*Remarks about Fireflies and other matters.*)

It was formerly supposed that the light of the firefly (in any family possessing the luminous power)
was a safeguard against the attacks of other insects,
rapacious and nocturnal in their habits. This was
Kirby and Spence's notion, but it might just as well
be Pliny's for all the attention it would receive from
modern entomologists : just at present any observer who lived in the pre-Darwin days is regarded
as one of the ancients. The reasons given for the
notion or theory in the celebrated *Introduction to
Entomology* were not conclusive; nevertheless it
was not an improbable supposition of the authors';
while the theory which has taken its place in recent
zoological writings seems in every way even less
satisfactory.

Let us first examine the antiquated theory, as it
must now be called. By bringing a raptorial insect
and a firefly together, we find that the flashing light
of the latter does actually scare away the former,
and is therefore, for the moment, a protection as
effectual as the camp-fire the traveller lights in a
district abounding with beasts of prey. Notwith-

standing this fact, and assuming that we have here
the whole reason of the existence of the light-
emitting power, a study of the firefly's habits compels us to believe that the insect would be just as
well off without the power as with it. Probably it
experiences some pleasure in emitting flashes of
light during its evening pastimes, but this could
scarcely be considered an advantage in its struggle
for existence, and it certainly does not account for
the possession of the faculty.

About the habits of Pyrophorus, the large tropical
firefly which has the seat of its luminosity on the
upper surface of the thorax, nothing definite appears
to be known; but it has been said that this instinct
is altogether nocturnal. The Pyrophorus is only
found in the sub-tropical portion of the Argentine
country, and I have never met with it. With the
widely-separated Cratomorphus, and the tortoise-
shaped Aspisoma, which emit the light from the
abdomen, I am familiar; one species of Cratomorphus—a long slender insect with yellow wing-
cases marked with two parallel black lines—is "the
firefly" known to every one and excessively abundant in the southern countries of La Plata. This
insect is strictly diurnal in its habits—as much so,
in fact, as diurnal butterflies. They are seen flying
about, wooing their mates, and feeding on composite
and umbelliferous flowers at all hours of the day,
and are as active as wasps during the full glare of
noon. Birds do not feed on them, owing to the
disagreeable odour, resembling that of phosphorus,
which they emit, and probably because they are
found to be uneatable; but their insect enemies are

not so squeamish, and devour them readily, just as they also do the blister-fly, which one would imagine a morsel fitted to disagree with any stomach. One of their enemies is the Monedula wasp ; another, a fly, of the rapacious Asilidæ family ; and this fly is also a wasp in appearance, having a purple body and bright red wings, like a Pepris, and this mimetic resemblance doubtless serves it as a protection against birds. A majority of raptorial insects are, however, nocturnal, and from all these enemies that go about under cover of night, the firefly, as Kirby and Spence rightly conjectured, protects itself, or rather is involuntarily protected, by means of its frequent flashing light. We are thus forced to the conclusion that, while the common house fly and many other diurnal insects spend a considerable portion of the daylight in purely sportive exercises, the firefly, possessing in its light a protection from nocturnal enemies, puts off its pastimes until the evening ; then, when its carnival of two or three hours' duration is over, retires also to rest, putting out its candle, and so exposing itself to the dangers which surround other diurnal species during the hours of darkness. I have spoken of the firefly's pastimes advisedly, for I have really never been able to detect it doing anything in the evening beyond flitting aimlessly about, like house flies in a room, hovering and revolving in company by the hour, apparently for amusement. Thus, the more closely we look at the facts, the more unsatisfactory does the explanation seem. That the firefly should have become possessed of so elaborate a machinery, producing incidentally such splendid results, meraly as a protection against one set of enemies for a portion only of the period during which they are active, is altogether incredible.

The current theory, which we owe to Belt, is a prettier one. Certain insects (also certain Batrachians, reptiles, &c.) are unpalatable to the rapacious kinds; it is therefore a direct advantage to these unpalatable species to be distinguishable from all the persecuted, and the more conspicuous and well-known they are, the less likely are they to be mistaken by birds, insectivorous mammals, &c., for eatable kinds and caught or injured. Hence we find that many such species have acquired for their protection very brilliant or strongly-contrasted colours--warning colours—which insect-eaters come to know.

The firefly, a soft-bodied, slow-flying insect, is easily caught and injured, but it is not fit for food, and, therefore, says the theory, lest it should be injured or killed by mistake, it has a fiery spark to warn enemies—birds, bats, and rapacious insects—that it is uneatable.

The theory of warning colours is an excellent one, but it has been pushed too far. We have seen that one of the most common fireflies is diurnal in habits, or, at any rate, that it performs all the important business of its life by day, when it has neither bright colour nor light to warn its bird enemies ; and out of every hundred species of insect-eating birds at least ninety-nine are diurnal. Raptorial insects, as I have said, feed freely on fireflies, so that the supposed warning is not for them, and it would be hard to believe that the magnificent display made by luminous insects is useful only in preventing accidental injuries to them from a few crepuscular bats and goatsuckers. And to believe even this we should first have to assume that bats and goatsuckers are differently constituted from all other creatures; for in other animals—insects, birds, and mammalians—the appearance of fire by night seems to confuse and frighten, but it certainly cannot be said to *warn*, in the sense in which that word is used when we speak of the brilliant colours of some butterflies, or even of the gestures of some venomous snakes, and of the sounds they emit.

Thus we can see that, while the old theory of Kirby and Spence had some facts to support it, the one now in vogue is purely fanciful. Until some better suggestion is made, it would perhaps be as well to consider the luminous organ as having " no very close and direct relation to present habits of life." About their present habits, however, especially their crepuscular habits, there is yet much to learn. One thing I have observed in them has always seemed very strange to me. Occasionally an individual insect is seen shining with a very large and steady light, or with a light which very gradually decreases and increases in power, and at such times it is less active than at others, remaining for long intervals motionless on the leaves, or moving with a very slow flight. In South America a firefly displaying this abnormal splendour is said to be dying, and it is easy to imagine how such a notion originated. The belief is, however, erroneous, for sometimes, on very rare occasions, all the insects in one place are simultaneously affected in the same way, and at such times they mass themselves together in myriads, as if for migration, or for some other great purpose. Mr. Bigg-Wither, in South Brazil, and D'Albertis, in New Guinea, noticed these firefly gatherings; I also once had the rare good fortune to witness a phenomenon of the kind on a very grand scale. Riding on the pampas one dark evening an hour after sunset, and passing from high ground overgrown with giant thistles to a low plain covered with long grass, bordering a stream of water, I found it all ablaze with myriads of fireflies. I noticed that all the insects gave out an exceptionally large, brilliant light, which shone almost steadily. The long grass was thickly studded with them, while they literally swarmed in the air, all moving up the valley with a singularly slow and languid flight. When I galloped down into this river of phosphorescent fire, my horse plunged and snorted with alarm. I succeeded at length in quieting him, and then rode slowly through, compelled to keep my mouth and eyes closed, so thickly did the insects rain on to my face. The air was laden with the sickening phosphorous smell they emit, but when I had once got free of the broad fiery zone, stretching away on either hand for miles along the moist valley, I stood still and gazed back for some time on a scene the most wonderful and enchanting I have ever witnessed.

The fascinating and confusing effect which the appearance of fire at night has on animals is a most

interesting subject ; and although it is not probable that anything very fresh remains to be said
about it, I am tempted to add here the results of
my own experience.

When travelling by night, I have frequently
been struck with the behaviour of my horse at the
sight of natural fire, or appearance of fire, always
so different from that caused by the sight of fire
artificially created. The steady gleam from the
open window or door of a distant house, or even
the unsteady wind-tossed flame of some lonely
camp-fire, has only served to rouse a fresh spirit in
him and the desire to reach it ; whereas those infrequent displays of fire which nature exhibits, such
as lightning, or the ignis fatuus, or even a cloud of
fireflies, has always produced a disquieting effect.
Experience has evidently taught the domestic horse
to distinguish a light kindled by man from all
others ; and, knowing its character, he is just as
well able as his rider to go towards it without experiencing that confusion of mind caused by a glare
in the darkness, the origin and nature of which is
a mystery. The artificially-lighted fire is to the
horse only the possible goal of the journey, and is
associated with the thought of rest and food. Wild
animals, as a rule, at any rate in thinly-settled
districts, do not know the meaning of any fire ; it
only excites curiosity and fear in them; and they
are most disturbed at the sight of fires made by
man, which are brighter and steadier than most
natural fires. We can understand this sensation
in animals, since we ourselves experience a similar
one (although in a less degree and not associated

with fear) in the effect which mere brightness has on us, both by day and night.

On riding across the monotonous grey Patagonian uplands, where often for hours one sees not the faintest tinge of bright colour, the intense glowing crimson of a cactus-fruit, or the broad shining white bosom of the Patagonian eagle-buzzard (Buteo erythronotus), perched on the summit of a distant bush, has had a strangely fascinating effect on me, so that I have been unable to take my eyes off it as long as it continued before me. Or in passing through extensive desolate marshes, the dazzling white plumage of a stationary egret has exercised the same attraction. At night we experience the sensation in a greater degree, when the silver sheen of the moon makes a broad path on the water; or when a meteor leaves a glowing track across the sky; while a still more familiar instance is seen in the powerful attraction on the sight of glowing embers in a darkened room. The mere brightness, or vividness of the contrast, fascinates the mind; but the effect on man is comparatively weak, owing to his fiery education and to his familiarity with brilliant dyes artificially obtained from nature. How strong this attraction of mere brightness, even where there is no mystery about it, is to wild animals is shown by birds of prey almost invariably singling out white or bright-plumaged birds for attack where bright and sober-coloured kinds are mingled together. By night the attraction is immeasurably greater than by day, and the light of a fire steadily gazed at quickly confuses the mind. The fires which travellers make

for their protection actually serve to attract the
beasts of prey, but the confusion and fear caused by
the bright glare makes it safe for the traveller to
lie down and sleep in the light. Mammals do not
lose their heads altogether, because they are walking
on firm ground where muscular exertion and an
exercise of judgment are necessary at every step ;
whereas birds floating buoyantly and with little
effort through the air are quickly bewildered.
Incredible numbers of migratory birds kill themselves by dashing against the windows of light-
houses ; on bright moonlight nights the voyagers
are comparatively safe ; but during dark cloudy
weather the slaughter is very great; over six
hundred birds were killed by striking a lighthouse
in Central America in a single night. On insects
the effect is the same as on the higher animals : on
the ground they are attracted by the light, but
keep, like wolves and tigers, at a safe distance
from it ; when rushing through the air and unable
to keep their eyes from it they fly into it, or else
revolve about it, until, coming too close, their
wings are singed.

I find that when I am on horseback, going at a
swinging gallop, a bright light affects me far more
powerfully than when I am trudging along on foot.
A person mounted on a bicycle and speeding over
a level plain on a dark night, with nothing to guide
him except the idea of the direction in his mind,
would be to some extent in the position of the
migratory bird. An exceptionally brilliant ignis
fatuus flying before him would affect him as the
gleam of a lamp placed high above the surface

affects the migrants : he would not be able to keep his eyes from it, but would quickly lose the sense of direction, and probably end his career much as the bird does, by breaking his machine and perhaps his bones against some unseen obstruction in the way.

CHAPTER XIV.

SOME time ago, while turning over a quantity of
rubbish in a little-used room, I disturbed a large
black spider. Rushing forth, just in time to save
itself from destruction through the capsizing of a
pile of books, it paused for one moment, took a
swift comprehensive glance at the position, then
scuttled away across the floor, and was lost in an
obscure corner of the room. This incident served
to remind me of a fact I was nearly forgetting, that
England is not a spiderless country. A foreigner,
however intelligent, coming from warmer regions,
might very easily make that mistake. In Buenos
Ayres, the land of my nativity, earth teems with
these interesting little creatures. They abound in
and on the water, they swarm in the grass and
herbage, which everywhere glistens with the silvery
veil they spin over it. Indeed it is scarcely an
exaggeration to say that there is an atmosphere of
spiders, for they are always floating about invisible
in the air; their filmy threads are unfelt when they
fly against you; and often enough you are not even
aware of the little arrested aeronaut hurrying over
your face with feet lighter than the lightest thistle-
down.

It is somewhat strange that although, where
other tribes of living creatures are concerned, I am
something of a naturalist, spiders I have always
observed and admired in a non-scientific spirit, and
this must be my excuse for mentioning the habits
of some spiders without giving their specific names
—an omission always vexing to the severely-techni-
cal naturalist. They have ministered to the love of
the beautiful, the grotesque, and the marvellous in
me; but I have never *collected* a spider, and if I
wished to preserve one should not know how to do
it. I have been "familiar with the face" of these
monsters so long that I have even learnt to love
them; and I believe that if Emerson rightly predicts
that spiders are amongst the things to be expelled
from earth by the perfected man of the future, then
a great charm and element of interest will be lost
to nature. Though loving them, I cannot, of
course, feel the same degree of affection towards all
the members of so various a family. The fairy
gossamer, scarce seen, a creature of wind and sunshine; the gem-like Epeïra in the centre of its
starry web; even the terrestrial Salticus, with its
puma-like strategy, certainly appeal more to our
æsthetic feelings than does the slow heavy Mygale,
looking at a distance of twenty yards away, as he
approaches you, like a gigantic cockroach mounted
on stilts. The rash fury with which the female
wolf-spider defends her young is very admirable;
but the admiration she excites is mingled with other
feelings when we remember that the brave mother
proves to her consort a cruel and cannibal spouse.

Possibly my affection for spiders is due in a great

measure to the compassion I have always felt for
them.   Pity, 'tis said, is akin to love; and who can
help experiencing that tender emotion that considers
the heavy affliction nature has laid on the spiders
in compensation for the paltry drop of venom with
which she, unasked, endowed them!   And here, of
course, I am alluding to the wasps.   These insects,
with a refinement of cruelty, prefer not to kill their
victims outright, but merely maim them, then house
them in cells where the grubs can vivisect them at
leisure.   This is one of those revolting facts the
fastidious soul cannot escape from in warm climates ;
for in and out of open windows and doors, all day
long, all the summer through, comes the busy
beautiful mason-wasp.   A long body, wonderfully
slim at the waist, bright yellow legs and thorax,
and a dark crimson abdomen,—what object can be
prettier to look at ?   But in her life this wasp is
not beautiful.   At home in summer they were the
pests of my life, for nothing would serve to keep
them out.   One day, while we were seated at dinner,
a clay nest, which a wasp had succeeded in complet-
ing unobserved, detached itself from the ceiling and
fell with a crash on to the table, where it was
shattered to pieces, scattering a shower of green
half-living spiders round it.   I shall never forget
the feeling of intense repugnance I experienced at
the sight, coupled with detestation of the pretty
but cruel little architect.   There is, amongst our
wasps, even a more accomplished spider-scourge
than the mason-wasp, and I will here give a brief
account of its habits.   On the grassy pampas, dry
bare spots of soil are resorted to by a class of

spiders that either make or take little holes in the
ground to reside in, and from which they rush forth
to seize their prey. They also frequently sit inside
their dens and patiently wait there for the intrusion
of some bungling insect. Now, in summer, to a
dry spot of ground like this, comes a small wasp,
scarcely longer than a blue-bottle fly, body and
wings of a deep shining purplish blue colour, with
only a white mark like a collar on the thorax. It
flirts its blue wings, hurrying about here and there,
and is extremely active, and of a slender graceful
figure—the type of an assassin. It visits and
explores every crack and hole in the ground, and,
if you watch it attentively, you will at length see
it, on arriving at a hole, give a little start backwards. It knows that a spider lies concealed
within. Presently, having apparently matured a
plan of attack, it disappears into the hole and
remains there for some time. Then, just when you
are beginning to think that the little blue explorer
has been trapped, out it rushes, flying in terror,
apparently, from the spider who issues close behind
in hot pursuit; but, before they are three inches
away from the hole, quick as lightning the wasp
turns on its follower, and the two become locked
together in a deadly embrace. Looking like one
insect, they spin rapidly round for a few moments,
then up springs the wasp — victorious. The
wretched victim is not dead; its legs move a
little, but its soft body is paralyzed, and lies
collapsed, flabby, and powerless as a stranded jelly-
fish. And this is the invariable result of every
such conflict. In other classes of beings, even the

weakest hunted thing occasionally succeeds in inflicting pain on its persecutor, and the small trembling mouse, unable to save itself, can sometimes make the cat shriek with pain ; but there is no weak spot in the wasp's armour, no fatal error of judgment, not even an accident, ever to save the wretched victim from its fate. And now comes the most iniquitous part of the proceeding. When the wasp has sufficiently rested after the struggle, it deliberately drags the disabled spider back into its own hole, and, having packed it away at the extremity, lays an egg alongside of it, then, coming out again, gathers dust and rubbish with which it fills up and obliterates the hole; and, having thus concluded its Machiavellian task, it flies cheerfully off in quest of another victim.

The extensive Epeïra family supply the mason-wasps and other spider-killers with the majority of their victims. These spiders have soft, plump, succulent bodies like pats of butter ; they inhabit trees and bushes chiefly, where their geometric webs betray their whereabouts ; they are timid, comparatively innocuous, and reluctant to quit the shelter of their green bower, made of a rolled-up leaf; so that there are many reasons why they should be persecuted. They exhibit a great variety of curious forms; many are also very richly coloured; but even their brightest hues—orange, silver, scarlet —have not been given without regard to the colouring of their surroundings. Green-leafed bushes are frequented by vividly green Epeïras, but the imitative resemblance does not quite end here. The green spider's method of escape, when the bush is roughly shaken, is to drop itself down on the earth, where it lies simulating death. In falling, it drops just as a green leaf would drop, that is, not quite so rapidly as a round, solid body like a beetle or spider. Now in the bushes there is another Epeïra, in size and form like the last, but differing in colour; for instead of a vivid green, it is of a faded yellowish white—the exact hue of a dead, dried-up leaf. This spider, when it lets itself drop—for it has the same protective habit as the other—falls not so rapidly as a green freshly broken off leaf or as the green spider would fall, but with a slower motion, precisely like a leaf withered up till it has become almost light as a feather. It is not difficult to imagine how this comes about : either a thicker line, or a greater stiffness or tenacity of the viscid fluid composing the web and attached to the point the spider drops from, causes one to fall slower than the other. But how many tentative variations in the stiffness of the web material must there have been before the precise degree was attained enabling the two distinct species, differing in colour, to complete their resemblance to falling leaves—a fresh green leaf in one case and a dead, withered leaf in the other !

The Tetragnatha—a genus of the Epeïra family, and known also in England—are small spiders found on the margin of streams. Their bodies are slender, oblong, and resembling a canoe in shape ; and when they sit lengthwise on a stem or blade of grass, their long, hair-like legs arranged straight before and behind them, it is difficult to detect them, so closely do they resemble a discoloured stripe on the herbage. A species of Tetragnatha

with a curious modification of structure abounds on
the pampas. The long leg of this spider is no
thicker than a bristle from a pig's back, but at the
extremity it is flattened and broad, giving it a
striking resemblance to an oar. These spiders are
only found in herbage overhanging the borders of
streams : they are very numerous, and, having a
pugnacious temper, are incessantly quarrelling ; and
it frequently happens that in these encounters, or
where they are pursuing each other through the
leaves, they drop into the water below. I believe,
in fact, that they often drop themselves purposely
into it as the readiest means of escape when hard
pressed. When this happens, the advantage of the
modified structure of the legs is seen. The fallen
spider, sitting boat-like on the surface, throws out
its long legs, and, dipping the broad ends into the
water, literally rows itself rapidly to land.

The gossamer-spider, most spiritual of living things,
of which there are numerous species, some extremely
beautiful in colouring and markings, is the most
numerous of our spiders. Only when the declining
sun flings a broad track of shiny silver light on the
plain does one get some faint conception of the un-
numbered millions of these buoyant little creatures
busy weaving their gauzy veil over the earth and
floating unseen, like an ethereal vital dust, in the
atmosphere.

This spider carries within its diminutive abdomen
a secret which will possibly serve to vex subtle
intellects for a long time to come ; for it is hard
to believe that merely by mechanical force, even aided
by currents of air, a creature half as big as a barley

grain can instantaneously shoot out filaments twenty or thirty inches long, and by means of which it floats itself in the air.

Naturalists are now giving a great deal of attention to the migrations of birds in different parts of the world: might not insect and spider migrations be included with advantage to science in their observations? The common notion is that the gossamer makes use of its unique method of locomotion only to shift its quarters, impelled by want of food or unfavourable conditions—perhaps only by a roving disposition. I believe that besides these incessant flittings about from place to place throughout the summer the gossamer-spiders have great periodical migrations which are, as a rule, invisible, since a single floating web cannot be remarked, and each individual rises and floats away by itself from its own locality when influenced by the instinct. When great numbers of spiders rise up simultaneously over a large area, then, sometimes, the movement forces itself on our attention ; for at such times the whole sky may be filled with visible masses of floating web. All the great movements of gossamers I have observed have occurred in the autumn, or, at any rate, several weeks after the summer solstice ; and, like the migrations of birds at the same season of the year, have been in a northerly direction. I do not assert or believe that the migratory instinct in the gossamer is universal. In a moist island, like England, for instance, where the condition of the atmosphere is seldom favourable, and where the little voyagers would often be blown by adverse winds to perish far out at sea, it is difficult to believe that such migrations take place. But where they inhabit a vast area of land, as in South America, extending without interruption from the equator to the cold Magellanic regions, and where there is a long autumn of dry, hot weather, then such an instinct as migration might have been developed. For this is not a faculty merely of a few birds : the impulse to migrate at certain seasons affects birds, insects, and even mammals. In a few birds only is it highly developed, but the elementary feeling, out of which the wonderful habit of the swallow has grown, exists widely throughout animated nature. On the continent of Europe it also seems probable that a great autumnal movement of these spiders takes place ; although, I must confess, I have no grounds for this statement, except that the floating gossamer is called in Germany " Der fliegender Summer "—the flying or departing summer.

I have stated that all migrations of gossamers I have witnessed have been in the autumn ; excepting in one instance, these flights occurred when the weather was still hot and dry. The exceptionally late migration was on March 22—a full month after the departure of martins, humming-birds, flycatchers, and most other true bird-migrants. It struck me as being so remarkable, and seems to lend so much force to the idea I have suggested, that I wish to give here an exact copy of the entries made at the time and on the spot in my notebook.

" March 22. This afternoon, while I was out shooting, the gossamer-spiders presented an appearance quite new to me. Walking along a stream

(the Conchitas, near Buenos Ayres), I noticed a
broad white line skirting the low wet ground. This
I found was caused by gossamer web lying in such
quantities over the earth as almost to hide the grass
and thistles under it. The white zone was about
twenty yards wide, and outside it only a few
scattered webs were visible on the grass; its exact
length I did not ascertain, but followed it for about
two miles without finding the end. The spiders
were so numerous that they continually baulked
one another in their efforts to rise in the air. As
soon as one threw out its lines they would become
entangled with those of another spider, lanced out
at the same moment; both spiders would immediately seem to know the cause of the trouble, for
as soon as their lines fouled they would rush
angrily towards each other, each trying to drive
the other from the elevation. Notwithstanding
these difficulties, numbers were continually floating
off on the breeze which blew from the south.

"I noticed three distinct species: one with a
round scarlet body; another, velvet black, with
large square cephalothorax and small pointed abdomen; the third and most abundant kind were of
different shades of olive green, and varied greatly
in size, the largest being fully a quarter of an inch
in length. Apparently these spiders had been
driven up from the low ground along the stream
where it was wet, and had congregated along the
borders of the dry ground in readiness to migrate.

"25th. Went again to visit the spiders, scarcely
expecting to find them, as, since first seeing them,
we have had much wind and rain. To my surprise

I found them in greatly increased numbers : on the
tops of cardoons, posts, and other elevated situations they were literally lying together in heaps.
Most of them were large and of the olive-coloured
species ; their size had probably prevented them
from getting away earlier, but they were now floating off in great numbers, the weather being calm
and tolerably dry. To-day I noticed a new species
with a grey body, elegantly striped with black, and
pink legs—a very pretty spider.

" 26th. Went again to-day and found that the
whole vast army of gossamers, with the exception
of a few stragglers sitting on posts and dry stalks,
had vanished. They had taken advantage of the
short spell of fine weather we are now having, after
an unusually wet and boisterous autumn, to make
their escape."

Here it seemed to me that a conjunction of circumstances—first, the unfavourable season preventing migration at the proper time, and secondly, the
strip of valley out of which the spiders had been
driven to the higher ground till they were massed
together—only served to make visible and evident
that a vast annual migration takes place which we
have only to look closely for to discover.

One of the most original spiders in Buenos Ayres
—mentally original, I mean—is a species of
Pholcus ; a quiet, inoffensive creature found in
houses, and so abundant that they literally swarm
where they are not frequently swept away from
ceilings and obscure corners. Certainly it seems a
poor spider after the dynamical and migratory
gossamer ; but it happens, curiously enough, that a

study of the habits of this dusty domestic creature
leads us incidentally into the realms of fable and
romance. It is remarkable for the extreme length
of its legs, and resembles in colour and general appearance a crane fly, but is double the size of that
insect. It has a singular method of protecting
itself: when attacked or approached even, gathering
its feet together and fastening them to the centre
of its web, it swings itself round and round with
the velocity of a whirligig, so that it appears like a
mist on the web, offering no point for an enemy to
strike at. When a fly is captured the spider
approaches it cautiously and spins a web round it,
continually narrowing the circle it describes, until
the victim is inclosed in a cocoon-like covering.
This is a common method with spiders; but the
intelligence—for I can call it by no other word—of
the Pholcus has supplemented this instinctive pro-
cedure with a very curious and unique habit. The
Pholcus, in spite of its size, is a weak creature,
possessing little venom to despatch its prey with,
so that it makes a long and laborious task of killing
a fly. A fly when caught in a web is a noisy creature, and it thus happens that when the Daddy-
longlegs—as Anglo-Argentines have dubbed this
species—succeeds in snaring a captive the shrill
outrageous cries of the victim are heard for a long
time—often for ten or twelve minutes. This noise
greatly excites other spiders in the vicinity, and
presently they are seen quitting their webs and
hurrying to the scene of conflict. Sometimes the
captor is driven off, and then the strongest or most
daring spider carries away the fly. But where a

large colony are allowed to continue for a long
time in undisturbed possession of a ceiling, when
one has caught a fly he proceeds rapidly to throw a
covering of web over it, then, cutting it away, drops
it down and lets it hang suspended by a line at a
distance of two or three feet from the ceiling. The
other spiders arrive on the scene, and after a short
investigation retreat to their own webs, and when
the coast is clear our spider proceeds to draw up
the captive fly, which is by this time exhausted
with its struggles.

Now, I have repeatedly remarked that all spiders,
when the shrill humming of an insect caught in a
web is heard near them, become agitated, like the
Pholcus, and will, in the same way, quit their own
webs and hurry to the point the sound proceeds
from. This fact convinced me many years ago that
spiders are attracted by the sound of musical in-
struments, such as violins, concertinas, guitars, &c.,
simply because the sound produces the same effect
on them as the shrill buzzing of a captive fly. I
have frequently seen spiders come down walls or
from ceilings, attracted by the sound of a guitar,
softly played ; and by gently touching metal strings,
stretched on a piece of wood, I have succeeded in
attracting spiders on to the strings, within two or
three inches of my fingers ; and I always noticed
that the spiders seemed to be eagerly searching for
something which they evidently expected to find
there, moving about in an excited manner and looking very hungry and fierce. I have no doubt that
Pelisson's historical spider in the Bastille came
down in a mood and with a manner just as ferocious

when the prisoner called it with musical sounds to
be fed.

The spiders I have spoken of up till now are
timid, inoffensive creatures, chiefly of the Epeïra
family; but there are many others exceedingly
high-spirited and, like some of the most touchy
hymenopteras, always prepared to "greatly quarrel"
over matters of little moment. The Mygales, of

Mygale fusca, threatening.

which we have several species, are not to be treated
with contempt. One is extremely abundant on the
pampas, the Mygale fusca, a veritable monster,
covered with dark brown hair, and called in the
vernacular *aranea peluda*—hairy spider. In the
hot month of December these spiders take to roaming about on the open plain, and are then everywhere seen travelling in a straight line with a slow

even pace. They are very great in attitudes, and
when one is approached it immediately throws itself
back, like a pugilist preparing for an encounter,
and stands up so erect on its four hind feet that the
under surface of its body is displayed. Humble-
bees are commonly supposed to carry the palm in
attitudinizing ; and it is wonderful to see the
grotesque motions of these irascible insects when
their nest is approached, elevating their abdomens
and two or three legs at a time, so that they resemble a troupe of acrobats balancing themselves
on their heads or hands, and kicking their legs
about in the air. And to impress the intruder with
the dangerous significance of this display they hum
a shrill warning or challenge, and stab at the air
with their naked stings, from which limpid drops of
venom are seen to exude. These threatening
gestures probably have an effect. In the case of
the hairy spider, I do not think any creature, however stupid, could mistake its meaning when it
stands suddenly up, a figure horribly grotesque ;
then, dropping down on all eights, charges violently
forwards. Their long, shiny black, sickle-shaped
falces are dangerous weapons. I knew a native
woman who had been bitten on the leg, and who,
after fourteen years, still suffered at intervals acute
pains in the limb.

The king of the spiders on the pampas is, however, not a Mygale, but a Lycosa of extraordinary
size, light grey in colour, with a black ring round
its middle. It is active and swift, and irritable to
such a degree that one can scarcely help thinking
that in this species nature has overshot her mark.

When a person passes near one—say, within three
or four yards of its lurking-place—it starts up and
gives chase, and will often follow for a distance of
thirty or forty yards. I came once very nearly
being bitten by one of these savage creatures
Riding at an easy trot over the dry grass, I suddenly
observed a spider pursuing me, leaping swiftly along
and keeping up with my beast. I aimed a blow
with my whip, and the point of the lash struck the
ground close to it, when it instantly leaped upon
and ran up the lash, and was actually within three
or four inches of my hand when I flung the whip
from me.

The gauchos have a very quaint ballad which tells
that the city of Cordova was once invaded by an
army of monstrous spiders, and that the towns-
people went out with beating drums and flags flying
to repel the invasion, and that after firing several
volleys they were forced to turn and fly for their
lives. I have no doubt that a sudden great increase
of the man-chasing spiders, in a year exceptionally
favourable to them, suggested this fable to some
rhyming satirist of the town.

In conclusion of this part of my subject, I will
describe a single combat of a very terrible nature
I once witnessed between two little spiders belonging to the same species. One had a small web
against a wall, and of this web the other coveted
possession. After vainly trying by a series of
strategic movements to drive out the lawful owner,
it rushed on to the web, and the two envenomed
little duellists closed in mortal combat. They did
nothing so vulgar and natural as to make use of

their falces, and never once actually touched each
other, but the fight was none the less deadly.
Rapidly revolving about, or leaping over, or passing
under, each other, each endeavoured to impede or
entangle his adversary, and the dexterity with
which each avoided the cunningly thrown snare,
trying at the same time to entangle its opponent,
was wonderful to see. At length, after this equal
battle had raged for some time, one of the combatants made some fatal mistake, and for a moment
there occurred a break in his motions; instantly
the other perceived his advantage, and began leaping backwards and forwards across his struggling
adversary with such rapidity as to confuse the sight,
producing the appearance of two spiders attacking
a third one lying between them. He then changed
his tactics, and began revolving round and round
his prisoner, and very soon the poor vanquished
wretch—the aggressor, let us hope, in the interests
of justice—was closely wrapped in a silvery cocoon,
which, unlike the cocoon the caterpillar weaves for
itself, was also its winding-sheet.

In the foregoing pages I have thrown together
some of the most salient facts I have noted ; but
the spider-world still remains to me a wonderland
of which I know comparatively nothing. Nor is
any very intimate knowledge of spiders to be got
from books, though numberless lists of new species
are constantly being printed ; for they have not yet
had, like the social bees and ants, many loving and
patient chroniclers of their ways. The Hubers and

Lubbocks have been many; the Moggridges few. But even a very slight study of these most versatile and accomplished of nature's children gives rise to some interesting reflections. One fact that strikes the mind very forcibly is the world-wide distribution of groups of species possessing highly developed instincts. One is the zebra-striped Salticus, with its unique strategy—that is to say, unique amongst spiders. It is said that the Australian savage approaches a kangaroo in the open by getting up in sight of its prey and standing perfectly motionless till he is regarded as an inanimate object, and every time the animal's attention wanders advancing a step or two until sufficiently near to hurl his spear. The Salticus approaches a fly in the same manner, till near enough to make its spring. Another is the Trapdoor spider. Another the Dolomedes, that runs over the surface of the water in pursuit of its prey, and dives down to escape from its enemies; and, strangest of all, the Argyroneta, that has its luminous dwelling at the bottom of streams; and just as a mason carries bricks and mortar to its building, so does this spider carry down bubbles of air from the surface to enlarge its mysterious house, in which it lays its eggs and rears its young. Community of descent must be supposed of species having such curious and complex instincts; but how came these feeble creatures, unable to transport themselves over seas and continents like the aërial gossamer, to be so widely distributed, and inhabiting regions with such different conditions? This can only be attributed to the enormous antiquity of the species, and of this antiquity the earliness in which the instinct manifests itself in the young spiders is taken as evidence.

A more important matter, the intelligence of spiders, has not yet received the attention it deserves. The question of insect intelligence—naturalists are agreed that insects do possess intelligence—is an extremely difficult one ; probably some of our conclusions on this matter will have to be reconsidered. For instance, we regard the Order Hymenoptera as the most intelligent because most of the social insects are included in it ; but it has not yet been proved, probably never will be proved, that the social instincts resulted from intelligence which has "lapsed." Whether ants and bees were more intelligent than other insects during the early stages of their organic societies or not, it will hardly be disputed by any naturalist who has observed insects for long that many solitary species display more intelligence in their actions than those that live in communities.

The nature of the spider's food and the difficulties in the way of providing for their wants impose on them a life of solitude : hunger, perpetual watchfulness, and the sense of danger have given them a character of mixed ferocity and timidity. But these very conditions, which have made it impossible for them to form societies like some insects and progress to a state of things resembling civilization in men, have served to develop the mind that is in a spider, making of him a very clever barbarian. The spider's only weapon of defence—his falces— are as poor a protection against the assaults of his insect foes as are teeth and finger-nails in man employed against wolves, bears, and tigers. And the spider is here even worse off than man, since his enemies are winged and able to sweep down instantly on him from above; they are also protected with an invulnerable shield, and are armed with deadly stings. Like man, also, the spider has a soft, unprotected body, while his muscular strength, compared with that of the insects he has to contend with, is almost *nil*. His position in nature then, with relation to his enemies, is like that of man; only the spider has this disadvantage, that he cannot combine with others for protection. That he does protect himself and maintains his place in nature is due, not to special instincts, which are utterly insufficient, but to the intelligence which supplements them. At the same time this superior cunning is closely related with, and probably results indirectly from, the web he is provided with, and which is almost of the nature of an artificial aid. Let us take the imaginary case of a man-like monkey, or of an arboreal man, born with a cord of great length attached to his waist, which could be either dragged after him or carried in a coil. After many accidents, experience would eventually teach him to put it to some use; practice would make him more and more skilful in handling it, and, indirectly, it would be the means of developing his latent mental faculties. He would begin by using it, as the monkey does its prehensile tail, to swing himself from branch to branch, and finally, to escape from an enemy or in pursuit of his prey, he would be able by means of his cord to drop himself with safety from the tallest trees, or fly down the steepest precipices. He would coil up his cord to make a bed to lie on, and also use it for binding branches together when building himself a refuge. In a close fight, he would endeavour to entangle an adversary, and at last he would learn to make a snare with it to capture his prey. To all these, and to a hundred other uses, the spider has put his web. And when we see him spread his beautiful geometric snare, held by lines fixed to widely separated points, while he sits concealed in his web-lined retreat amongst the leaves where every touch on the far-reaching structure is telegraphed to him by the communicating line faithfully as if a nerve had been touched, we must admire the wonderful perfection to which he has attained in the use of his cord. By these means he is able to conquer creatures too swift and strong for him, and make them his prey. When we see him repairing damages, weighting his light fabric in windy weather with pebbles or sticks, as a fisher weights his net, and cutting loose a captive whose great strength threatens the destruction of the web, then we begin to suspect that he has, above his special instinct, a reason that guides, modifies, and in many ways supplements it. It is not, however, only on these great occasions, when the end is sought by unusual means, that spiders show their intelligence; for even these things might be considered by some as merely parts of one great complex instinct; but at all times, in all things, the observer who watches them closely cannot fail to be convinced that they possess a guiding principle which is not mere instinct. What the stick or stone was to primitive man, when he had made the discovery that by holding it in his hand he greatly increased the force of his blow, the possession of a web has been to the spider in developing that spark of intellect which it possesses in common with all animal organisms.

CHAPTER XV.

MOST people are familiar with the phenomenon of " death-feigning," commonly seen in coleopterous insects, and in many spiders. This highly curious instinct is also possessed by some vertebrates. In insects it is probably due to temporary paralysis occasioned by sudden concussion, for when beetles alight abruptly, though voluntarily, they assume that appearance of death, which lasts for a few moments. Some species, indeed, are so highly sensitive that the slightest touch, or even a sudden menace, will instantly throw them into this motionless, death-simulating condition. Curiously enough, the same causes which produce this trance in slow-moving species, like those of Scarabæus for example, have a precisely contrary effect on species endowed with great activity. Rapacious beetles, when disturbed, scuttle quickly out of sight, and some water-beetles spin about the surface, in circles or zigzag lines, so rapidly as to confuse the eye. Our common long-legged spiders (Pholcus) when approached draw their feet together in the middle of the web, and spin the body round with such velocity as to resemble a whirligig.

Certain mammals and birds also possess the death-simulating instinct, though it is hardly possible to believe that the action springs from the same immediate cause in vertebrates and in insects. In the latter it appears to be a purely physical instinct, the direct result of an extraneous cause, and resembling the motions of a plant. In mammals and birds it is evident that violent emotion, and not the rough handling experienced, is the final cause of the swoon.

Passing over venomous snakes, skunks, and a few other species in which the presence of danger excites only anger, fear has a powerful, and in some cases a disabling, effect on animals; and it is this paralyzing effect of fear on which the death-feigning instinct, found only in a few widely-separated species, has probably been built up by the slow cumulative process of natural selection.

I have met with some curious instances of the paralyzing effect of fear. I was told by some hunters in an outlying district of the pampas of its effect on a jaguar they started, and which took refuge in a dense clump of dry reeds. Though they could see it, it was impossible to throw the lasso over its head, and, after vainly trying to dislodge it, they at length set fire to the reeds. Still it refused to stir, but lay with head erect, fiercely glaring at them through the flames. Finally it disappeared from sight in the black smoke; and when the fire had burnt itself out, it was found, dead and charred, in the same spot.

On the pampas the gauchos frequently take the black-necked swan by frightening it. When the birds are feeding or resting on the grass, two or three men or boys on horseback go quietly to leeward of the flock, and when opposite to it suddenly wheel and charge it at full speed, uttering loud shouts, by which the birds are thrown into such terror that they are incapable of flying, and are quickly despatched.

I have also seen gaucho boys catch the Silver-bill (Lichenops perspicillata) by hurling a stick or stone at the bird, then rushing at it, when it sits perfectly still, disabled by fear, and allows itself to be taken. I myself once succeeded in taking a small bird of another species in the same way.

Amongst mammals our common fox (Canis azaræ), and one of the opossums (Didelphys azaræ), are strangely subject to the death-simulating swoon. For it does indeed seem strange that animals so powerful, fierce, and able to inflict such terrible injury with their teeth should also possess this safe-guard, apparently more suited to weak inactive creatures that cannot resist or escape from an enemy and to animals very low down in the scale of being. When a fox is caught in a trap or run down by dogs he fights savagely at first, but by-and-by relaxes his efforts, drops on the ground, and apparently yields up the ghost. The deception is so well carried out, that dogs are constantly taken in by it, and no one, not previously acquainted with this clever trickery of nature, but would at once pro-nounce the creature dead, and worthy of some praise for having perished in so brave a spirit. Now, when in this condition of feigning death, I am quite sure that the animal does not altogether lose conscious-ness. It is exceedingly difficult to discover any evidence of life in the opossum; but when one withdraws a little way from the feigning fox, and watches him very attentively, a slight opening of the eye may be detected; and, finally, when left to himself, he does not recover and start up like an animal that has been stunned, but slowly and cautiously raises his head first, and only gets up when his foes are at a safe distance. Yet I have seen gauchos, who are very cruel to animals, practise the most barbarous experiments on a captive fox without being able to rouse it into exhibiting any sign of life. This has greatly puzzled me, since, if death-feigning is simply a cunning habit, the animal could not suffer itself to be mutilated without wincing. I can only believe that the fox, though not insensible, as its behaviour on being left to itself appears to prove, yet has its body thrown by extreme terror into that benumbed condition which simulates death, and during which it is unable to feel the tortures practised on it.

The swoon sometimes actually takes place before the animal has been touched, and even when the exciting cause is at a considerable distance. I was once riding with a gaucho, when we saw, on the open level ground before us, a fox, not yet fully grown, standing still and watching our approach. All at once it dropped, and when we came up to the spot it was lying stretched out, with eyes closed, and apparently dead. Before passing on my companion, who said it was not the first time he had seen such a thing, lashed it vigorously with his whip for some moments, but without producing the slightest effect.

The death-feigning instinct is possessed in a very marked degree by the spotted tinamou or common

partridge of the pampas (Nothura maculosa). When
captured, after a few violent struggles to escape, it
drops its head, gasps two or three times, and to all
appearances dies. If, when you have seen this, you
release your hold, the eyes open instantly, and, with
startling suddenness and a noise of wings, it is up
and away, and beyond your reach for ever. Possibly, while your grasp is on the bird it does actually
become insensible, though its recovery from that
condition is almost instantaneous. Birds when
captured do sometimes die in the hand, purely from
terror. The tinamou is excessively timid, and sometimes when birds of this species are chased—for
gaucho boys frequently run them down on horseback—and when they find no burrows or thickets
to escape into, they actually drop down dead on the
plain. Probably, when they feign death in their
captor's hand, they are in reality very near to
death.

CHAPTER XVI.

HUMMING-BIRDS are perhaps the very loveliest things
in nature, and many celebrated writers have exhausted
their descriptive powers in vain efforts to picture
them to the imagination. The temptation was
certainly great, after describing the rich setting of
tropical foliage and flower, to speak at length of
the wonderful gem contained within it; but they
would in this case have been wise to imitate that
modest novel-writer who introduced a blank space
on the page where the description of his matchless
heroine should have appeared. After all that has
been written, the first sight of a living humming-bird,
so unlike in its beauty all other beautiful things,
comes like a revelation to the mind. To give any
true conception of it by means of mere word-painting
is not more impossible than it would be to bottle
up a supply of the " living sunbeams " themselves,
and convey them across the Atlantic to scatter them
in a sparkling shower over the face of England.

Doubtless many who have never seen them in a
state of nature imagine that a tolerably correct idea
of their appearance can be gained from Gould's
colossal monograph. The pictures there, however,
only represent dead humming-birds. A dead robin

is, for purposes of bird-portraiture, as good as a live
robin ; the same may be said of even many brilliant-
plumaged species less aërial in their habits than
humming-birds.   In butterflies the whole beauty is
seldom seen until the insect is dead, or, at any rate,
captive.   It was not when Wallace saw the
Ornithoptera crœsus flying about, but only when
he held it in his hands, and opened its glorious
wings, that the sight of its beauty overcame him so
powerfully.   The special kind of beauty which
makes the first sight of a humming-bird a revelation
depends on the swift singular motions as much as
on the intense gem-like and metallic brilliancy of
the plumage.

The minute exquisite form, when the bird hovers
on misty wings, probing the flowers with its coral
spear, the fan-like tail expanded, and poising
motionless, exhibits the feathers shot with many
hues ; and the next moment vanishes, or all but
vanishes, then reappears at another flower only to
vanish again, and so on successively, showing its
splendours not continuously, but like the intermitted
flashes of the firefly—this forms a picture of airy
grace and loveliness that baffles description.   All
this glory disappears when the bird is dead, and
even when it alights to rest on a bough.   Sitting
still, it looks like an exceedingly attenuated kingfisher, without the pretty plumage of that bird, but
retaining its stiff artificial manner.   No artist has
been so bold as to attempt to depict the bird as it
actually appears, when balanced before a flower the
swift motion of the wings obliterates their form,
making them seem like a mist encircling the body ;

yet it is precisely this formless cloud on which the glittering body hangs suspended, which contributes most to give the humming-bird its wonderful sprite-like or extra-natural appearance. How strange, then, to find bird-painters persisting in their efforts to show the humming-bird flying! When they draw it stiff and upright on its perch the picture is honest, if ugly; the more ambitious representation is a delusion and a mockery.

Coming to the actual colouring—the changeful tints that glow with such intensity on the scale-like feathers, it is curious to find that Gould seems to have thought that all difficulties here had been successfully overcome. The "new process" he spoke so confidently about might no doubt be used with advantage in reproducing the coarser metallic reflections on a black plumage, such as we see in the corvine birds; but the glittering garment of the humming-bird, like the silvery lace woven by the Epeïra, gemmed with dew and touched with rainbow-coloured light, has never been and never can be imitated by art.

On this subject one of the latest observers of humming-birds, Mr. Everard im Thurn, in his work on British Guiana, has the following passage:—
"Hardly more than one point of colour is in reality ever visible in any one humming-bird at one and the same time, for each point only shows its peculiar and glittering colour when the light falls upon it from a particular direction. A true representation of one of these birds would show it in somewhat sombre colours, except just at the one point which, when the bird is in the position chosen

for representation, meets the light at the requisite
angle, and that point alone should be shown in full
brilliance of colour. A flowery shrub is sometimes
seen surrounded by a cloud of humming-birds, all
of one species, and each, of course, in a different
position. If someone would draw such a scene
as that, showing a different detail of colour in each
bird, according to its position, then some idea of
the actual appearance of the bird might be given
to one who had never seen an example."

It is hardly to be expected that anyone will carry
out the above suggestion, and produce a monograph
with pages ten or fifteen feet wide by eighteen feet
long, each one showing a cloud of humming-birds
of one species flitting about a flowery bush; but
even in such a picture as that would be, the birds,
suspended on unlovely angular projections instead
of "hazy semicircles of indistinctness," and each
with an immovable fleck of brightness on the otherwise sombre plumage, would be as unlike living
humming-birds as anything in the older monographs.

Whether the glittering iridescent tints and
singular ornaments for which this family is famous
result from the cumulative process of conscious or
voluntary sexual selection, as Darwin thought,
or are merely the outcome of a superabundant
vitality, as Dr. A. R. Wallace so strongly maintains,
is a question which science has not yet answered
satisfactorily. The tendency to or habit of varying
in the direction of rich colouring and beautiful or
fantastic ornament, might, for all we know to the
contrary, have descended to humming-birds from

some diminutive, curiously-shaped, bright-tinted,
flying reptile of arboreal habits that lived in some
far-off epoch in the world's history. It is not, at
all events, maintained by anyone that *all* birds
sprang originally from one reptilian stock; and the
true position of humming-birds in a natural classi-
fication has not yet been settled, for no intermediate
forms exist connecting them with any other group.
To the ordinary mind they appear utterly unlike all
other feathered creatures, and as much entitled to
stand apart as, for instance, the pigeon and ostrich
families. It has been maintained by some writers
that they are anatomically related to the swifts,
although the differences separating the two families
appear so great as almost to stagger belief in this
notion. Now, however, the very latest authority
on this subject, Dr. Schufeldt, has come to the
conclusion that swifts are only greatly modified
Passeres, and that the humming-birds should form
an order by themselves.

Leaving this question, and regarding them simply
with the ornithological eye that does not see far
below the surface of things, when we have sufficiently
admired the unique beauty and marvellous velocity
of humming-birds, there is little more to be said
about them. They are lovely to the eye—in-
describably so ; and it is not strange that Gould
wrote rapturously of the time when he was at length
"permitted to revel in the delight of seeing the
humming-bird in a state of nature." The feeling,
he wrote, which animated him with regard to these
most wonderful works of creation it was impossible
to describe, and could only be appreciated by those

who have made natural history a study, and who " pursue the investigations of her charming mysteries with ardour and delight." This we can understand ; but to what an astonishing degree the feeling was carried in him, when, after remarking that enthusiasm and excitement with regard to most things in life become lessened and eventually deadened by time in most of us, he was able to add, " not so, however, I believe, with those who take up the study of the Family of Humming-birds ! " It can only be supposed that he regarded natural history principally as a " science of dead animals— a *necrology*," and collected humming-birds just as others collect Roman coins, birds' eggs, old weapons, or blue china, their zeal in the pursuit and faith in its importance increasing with the growth of their treasures, until they at last come to believe that though all the enthusiasms and excitements which give a zest to the lives of other men fade and perish with time, it is not so with their particular pursuit.

The more rational kind of pleasure experienced by the ornithologist in studying habits and disposition no doubt results in a great measure from the fact that the actions of the feathered people have a savour of intelligence in them. Whatever his theory or conviction about the origin of instincts may happen to be, or even if he has no convictions on the subject, it must nevertheless seem plain to him that intelligence is, after all, in most cases, the guiding principle of life, supplementing and modifying habits to bring them into closer harmony with the environment, and enlivening every day with countless little acts which result from judgment and experience, and form no part of the inherited complex instincts. The longer he observes any one species or individual, the more does he find in it to reward his attention ; this is not the case, however, with humming-birds, which possess the avian body but do not rank mentally with birds. The pleasure one takes in their beauty soon evaporates, and is succeeded by no fresh interest, so monotonous and mechanical are all their actions ; and we accordingly find that those who are most familiar with them from personal observation have very little to say about them. A score of humming-birds, of as many distinct species, are less to the student of habits than one little brown-plumaged bird haunting his garden or the rush-bed of a neighbouring stream; and, doubtless, for a reason similar to that which makes a lovely human face uninformed by intellect seem less permanently attractive than many a homelier countenance. He grows tired of seeing the feathered fairies per- petually weaving their aërial ballet-dance about the flowers, and finds it a relief to watch the little finch or wren or flycatcher of shy temper and obscure protective colouring. Perhaps it possesses a graceful form and melodious voice to give it æsthetic value, but even without such accessories he can observe it day by day with increasing interest and pleasure ; and it only adds piquancy to the feeling to know that the little bird also watches him with a certain amount of intelligent curiosity and a great deal of suspicion, and that it studiously endeavours to conceal from him all the little secrets of its life which he is bent on discovering.

It has frequently been remarked that humming-birds are more like insects than birds in disposition. Some species, on quitting their perch, perform wide bee-like circles about the tree before shooting away in a straight line. Their aimless attacks on other species approaching or passing near them, even on large birds like hawks and pigeons, is a habit they have in common with many solitary wood-boring bees. They also, like dragon-flies and other insects, attack each other when they come together while feeding; and in this case their action strangely resembles that of a couple of butterflies, as they revolve about each other and rise vertically to a great height in the air. Again, like insects, they are undisturbed at the presence of man while feeding, or even when engaged in building and incubation; and like various solitary bees, wasps, &c., they frequently come close to a person walking or standing, to hover suspended in the air within a few inches of his face; and if then struck at they often, insect-like, return to circle round his head. All other birds, even those which display the least versatility, and in districts where man is seldom seen, show as much caution as curiosity in his presence; they recognize in the upright unfamiliar form a living being and a possible enemy. Mr. Whiteley, who observed humming-birds in Peru, says it is an amusing sight to watch the Lesbia nuna attempting to pass to a distant spot in a straight line during a high wind, which, acting on the long tail feathers, carries it quite away from the point aimed at. Insects presenting a large surface to the wind are always blown from their course in the

same way, for even in the most windy districts they
never appear to learn to guide themselves; and I
have often seen a butterfly endeavouring to reach
an isolated flower blown from it a dozen times
before it finally succeeded or gave up the contest.
Birds when shaping their course, unless young and
inexperienced, always make allowance for the force
of the wind. Humming-birds often fly into open
rooms, impelled apparently by a fearless curiosity,
and may then be chased about until they drop exhausted or are beaten down and caught, and, as
Gould says, "if then taken into the hand, they
almost immediately feed on any sweet, or pump up
any liquid that may be offered to them, without
betraying either fear or resentment at the previous
treatment." Wasps and bees taken in the same
way endeavour to sting their captor, as most people
know from experience, nor do they cease struggling
violently to free themselves; but the dragon-fly is
like the humming-bird, and is no sooner caught
after much ill-treatment, than it will greedily devour
as many flies and mosquitoes as one likes to offer
it. Only in beings very low in the scale of nature
do we see the instinct of self-preservation in this
extremely simple condition, unmixed with reason or
feeling, and so transient in its effects. The same
insensibility to danger is seen when humming-birds
are captured and confined in a room, and when,
before a day is over, they will flutter about their
captor's face and even take nectar from his lips.

Some observers have thought that humming-
birds come nearest to humble-bees in their actions.
I do not think so. Mr. Bates writes : " They do

not proceed in that methodical manner which bees
follow, taking the flowers seriatim, but skip about
from one part of a tree to another in the most
capricious manner." I have observed humble-bees
a great deal, and feel convinced that they are
among the most highly intelligent of the social
hymenoptera. Humming-birds, to my mind, have
a much closer resemblance to the solitary wood-
boring bees and to dragon-flies. It must also be
borne in mind that insects have very little time in
which to acquire experience, and that a large
portion of their life, in the imago state, is taken up
with the complex business of reproduction.

The Trochilidæ, although confined to one continent, promise to exceed all other families—even
the cosmopolitan finches and warblers—in number
of species. At present over five hundred are
known, or as many as all the species of birds in
Europe together; and good reasons exist for believing that very many more—not less perhaps
than one or two hundred species—yet remain to be
discovered. The most prolific region, and where
humming-birds are most highly developed, is known
to be West Brazil and the eastern slopes of the
Bolivian and Peruvian Andes. This is precisely
the least known portion of South America; the
few naturalists and collectors who have reached it
have returned laden with spoil, to tell us of a
region surpassing all others in the superabundance
and beauty of its bird life. Nothing, however,
which can be said concerning these vast unexplored
areas of tropical mountain and forest so forcibly
impresses us with the idea of the unknown riches

contained in them as the story of the Loddigesia mirabilis. This is perhaps the most wonderful humming-bird known, and no one who had not previously seen it figured could possibly form an idea of what it is like from a mere description. An outline sketch of it would probably be taken by most people as a fantastic design representing a

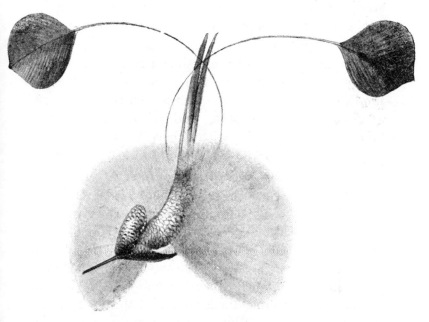

Loddigesia Mirabilis.

bird-form in combination with leaves, in size and shape resembling poplar leaves, but on leaf-stalks of an impossible length, curving and crossing each other so as to form geometrical figures unlike anything in nature. Yet this bird (a single specimen) was obtained in Peru half a century ago, and for upwards of twenty years after its discovery

Gould tried to obtain others, offering as much as fifty pounds for one; but no second specimen ever gladdened his eyes, nor was anything more heard of it until Stolzmann refound it in the year 1880. The addition of many new species to the long list would, however, be a matter of small interest, unless fresh facts concerning their habits and structure were at the same time brought to light; but we can scarcely expect that the as yet unknown species will supply any link connecting the Trochilidæ with other existing families of birds. The eventual conclusion will perhaps be that this family has come down independently from an exceedingly remote past, and with scarcely any modification. While within certain very narrow limits humming-birds vary more than other families, outside of these limits they appear relatively stationary; and, conversely, other birds exhibit least variability in the one direction in which humming-birds vary excessively. On account of a trivial difference in habit they have sometimes been separated in two sub-families: the Phaëthornithinæ, found in shady tropical forests; and the Trochilinæ, comprising humming-birds which inhabit open sunny places—and to this division they mostly belong. In both of these purely arbitrary groups, however, the aërial habits and manner of feeding poised in the air are identical, although the birds living in shady forests, where flowers are scarce, obtain their food principally from the under surfaces of leaves. In their procreant habits the uniformity is also very great. In all cases the nest is small, deep, cup-shaped, or conical, composed of soft felted materials, and lined inside with vegetable down. The eggs are white, and never exceed two in number. Broadly speaking, they resemble each other as closely in habits as in structure; the greatest differences in habit in the most widely separated genera being no greater than may be found in two wrens or sparrows of the same genus.

This persistence of character in humming-birds, both as regards structure and habit, seems the more remarkable when we consider their very wide distribution over a continent so varied in its conditions, and where they range from the lowest levels to the limit of perpetual snow on the Andes, and from the tropics to the wintry Magellanic district; also that a majority of genera inhabit very circumscribed areas—these facts, as Dr. Wallace remarks, clearly pointing to a very high antiquity.

It is perhaps a law of nature that when a species (or group) fits itself to a place not previously occupied, and in which it is subject to no opposition from beings of its own class, or where it attains so great a perfection as to be able easily to overcome all opposition, the character eventually loses its original plasticity, or tendency to vary, since improvement in such a case would be superfluous, and becomes, so to speak, crystallized in that form which continues thereafter unaltered. It is, at any rate, clear that while all other birds rub together in the struggle for existence, the humming-bird, owing to its aërial life and peculiar manner of seeking its food, is absolutely untouched by this kind of warfare, and is accordingly as far removed

from all competition with other birds as the solitary
savage is removed from the struggle of life affecting and modifying men in crowded communities.
The lower kind of competition affecting humming-
birds, that with insects and, within the family, of
species with species, has probably only served to
intensify their unique characteristics, and, perhaps,
to lower their intelligence.

Not only are they removed from that indirect
struggle for existence which acts so powerfully on
other families, but they are also, by their habits
and the unequalled velocity of their flight, placed
out of reach of that direct war waged on all other
small birds by the rapacious kinds—birds, mammals,
and reptiles. One result of this immunity is that
humming-birds are excessively numerous, albeit such
slow breeders; for, as we have seen, they only lay
two eggs, and not only so, but the second egg is
often dropped so long after incubation has begun
in the first that only one is really hatched. Yet
Belt expressed the opinion that in Nicaragua, where
he observed humming-birds, they out-numbered all
the other birds together. Considering how abundant birds of all kinds are in that district, and that
most of them have a protective colouring and lay
several eggs, it would be impossible to accept such
a statement unless we believed that humming-birds
have, practically, no enemies.

Another result of their immunity from persecution is the splendid colouring and strange and
beautiful feather ornaments distinguishing them
above all other birds; and excessive variation in
this direction is due, it seems to me, to the very

causes which serve to check variation in all other
directions. In their plumage, as Martin long ago
wrote, nature has strained at every variety of effect
and revelled in an infinitude of modifications. How
wonderful their garb is, with colours so varied, so
intense, yet seemingly so evanescent!—the glittering mantle of powdered gold ; the emerald green
that changes to velvet black; ruby reds and
luminous scarlets ; dull bronze that brightens and
burns like polished brass, and pale neutral tints
that kindle to rose and lilac-coloured flame. And
to the glory of prismatic colouring are added feather
decorations, such as the racket-plumes and downy
muffs of Spathura, the crest and frills of Lophornis,
the sapphire gorget burning on the snow-white
breast of Oreotrochilus, the fiery tail of Cometes,
and, amongst grotesque forms, the long pointed
crest-feathers, representing horns, and flowing
white beard adorning the piebald goat-like face of
Oxypogon.

Excessive variation in this direction is checked
in nearly all other birds by the need of a protective
colouring, few kinds so greatly excelling in strength
and activity as to be able to maintain their existence without it. Bright feathers constitute a
double danger, for not only do they render their
possessor conspicuous, but, just as the butterfly
chooses the gayest flower, so do hawks deliberately
single out from many obscure birds the one with
brilliant plumage ; but the rapacious kinds do not
waste their energies in the vain pursuit of humming-
birds. These are in the position of neutrals, free
to range at will amidst the combatants, insulting

all alike, and flaunting their splendid colours with impunity. They are nature's favourites, endowed with faculties bordering on the miraculous, and all other kinds, gentle or fierce, ask only to be left alone by them.

CHAPTER XVII.

THE CRESTED SCREAMER.

(*Chauna chavarria.*)

AMONGST the feathered notables from all parts of the world found gathered at the Zoological Gardens in London is the Crested Screamer from South America. It is in many respects a very singular species, and its large size, great strength, and majestic demeanour, with the surprising docility and intelligence it displays when domesticated, give it a character amongst birds somewhat like that of the elephant amongst mammals. Briefly and roughly to describe it: in size it is like a swan, in shape like a lapwing, only with a powerful curved gallinaceous beak. It is adorned with a long pointed crest and a black neck-ring, the plumage being otherwise of a pale slaty blue, while the legs and the naked skin about the eyes are bright red. On each wing, in both sexes, there are two formidable spurs; the first one, on the second joint, is an inch and a half long, nearly straight, triangular, and exceedingly sharp; the second spur, on the last joint, being smaller, broad, and curved, and roughly resembling in shape and size a lion's claw. There is another striking peculiarity. The skin is *emphy-*

sematous—that is, bloated and yielding to pressure.
It crackles when touched, and the surface, when
the feathers are removed, presents a swollen bubbly
appearance; for under the skin there is a layer of
air-bubbles extending over the whole body and even
down the legs under the horny tesselated skin to
the toes, the legs thus having a somewhat massive
appearance.

And now just a few words about the position
of the screamer in systematic zoology. It is placed
in the Family Palamedeidæ, which contains only
three species, but about the Order it belongs to
there is much disagreement. It was formerly
classed with the rails, and in popular books of
Natural History still keeps its place with them.
" Now the rail-tribe," says Professor Parker, speaking on this very matter, " has for a long time been
burdened (on paper) with a very false army list.
Everything alive that has had the misfortune to be
possessed of large unwieldy feet has been added to
this feeble-minded cowardly group, until it has
become a mixed multitude with discordant voices
and with manners and customs having no consonance
or relation." He takes the screamer from the rail-
tribe and classes it with the geese (as also does
Professor Huxley), and concludes his study with
these words :—" Amongst living birds there is not
one possessing characters of higher interest, none
that I am acquainted with come nearer, in some
important points, to the lizard ; and there are parts
of the organization which make it very probable
that it is one of the nearest living relations of the
marvellous *Archæopteryx* "—an intermediate form

between birds and reptiles belonging to the Upper Jurassic period.

The screamer's right to dwell with the geese has not been left unchallenged. The late Professor Garrod finds that " from considerations of pterylosis, visceral anatomy, myology, and osteology the screamer cannot be placed along with the Anserine birds." He finds that in some points it resembles the ostrich and rhea, and concludes : " It seems therefore to me that, summing these results, the screamer must have sprung from the primary avian stock as an independent offshoot at much the same time as did most of the other important families." This time, he further tells us, was when there occurred a general break-up of the ancient terrestrial bird-type, when the acquisition of wings brought many intruders into domains already occupied, calling forth a new struggle for existence, and bringing out many special qualities by means of natural selection.

With this archæological question I have little to do, and only quote the above great authorities to show that the screamer appears to be nearly the last descendant of an exceedingly ancient family, with little or no relationship to other existing families, and that its pedigree has been hopelessly lost in the night of an incalculable antiquity. I have only to speak of the bird as a part of the visible world and as it appears to the non-scientific lover of nature ; for, curiously enough, while anatomists have been laboriously seeking for the screamer's affinities in that " biological field which is as wide as the earth and deep as the sea," travellers and ornithologists have told us almost nothing about its strange character and habits.

Though dressed with Quaker-like sobriety, and without the elegance of form distinguishing the swan or peacock, this bird yet appeals to the æsthetic feelings in man more than any species 1 am acquainted with. Voice is one of its strong points, as one might readily infer from the name : never-

Crested Screamer.

theless the name is not an appropriate one, for though the bird certainly does scream, and that louder than the peacock, its scream is only a powerful note of alarm uttered occasionally, while the notes uttered at intervals in the night, or in the day-time, when it soars upwards like the lark of some far-off imaginary epoch in the world's history when all things, larks included, were on a gigantic scale, are, properly speaking, singing notes and in quality utterly unlike screams. Sometimes when walking across Regent's Park I hear the resounding cries of the bird confined there attempting to sing; above the concert of cranes, the screams of eagles and macaws, the howling of dogs and wolves and the muffled roar of lions, one can hear it all over the park. But those loud notes only sadden me. Exile and captivity have taken all joyousness from the noble singer, and a moist climate has made him hoarse; the long clear strains are no more, and he hurries through his series of confused shrieks as quickly as possible, as if ashamed of the performance. A lark singing high up in a sunny sky and a lark singing in a small cage hanging against a shady wall in a London street produce very different effects; and the spluttering medley of shrill and harsh sounds from the street singer scarcely seems to proceed from the same kind of bird as that matchless melody filling the blue heavens. There is even a greater difference in the notes of the crested screamer when heard in Regent's Park and when heard on the pampas, where the bird soars upwards until its bulky body disappears from sight, and from that vast elevation pours down a perpetual rain of jubilant sound.

Screamer being a misnomer, I prefer to call the bird by its vernacular name of *chajá*, or *chakar*, a more convenient spelling.

With the chakar the sexes are faithful, even in very large flocks the birds all being ranged in couples. When one bird begins to sing its partner immediately joins, but with notes entirely different in quality. Both birds have some short deep notes,

the other notes of the female being long powerful
notes with a trill in them; but over them sounds
the clear piercing voice of the male, ringing forth
at the close with great strength and purity. The
song produces the effect of harmony, but, comparing
it with human singing, it is less like a *duo* than a
terzetto composed of bass, contralto, and soprano.

At certain times, in districts favourable to them,
the chakars often assemble in immense flocks,
thousands of individuals being sometimes seen congregated together, and in these gatherings the birds
frequently all sing in concert. They invariably—
though without rising—sing at intervals during the
night, "counting the hours," as the gauchos say;
the first song being at about nine o'clock, the
second at midnight, and the third just before dawn,
but the hours vary in different districts.

I was once travelling with a party of gauchos
when, about midnight, it being intensely dark, a
couple of chakars broke out singing right ahead of
us, thus letting us know that we were approaching
a watercourse, where we intended refreshing our
horses. We found it nearly dry, and when we
rode down to the rill of water meandering over the
broad dry bed of the river, a flock of about a thousand chakars set up a perfect roar of alarm notes,
all screaming together, with intervals of silence
after; then they rose up with a mighty rush of
wings. They settled down again a few hundred
yards off, and all together burst forth in one of
their grand midnight songs, making the plains echo
for miles around.

There is something strangely impressive in these

spontaneous outbursts of a melody so powerful from
one of these large flocks, and though accustomed
to hear these birds from childhood, I have often
been astonished at some new effect produced by a
large multitude singing under certain conditions.
Travelling alone one summer day, I came at noon
to a lake on the pampas called Kakel—a sheet
of water narrow enough for one to see across.
Chakars in countless numbers were gathered along
its shores, but they were all ranged in well-defined
flocks, averaging about five hundred birds in each
flock. These flocks seemed to extend all round
the lake, and had probably been driven by the
drought from all the plains around to this spot.
Presently one flock near me began singing, and
continued their powerful chant for three or four
minutes ; when they ceased the next flock took up
the strains, and after it the next, and so on until
the notes of the flocks on the opposite shore came
floating strong and clear across the water—then
passed away, growing fainter and fainter, until
once more the sound approached me travelling
round to my side again. The effect was very
curious, and I was astonished at the orderly way
with which each flock waited its turn to sing,
instead of a general outburst taking place after the
first flock had given the signal. On another occasion I was still more impressed, for here the largest
number of birds I have ever found congregated at
one place all sung together. This was on the
southern pampas, at a place called Gualicho, where
I had ridden for an hour before sunset over a
marshy plain where there was still much standing

water in the rushy pools, though it was at the
height of the dry season.   This whole plain was
covered with an endless flock of chakars, not in
close order, but scattered about in pairs and small
groups.   In this desolate spot I found a small
rancho inhabited by a gaucho and his family, and I
spent the night with them.   The birds were all
about the house, apparently as tame as the domestic
fowls, and when I went out to look for a spot for
my horse to feed on, they would not fly away from
me, but merely moved a few steps out of my path
About nine o'clock we were eating supper in the
rancho when suddenly the entire multitude of birds
covering the marsh for miles around burst forth
into a tremendous evening song.   It is impossible
to describe the effect of this mighty rush of sound ;
but let the reader try to imagine half-a-million
voices, each far more powerful than that one which
makes itself heard all over Regent's Park, bursting
forth on the silent atmosphere of that dark lonely
plain.   One peculiarity was that in this mighty
noise, which sounded louder than the sea thundering on a rocky coast, I seemed to be able to distinguish hundreds, even thousands, of individual
voices.   Forgetting my supper, I sat motionless
and overcome with astonishment, while the air, and
even the frail rancho, seemed to be trembling in
that tempest of sound.   When it ceased my host
remarked with a smile, " We are accustomed to
this, señor—every evening we have this concert."
It was a concert well worth riding a hundred miles
to hear.   But the chakar country is just now in a
transitional state, and the precise conditions which

made it possible for birds so large in size to form such immense congregations are rapidly passing away. In desert places, the bird subsists chiefly on leaves and seeds of aquatic plants; but when the vast level area of the pampas was settled by man, the ancient stiff grass-vegetation gave place to the soft clovers and grasses of Europe, and to this new food the birds took very kindly. Other circumstances also favoured their increase. They were never persecuted, for the natives do not eat them, though they are really very good—-the flesh being something like wild goose in flavour. A *higher* civilization is changing all this : the country is becoming rapidly overrun with emigrants, especially by Italians, the pitiless enemies of all bird-life.

The chakars, like the skylark, love to soar upwards when singing, and at such times when they have risen till their dark bulky bodies appear like floating specks on the blue sky, or until they disappear from sight altogether, the notes become wonderfully etherealized by distance to a soft silvery sound, and it is then very delightful to listen to them.

It seems strange that so ponderous a fowl with only six feet and a half spread of wings should possess a power of soaring equal to that of vultures and eagles. Even the vulture with its marvellous wing power soars chiefly from necessity, and when its crop is full finds no pleasure in "scaling the heavens by invisible stairs." The chakar leaves its grass-plot after feeding and soars purely for re-creation, taking so much pleasure in its aërial

exercises that in bright warm weather, in winter
and spring, it spends a great part of the day in the
upper regions of the air. On the earth its air is
grave and its motions measured and majestic, and
it rises with immense labour, the wings producing
a sound like a high wind. But as the bird mounts
higher, sweeping round as it ascends, just as
vultures and eagles do, it gradually appears to
become more buoyant, describing each succeeding
circle with increasing grace. I can only account
for this magnificent flight, beginning so laboriously,
by supposing that the bubble space under the skin
becomes inflated with an air lighter than atmospheric air, enabling a body so heavy with wings
disproportionately short to float with such ease and
evident enjoyment at the vast heights to which the
bird ascends. The heavenward flight of a large
bird is always a magnificent spectacle ; that of the
chakar is peculiarly fascinating on account of the
resounding notes it sings while soaring, and in
which the bird seems to exult in its sublime power
and freedom.

I was once very much surprised at the behaviour
of a couple of chakars during a thunderstorm. On
a still sultry day in summer I was standing watching masses of black cloud coming rapidly over the
sky, while a hundred yards from me stood the two
birds also apparently watching the approaching
storm with interest. Presently the edge of the
cloud touched the sun, and a twilight gloom fell on
the earth. The very moment the sun disappeared
the birds rose up and soon began singing their long-
resounding notes, though it was loudly thundering

at the time, while vivid flashes of lightning lit the
black cloud overhead at short intervals. I watched
their flight and listened to their notes, till suddenly
as they made a wide sweep upwards they disappeared in the cloud, and at the same moment
their voices became muffled, and seemed to come
from an immense distance. The cloud continued
emitting sharp flashes of lightning, but the birds
never reappeared, and after six or seven minutes
once more their notes sounded loud and clear above
the muttering thunder. I suppose they had passed
through the cloud into the clear atmosphere above
it, but I was extremely surprised at their fearless-
ness ; for as a rule when soaring birds see a storm
coming they get out of its way, flying before it or
stooping to the earth to seek shelter of some kind,
for most living things appear to have a wholesome
dread of thunder and lightning.

When taken young the chakar becomes very
tame and attached to man, showing no inclination
to go back to a wild life. There was one kept at an
estancia called Mangrullos, on the western frontier
of Buenos Ayres, and the people of the house gave
me a very curious account of it. The bird was a
male, and had been reared by a soldier's wife at a
frontier outpost called La Esperanza, about twenty-
five miles from Mangrullos. Four years before I
saw the bird the Indians had invaded the frontier,
destroying the Esperanza settlement and all the
estancias for some leagues around. For some
weeks after the invasion the chakar wandered about
the country, visiting all the ruined estancias, apparently in quest of human beings, and on arriving

at Mangrullos, which had not been burnt and was
still inhabited, it settled down at once and never
afterwards showed any disposition to go away. It
was extremely tame, associating by day with the
poultry, and going to roost with them at night on
a high perch, probably for the sake of companionship, for in a wild state the bird roosts on the
ground. It was friendly towards all the members
of the household except one, a peon, and against
this person from the first the bird always displayed the greatest antipathy, threatening him
with its wings, puffing itself out, and hissing like
an angry goose. The man had a swarthy, beardless
face, and it was conjectured that the chakar associated him in its mind with the savages who had
destroyed its early home.

Close to the house there was a lagoon, never
dry, which was frequently visited by flocks of wild
chakars. Whenever a flock appeared the tame bird
would go out to join them ; and though the chakars
are mild-tempered birds and very rarely quarrel,
albeit so well provided with formidable weapons,
they invariably attacked the visitor with great fury,
chasing him back to the house, and not ceasing
their persecutions till the poultry-yard was reached.
They appeared to regard this tame bird that dwelt
with man as a kind of renegade, and hated him
accordingly.

Before he had been long at the estancia it began
to be noticed that he followed the broods of young
chickens about very assiduously, apparently taking
great interest in their welfare, and even trying to
entice them to follow him. A few newly-hatched

chickens were at length offered to him as an experiment, and he immediately took charge of them with every token of satisfaction, conducting them about in search of food and imitating all the actions of a hen. Finding him so good a nurse, large broods were given to him, and the more the foster-chickens were the better he seemed pleased. It was very curious to see this big bird with thirty or forty little animated balls of yellow cotton following him about, while he moved majestically along, setting down his feet with the greatest care not to tread on them, and swelling himself up with jealous anger at the approach of a cat or dog.

The intelligence, docility, and attachment to man displayed by the chakar in a domestic state, with perhaps other latent aptitudes only waiting to be developed by artificial selection, seem to make this species one peculiarly suited for man's protection, without which it must inevitably perish. It is sad to reflect that all our domestic animals have descended to us from those ancient times which we are accustomed to regard as dark or barbarous, while the effect of our modern so-called humane civilization has been purely destructive to animal life. Not one type do we rescue from the carnage going on at an ever-increasing rate over all the globe. To Australia and America, North and South, we look in vain for new domestic species, while even from Africa, with its numerous fine mammalian forms, and where England has been the conquering colonizing power for nearly a century, we take nothing. Even the sterling qualities of the elephant, the unique beauty of the zebra, appeal to us in vain. We are only teaching the tribes of that vast continent to exterminate a hundred noble species they would not tame. With grief and shame, even with dismay, we call to mind that our country is now a stupendous manufactory of destructive engines, which we are rapidly placing in the hands of all the savage and semi-savage peoples of the earth, thus ensuring the speedy destruction of all the finest types in the animal kingdom.

CHAPTER XVIII.

THE WOODHEWER FAMILY.

(*Dendrocolaptidæ.*)

THE South American Tree-creepers, or Woodhewers, as they are sometimes called, although confined exclusively to one continent, their range extending from Southern Mexico to the Magellanic islands, form one of the largest families of the order Passeres; no fewer than about two hundred and ninety species (referable to about forty-six genera) having been already described. As they are mostly small, inconspicuous, thicket-frequenting birds, shy and fond of concealment to excess, it is only reasonable to suppose that our list of this family is more incomplete than of any other family of birds known. Thus, in the southern Plata and north Patagonian districts, supposed to be exhausted, where my observations have been made, and where, owing to the open nature of the country, birds are more easily remarked than in the forests and marshes of the tropical region, I have made notes on the habits of five species, of which I did not preserve specimens, and which, as far as I know, have never been described and named. Probably long before the whole of South America has been "exhausted," there will be not less than four to five hundred Dendrocolaptine

species known. And yet with the exception of
that dry husk of knowledge, concerning size, form
and colouration, which classifiers and cataloguers obtain from specimens, very little indeed—scarcely anything, in fact—is known about the Tree-creepers; and
it would not be too much to say that there are many
comparatively obscure and uninteresting species in
Europe, any one of which has a larger literature
than the entire Tree-creeper family. No separate
work about these birds has seen the light, even in
these days of monographs; but the reason of this
comparative neglect is not far to seek. In the
absence of any knowledge, except of the most frag-
mentary kind, of the life-habits of exotic species, the
monograph-makers of the Old World naturally take
up only the most important groups—i.e. the groups
which most readily attract the traveller's eye with
their gay conspicuous colouring, and which have
acquired a wide celebrity. We thus have a succession of splendid and expensive works dealing
separately with such groups as woodpeckers, trogons,
humming-birds, tanagers, king-fishers, and birds of
paradise; for with these, even if there be nothing
to record beyond the usual dreary details and
technicalities concerning geographical distribution,
variations in size and markings of different species,
&c., the little interest of the letter-press is com-
pensated for in the accompanying plates, which are
now produced on a scale of magnitude, and with so
great a degree of perfection, as regards brilliant
colouring, spirited attitudes and general fidelity to
nature, that leaves little further improvement in this
direction to be looked for. The Tree-creepers, being

without the inferior charm of bright colour, offer no attraction to the bird-painter, whose share in the work of the pictorial monograph is, of course, all-important. Yet even the very slight knowledge we possess of this family is enough to show that in many respects it is one richly endowed, possessing characters of greater interest to the student of the instincts and mental faculties of birds, than any of the gaily-tinted families I have mentioned.

There is, in the Dendrocolaptidæ, a splendid harvest for future observers of the habits of South American birds : some faint idea of its richness may perhaps be gathered from the small collection of the most salient facts known to us about them I have brought together and put in order in this place. And I am here departing a little from the plan usually observed in this book, which is chiefly occupied with matters of personal knowledge, seasoned with a little speculation; but in this case I have thought it best to supplement my own observations with those of others who have collected and observed birds in South America,* so as to give as comprehensive a survey of the family as I could.

It is strange to find a Passerine family, numerous as the Tree-creepers, uniformly of one colour, or nearly so ; for, with few exceptions, these birds have a brown plumage, without a particle of bright colour. But although they possess no brilliant or metallic tints, in some species, as we shall see, there are tints approaching to brightness. Notwithstand-

* Azara ; D'Orbigny ; Darwin ; Bridges ; Frazer ; Leotaud ; Gaumer ; Wallace ; Bates ; Cunningham ; Stolzmann ; Jelski ; Durnford ; Gibson ; Burrows ; Döring ; White, &c.

ing this family likeness in colour, any person, not
an ornithologist, looking at a collection of specimens comprising many genera, would hear with
surprise and almost incredulity that they all belonged
to one family, so great is the diversity exhibited in
their structure. In size they vary from species
smaller than the golden-crested wren to others
larger than the woodcock; but the differences in
size are as nothing compared with those shown in
the form of the beak. Between the minute, straight,
conical, tit-like beaks of the Laptasthenura—a tit
in appearance and habits—and the extravagantly
long, sword-shaped bill of Nasica, or the excessively
attenuated, sickle-shaped organ in Xiphorynchus,
the divergence is amazing, compared with what is
found in other families; while between these two
extremes there is a heterogeneous assemblage of
birds with beaks like creepers, nuthatches, finches,
tyrant-birds, woodpeckers, crows, and even curlews
and ibises. In legs, feet and tails, there are corresponding differences. There are tails of all lengths
and all forms; soft and stiff, square, acuminated,
broad and fan-like, narrow and spine-like, and
many as in the woodpeckers, and used as in that
bird to support the body in climbing. An extremely
curious modification is found in Sittosoma : the tail-
feathers in this genus are long and graduated, and
the shafts, projecting beyond the webs at the ends,
curve downwards and form stiff hooks. Concerning the habits of these birds, it has only been
reported that they climb on the trunks of trees:
probably they are able to run vertically up or down
with equal facility, and even to suspend themselves

by their feather-hooks when engaged in dislodging insects. Another curious variation is found in Sylviothorhynchus, a small wren-like bird and the

Some Woodhewers' beaks.

only member known of the genus, with a tail resembling that of the lyre-bird, the extravagantly long feathers being so narrow as to appear almost

like shafts destitute of webs.   This tail appears to
be purely ornamental.

This extreme variety in structure indicates a
corresponding diversity in habits; and, assuming it
to be a true doctrine that habits vary first and
structure afterwards, anyone might infer from a
study of their forms alone that these birds possess
a singular plasticity, or tendency to vary, in their
habits—or, in other words, that they are exceptionally intelligent; and that such a conclusion would
be right I believe a study of their habits will serve
to show.

The same species is often found to differ in its
manner of life in different localities.   Some species
of Xenops and Magarornis, like woodpeckers, climb
vertically on tree-trunks in search of insect prey,
but also, like tits, explore the smaller twigs and
foliage at the extremity of the branches; so that the
whole tree, from its root to its topmost foliage, is
hunted over by them.   The Sclerurus, although an
inhabitant of the darkest forest, and provided with
sharply-curved claws, never seeks its food on trees,
but exclusively on the ground, among the decaying
fallen leaves ; but, strangely enough, when alarmed
it flies to the trunk of the nearest tree, to which it
clings in a vertical position, and, remaining silent
and motionless, escapes observation by means of
its dark protective colour.   The Drymornis, a large
bird, with feet and tail like a woodpecker, climbs on
tree-trunks to seek its food; but also possesses
the widely-different habit of resorting to the open
plain, especially after a shower, to feed on larvæ and
earthworms, extracting them from a depth of three

or four inches beneath the surface with its immense
curved probing beak.

Again, when we consider a large number of
species of different groups, we find that there is
not with the Tree-creepers, as with most families,
any special habit or manner of life linking them
together; but that, on the contrary, different
genera, and, very frequently, different species
belonging to one genus, possess habits peculiarly
their own. In other families, even where the
divergence is greatest, what may be taken as the
original or ancestral habit is seldom or never quite
obsolete in any of the members. This we see, for
instance, in the woodpeckers, some of which have
acquired the habit of seeking their food exclusively
on the ground in open places, and even of nesting
in the banks of streams. Yet all these wanderers,
even those which have been structurally modified
in accordance with their altered way of life, retain
the primitive habit of clinging vertically to the
trunks of trees, although the habit has lost its
use. With the tyrant birds—a family showing an
extraordinary amount of variation—it is the same;
for the most divergent kinds are frequently seen
reverting to the family habit of perching on an
elevation, from which to make forays after passing
insects, returning after each capture to the same
stand. The thrushes, ranging all over the globe,
afford another striking example. Without speaking
of their nesting habits, their relationship appears in
their love of fruit, in their gait, flight, statuesque
attitudes, and abrupt motions.

With the numerous Dendrocolaptine groups, so

widely separated and apparently unrelated, it would
be difficult indeed to say which of their most
striking habits is the ancestral one. Many of the
smaller species live in trees or bushes, and in their
habits resemble tits, warblers, wrens, and other
kinds that subsist on small caterpillars, spiders, &c.,
gleaned from the leaves and smaller twigs. The
Anumbius nests on trees, but feeds exclusively on
the ground in open places ; while other ground-
feeders seek their food among dead leaves in dense
gloomy forests. Coryphistera resembles the lark
and pipit in its habits ; Cinclodes, the wagtail ;
Geobates a Saxicola ; Limnornis lives in reed beds
growing in the water ; Henicornis in reed beds
growing out of the water ; and many other ground
species exist concealed in the grass on dry plains ;
Homorus seeks its food by digging in the loose soil
and dead leaves about the roots of trees ; while Geositta, Furnarius, and Upercerthia obtain a livelihood
chiefly by probing in the soil. It would not be possible within the present limits to mention in detail
all the different modes of life of those species or
groups which do not possess the tree-creeping
habit ; after them comes a long array of genera in
which this habit is ingrained, and in which the
greatly modified feet and claws are suited to a
climbing existence. As these genera comprise the
largest half of the family, also the largest birds in
it, we might expect to find in the tree-creeping
the parental habit of the Dendrocolaptidæ, and that
from these tropical forest groups have sprung the
widely-diverging thicket, ground, marsh, sea-beach,
and rock-frequenting groups. It happens, however,

that these birds resemble each other only in their
climbing feet; in the form of their beaks they are
as wide apart as are nuthatches, woodpeckers,
crows, and curlews. They also differ markedly in
the manner of seeking their food. Some dig like
woodpeckers in decayed wood; others probe only
in soft rotten wood; while the humming-bird-billed
Xiphorhynchus, with a beak too long and slender
for probing, explores the interior of deep holes in
the trunks to draw out nocturnal insects, spiders,
and centipedes from their concealment. Xiphoco-
laptes uses its sword-like beak as a lever, thrusting
it under and forcing up the loose bark; while
Dendrornis, with its stout corvine beak, tears the
bark off.

In the nesting habits the diversity is greatest.
Some ground species excavate in the earth like
kingfishers, only with greater skill, making cylin-
drical burrows often four to five feet deep, and
terminating in a round chamber. Others build a
massive oven-shaped structure of clay on a branch
or other elevated site. Many of those that creep on
trees nest in holes in the wood. The marsh-
frequenting kinds attach spherical or oval domed
nests to the reeds; and in some cases woven grass
and clay are so ingeniously combined that the
structure, while light as a basket, is perfectly
impervious to the wet and practically indestructible.
The most curious nests, however, are the large stick
structures on trees and bushes, in the building and
repairing of which the birds are in many cases
employed more or less constantly all the year
round. These stick nests vary greatly in form,

size, and in other respects. Some have a spiral
passage-way leading from the entrance to the nest
cavity, and the cavity is in many cases only large
enough to accommodate the bird ; but in the
gigantic structure of Homorus gutturalis it is so
large that, if the upper half of the nest or dome
were removed, a condor could comfortably hatch
her eggs and rear her young in it. This nest is
spherical. The allied Homorus lophotis builds a
nest equally large, but with a small cavity for the
eggs inside, and outwardly resembling a gigantic
powder-flask, lying horizontally among the lower
branches of a spreading tree. Pracellodomus sibila-
trix, a bird in size like the English house sparrow,
also makes a huge nest, and places it on the twigs
at the terminal end of a horizontal branch from
twelve to fifteen feet above the ground ; but when
finished, the weight of the structure bears down
the branch-end to within one or two feet of the
surface. Mr. Barrows, who describes this nest,
says : " When other branches of the same tree are
similarly loaded, and other trees close at hand bear
the same kind of fruit, the result is very picturesque."
Synallaxis phryganophila makes a stick nest about
a foot in depth, and from the top a tubular passage,
formed of slender twigs interlaced, runs down the
entire length of the nest, like a rain-pipe on the
wall of a house, and then becoming external slopes
upward, ending at a distance of two to three feet
from the nest. Throughout South America there
are several varieties of these fruit-and-stem or
watering-pot shaped nests ; they are not, however,
all built by birds of one genus, while in the genus

Synallaxis many species have no tubular passage-
ways attached to their nests. One species—ery-
throthorax—in Yucatan, makes so large a nest of
sticks, that the natives do not believe that so small
a bird can be the builder. They say that when the
tzapatan begins to sing, all the birds in the forest
repair to it, each one carrying a stick to add to the
structure; only one, a tyrant-bird, brings two sticks,
one for itself and one for the *urubú* or vulture, that
bird being considered too large, heavy, and ignorant of architecture to assist personally in the
work.

In the southern part of South America, where
scattered thorn trees grow on a dry soil, these big
nests are most abundant. " There are plains," Mr.
Barrows writes, " within two miles of the centre of
this town (Concepcion, Argentine Republic), where
I have stood and counted, from one point within a
radius of twenty rods, over two hundred of these
curious nests, varying in size from that of a small
pumpkin to more than the volume of a barrel.
Often a single tree will contain half a dozen nests
or more; and, not unfrequently, the nests of several
different species are seen crowding each other out
of shape on the same bush or tree."

It would be a mistake to think that the widely
different nesting habits I have mentioned are found
in different genera. I have just spoken of the big
stick nests, with or without passage-ways, of the
Synallaxes, yet the nest of one member of this
group is simply a small straight tube of woven
grass, the aperture only large enough to admit the
middle finger, and open at both ends, so that the

bird can pass in and out without turning round.
Another species scoops a circular hollow in the soil,
and builds over it a dome of fine woven grass. It
should be mentioned that the nesting habits of only
about fifteen out of the sixty-five species comprised
in this genus are known to us. In the genus
Furnarius the oven-shaped clay structure is known
to be made by three species; a fourth builds a nest
of sticks in a tree; a fifth burrows in the side of a
bank, like a kingfisher.

The explanation of the most striking features
of the Dendrocolaptidæ, their monotonous brown
plumage, diversity of structure, versatile habits,
and the marvellous development of the nest-making
instinct which they exhibit is to be found, it appears
to me, in the fact that they are the most defenceless
of birds. They are timid, unresisting creatures,
without strength or weapons; their movements are
less quick and vigorous than those of other kinds,
and their flight is exceedingly feeble. The arboreal
species flit at intervals from one tree to another;
those that frequent thickets refuse to leave their
chosen shelter; while those inhabiting grassy
plains or marshes study concealment, and, when
forced to rise, flutter away just above the surface,
like flying-fish frightened from the water, and,
when they have gone thirty or forty yards, dip into
the grass or reeds again. Their life is thus one of
perpetual danger in a far greater degree than with
other passerine families, such as warblers, tyrants,
finches, thrushes, &c. ; while an exclusively insect
diet, laboriously extracted from secret places, and
inability to change their climate, contribute to make

their existence a hard one. It has been with these
birds as with human beings, bred in " misfortune's
school," and subjected to keen competition. One
of their most striking characteristics is a methodical,
plodding, almost painful diligence of manner while
seeking their food, so that when viewed side by
side with other species, rejoicing in a gayer plumage
and stronger flight, they seem like sober labourers
that never rest among holiday people bent only on
enjoyment. That they are able not only to maintain their existence, but to rise to the position of a
dominant family, is due to an intelligence and
adaptiveness exceeding that of other kinds, and
which has been strengthened, and perhaps directly
results from the hard conditions of their life.

How great their adaptiveness and variability
must be when we find that every portion of the
South American continent is occupied by them;
for there is really no climate, and no kind of soil or
vegetation, which does not possess its appropriate
species, modified in colour, form, and habits to suit
the surrounding conditions. In the tropical region,
so rich in bird life of all kinds, in forest, marsh,
and savanna, they are everywhere abundant—food
is plentiful there; but when we go to higher
elevations and cold sterile deserts, where their
companion families of the tropics dwindle away and
disappear, the creepers are still present, for they
are evidently able to exist where other kinds would
starve. On the stony plateaus of the Andes, and
on the most barren spots in Patagonia, where no
other bird is seen, there are small species of Synallaxis, which, in their obscure colour and motions

on the ground, resemble mice rather than birds; indeed, the Quichua name for one of these Synallaxes is *ukatchtuka*, or mouse-bird. How different is the life habit here from what we see in the tropical groups—the large birds with immense beaks, that run vertically on the trunks of the great forest trees!

At the extreme southern extremity of the South American continent we find several species of Cinclodes, seeking a subsistence like sandpipers on the beach; they also fly out to sea, and run about on the floating kelp, exploring the fronds for the small marine animals on which they live. In the dreary forests of Tierra del Fuego another creeper, Oxyurus, is by far the commonest bird. "Whether high up or low down, in the most gloomy, wet, and scarcely penetrable ravines," says Darwin, "this little bird is to be met with;" and Dr. Cunningham also relates that in these wintry, savage woods he was always attended in his walks by parties of these little creepers, which assembled to follow him out of curiosity.

To birds placed at so great a disadvantage, by a feeble flight and other adverse circumstances, in the race of life bright colours would certainly prove fatal. It is true that brown is not in itself a protective colour, and the clear, almost silky browns and bright chestnut tints in several species are certainly not protective; but these species are sufficiently protected in other ways, and can afford to be without a strictly adaptive colour, so long as they are not conspicuous. In a majority of cases, however, the colour is undoubtedly protective, the brown hue being of a shade that assimilates very closely to the surroundings. There are pale yellowish browns, lined and mottled, in species living amidst a sere, scanty vegetation; earthy browns, in those frequenting open sterile or stony places; while the species that creep on trees in forests are dark brown in colour, and in many cases the feathers are mottled in such a manner as to make them curiously resemble the bark of a tree. The genera Lochmias and Sclerurus are the darkest, the plumage in these birds being nearly or quite black, washed or tinged with rhubarb yellow. Their black plumage would render them conspicuous in the sunshine, but they pass their lives in dense tropical forests, where the sun at noon sheds only a gloomy twilight.

If " colour is ever tending to increase and to appear where it is absent," as Dr. Wallace believes, then we ought to find it varying in the direction of greater brightness in some species in a family so numerous and variable as the Dendrocolaptidæ, however feeble and in need of a protective colouring these birds may be in a majority of cases. And this in effect we do find. In many of the dark-plumaged species that live in perpetual shade some parts are a very bright chestnut; while in a few that live in such close concealment as to be almost independent of protective colouring, the lower plumage has become pure white. A large number of species have a bright or nearly bright gular spot. This is most remarkable in Synallaxis phryganophila, the chin being sulphur-yellow, beneath which is a spot of velvet-black, and on either side a white

patch, the throat thus having three strongly contrasted colours, arranged in four divisions. The
presence of this bright throat spot in so many
species cannot very well be attributed to voluntary
sexual selection, although believers in that theory
are of course at liberty to imagine that when engaged in courtship, the male bird, or rather male
and female both, as both sexes possess the spot,
hold up their heads vertically to exhibit it. Perhaps it would be safer to look on it as a mere
casual variation, which, like the exquisitely pencilled
feathers and delicate tints on the concealed sides
and under surfaces of the wings of many species
possessing outwardly an obscure protective colouring, is neither injurious nor beneficial in any way,
either to the birds or to the theory. It is more
than probable, however, that in such small feeble-
winged, persecuted birds, this spot of colour would
prove highly dangerous on any conspicuous part of
the body. In some of the more vigorous, active
species, we can see a tendency towards a brighter
colouring on large, exposed surfaces. In Auto-
malus the tail is bright satiny rufous; in Pseudo-
colaptes the entire under surface is rufous of a
peculiar vivid tint, verging on orange or red; in
Magarornis the bosom is black, and beautifully
ornamented with small leaf-shaped spots of a
delicate straw-colour. There are several other
very pretty birds in this homely family; but the
finest of all is Thripodectes flammulatus, the whole
body being tortoise-shell colour, the wings and tail
bright chesnut. The powerful tanager-like beak of
this species seems also to show that it has diverged

from its timid shade-loving congeners in another direction by becoming a seed and fruit eater.

Probably the sober and generally protective colouring of the tree-creepers, even with the variability and adaptiveness displayed in their habits superadded, would be insufficient to preserve such feeble birds in the struggle of life without the further advantage derived from their wonderful nests. It has been said of domed nests that they are a danger rather than a protection, owing to their large size, which makes it easy for carnivorous species that prey on eggs and young birds to find them ; while small open nests are usually well concealed. This may be the case with covered nests made of soft materials, loosely put together ; but it cannot be said of the solid structure the tree-creeper builds, and which, as often as not, the bird erects in the most conspicuous place it can find, as if, writes Azara, it desired all the world to admire its work. The annual destruction of adult birds is very great—more than double that, I believe, which takes place in other passerine families. Their eggs and young are, however, practically safe in their great elaborate nests or deep burrows, and, as a rule, they lay more eggs than other kinds, the full complement being seldom less than five in the species I am acquainted with, while some lay as many as nine. Their nests are also made so as to keep out a greater pest than their carnivorous or egg-devouring enemies—namely, the parasitical starlings (Molothrus), which are found throughout South America, and are excessively abundant and destructive to birds' nests in some districts. In most cases, in the big, strong-domed nest or deep burrow, all the eggs are hatched and all the young reared, the thinning-out process commencing only after the brood has been led forth into a world beset with perils. With other families, on the contrary, the greatest amount of destruction falls on the eggs or fledglings. I have frequently kept a dozen or twenty pairs of different species—warblers, finches, tyrants, starlings, &c.—under observation during the breeding season, and have found that in some cases no young were reared at all; in other cases one or two young; while, as often as not, the young actually reared were only parasitical starlings after all.

I have still to speak of the voice of the tree-creepers, an important point in the study of these birds; for, though not accounted singers, some species emit remarkable sounds; moreover, language in birds is closely related to the social instinct. They seem to be rather solitary than gregarious; and this seems only natural in birds so timid, weak-winged, and hard pressed. It would also be natural to conclude from what has been said concerning their habits that they are comparatively silent; for, as a rule, vigorous social birds are loquacious and loud-voiced, while shy solitary kinds preserve silence, except in the love season. Nevertheless the creepers are loquacious and have loud resonant voices; this fact, however, does not really contradict a well-known principle, for the birds possess the social disposition in an eminent degree, only the social habit is kept down in them by the conditions of a life which makes solitude necessary. Thus, a large proportion of species are found to pair for life; and the only reasonable explanation of this habit in birds—one which is not very common in the mammalia—is that such species possess the social temper or feeling, and live in pairs only because they cannot afford to live in flocks. Strictly gregarious species pair only for the breeding season. In the creepers the attachment between the birds thus mated for life is very great, and, as Azara truly says of Anumbius, so fond of each other's society are these birds, that when one incubates the other sits at the entrance to the nest, and when one carries food to its young the other accompanies it, even if it has found nothing to carry. In these species that live in pairs, when the two birds are separated they are perpetually calling to each other, showing how impatient of solitude they are; while even from the more solitary kind, a high-pitched call-note is constantly heard in the woods, for these birds, debarred from associating together, satisfy their instinct by conversing with one another over long distances.

The foregoing remarks apply to the Dendrocolaptidæ throughout the temperate countries of South America—the birds inhabiting extensive grassy plains and marshes, and districts with a scanty or scattered tree and bush vegetation. In the forest areas of the hotter regions it is different; there the birds form large gatherings or " wandering bands," composed of all the different species found in each district, associated with birds of other families— wood-peckers, tyrant-birds, bush shrikes, and many others. These miscellaneous gatherings are not of rare occurrence, but out of the breeding season are formed daily, the birds beginning to assemble at about nine or ten o'clock in the morning, their number increasing through the day until it reaches its maximum between two and four o'clock in the afternoon, after which it begins to diminish, each bird going off to its customary shelter or dwelling-place. Mr. Bates, who first described these wandering bands, says that he could always find the particular band belonging to a district any day he wished, for when he failed to meet with it in one part of the forest he would try other paths, until he eventually found it. The great Amazonian forests, he tells us, appear strangely silent and devoid of bird life, and it is possible to ramble about for whole days without seeing or hearing birds. But now and then the surrounding trees and bushes appear suddenly swarming with them. " The bustling crowd loses no time, and, always moving in concert, each bird is occupied on its own account in searching bark, or leaf, or twig. In a few moments the host is gone, and the forest path remains deserted and silent as before." Stolzmann, who observed them in Peru, says that the sound caused by the busy crowd searching through the foliage, and the falling of dead leaves and twigs, resembles that produced by a shower of rain. The Indians of the Amazons, Mr. Bates writes, have a curious belief to explain these bird armies ; they say that the Papa-uirá, supposed to be a small grey bird, fascinates all the others, and leads them on a weary perpetual dance through the forest. It seems very wonderful that birds, at other times solitary, should thus combine daily in large numbers, includ-

ing in their bands scores of widely different species,
and in size ranging from those no larger than a
wren to others as big as a magpie. It is certainly
very advantageous to them. As Belt remarks, they
play into each other's hands; for while the larger
creepers explore the trunks of big trees, others run
over the branches and cling to the lesser twigs, so
that every tree in their route, from its roots to the
topmost foliage, is thoroughly examined, and every
spider and caterpillar taken, while the winged
insects, driven from their lurking-places, are seized
where they settle, or caught flying by the tyrant
birds.

I have observed the wandering bands only in
Patagonia, where they are on a very small scale
compared with those of the tropical forests. In the
Patagonia thickets the small tit-like creeper, Laptasthenura, is the prime mover ; and after a considerable number of these have gathered, creepers of
other species and genera unite with them, and
finally the band, as it moves through the thickets,
draws to itself other kinds—flycatchers, finches,
&c.—many of the birds running or hopping on the
ground to search for insects in the loose soil or
under dead leaves, while others explore the thorny
bushes. My observations of these small bands lead
me to believe that everywhere in South America
the Dendrocolaptidæ are the first in combining to
act in concert, and that the birds of other families
follow their march and associate with them, knowing from experience that a rich harvest may be
thus reaped. In the same way birds of various
kinds follow the movements of a column of hunting

ants, to catch the insects flying up from the earth
to escape from their enemies ; swallows also learn
to keep company with the traveller on horseback,
and, crossing and recrossing just before the hoofs,
they catch the small twilight moths driven up from
the grass.

To return to the subject of voice. The tree-creepers
do not possess melodious, or at any rate mellow
notes, although in so numerous a family there is
great variety of tone, ranging from a small reedy
voice like the faint stridulation of a grasshopper,
to the resounding, laughter-like, screaming concerts
of Homorus, which may be heard distinctly two
miles away. As a rule, the notes are loud ringing
calls ; and in many species the cry, rapidly reiterated,
resembles a peal of laughter. With scarcely an
exception, they possess no set song ; but in most
species that live always in pairs there are loud,
vehement, gratulatory notes uttered by the two
birds in concert when they meet after a brief
separation. This habit they possess in common
with birds of other families, as, for instance, the
tyrants ; but, in some creepers, out of this confused
outburst of joyous sound has been developed a
musical performance very curious, and perhaps
unique among birds. On meeting, the male and
female, standing close together and facing each
other, utter their clear ringing concert, one emitting
loud single measured notes, while the notes of its
fellow are rapid, rhythmical triplets ; their voices
have a joyous character, and seem to accord, thus
producing a kind of harmony. This manner of
singing is perhaps most perfect in the oven-bird,

Furnarius, and it is very curious that the young birds, when only partially fledged, are constantly heard in the nest or oven apparently practising these duets in the intervals when the parents are absent; single measured notes, triplets, and long concluding trills are all repeated with wonderful fidelity, although these notes are in character utterly unlike the hunger cry, which is like that of other fledglings.

I cannot help thinking that this fact of the young birds beginning to sing like the adults, while still confined in their dark cradle, is one of very considerable significance, especially when we consider the singular character of the performance; and that it might even be found to throw some light on the obscure question of the comparative antiquity of the different and widely separated Dendrocolaptine groups. It is a doctrine in evolutionary science that the early maturing of instincts in the young indicates a high antiquity for the species or group; and there is no reason why this principle should not be extended, in the case of birds at any rate, to language. It is true that Daines Barrington's notion that young song-birds learn to sing only by imitating the adults still holds its ground; and Darwin gives it his approval in his *Descent of Man*. It is perhaps one of those doctrines which are partially true, or which do not contain the whole truth; and it is possible to believe that, while many singing birds do so learn their songs, or acquire a greater proficiency in them from hearing the adults, in other species the song comes instinctively, and is, like other instincts and habits, purely an "inherited memory."

The case of a species in another order of birds
—Crypturi—strikes me as being similar to this of
the oven-bird, and seems to lend some force to the
suggestion I have made concerning the early development of voice in the young.

Birds peculiar to South America are said by
anatomists to be less specialized, lower, more
ancient, than the birds of the northern continents,
and among those which are considered lowest and
most ancient are the Tinamous (rail and partridge
like in their habits), birds that lead a solitary,
retiring life, and in most cases have sweet melancholy voices. Rhynchotus rufescens, a bird the
size of a fowl, inhabiting the pampas, is perhaps
the sweetest-voiced, and sings with great frequency.
Its song or call is heard oftenest towards the
evening, and is composed of five modulated notes,
flute-like in character, very expressive, and uttered
by many individuals answering each other as they
sit far apart concealed in the grass. As we might
have expected, the faculties and instincts of the
young of this species mature at a very early period;
when extremely small, they abandon their parents
to shift for themselves in solitude; and when not
more than one-fourth the size they eventually attain,
they acquire the adult plumage and are able to fly
as well as an old bird. I observed a young bird of
this species, less than a quail in size, at a house on
the pampas, and was told that it had been taken
from the nest when just breaking the shell; it had,
therefore, never seen or heard the parent birds.
Yet this small chick, every day at the approach of
evening, would retire to the darkest corner of the

dining room, and, concealed under a piece of furniture, would continue uttering its evening song for
an hour or longer at short intervals, and rendering it
so perfectly that I was greatly surprised to hear it ;
for a thrush or other songster at the same period of
life, when attempting to sing, only produces a
chirping sound.

The early singing of the oven-bird fledgling is
important, owing to the fact that the group it
belongs to comprises the least specialized forms in
the family. They are strong-legged, square-tailed,
terrestrial birds, generally able to perch, have
probing beaks, and build the most perfect mud or
stick nests, or burrow in the ground. In the
numerous tree-creeping groups, which seem as
unrelated to the oven-bird as the woodpecker is to
the hoopoe, we find a score of wonderfully different
forms of beak ; but many of them retain the probing character, and are actually used to probe in
rotten wood on trees, and to explore the holes and
deep crevices in the trunk. We have also seen that
some of these tree-creepers revert to the ancestral
habit (if I may so call it) of seeking their food by
probing in the soil. In others, like Dendrornis, in
which the beak has lost this character, and is used
to dig in the wood or to strip off the bark, it has
not been highly specialized, and, compared with the
woodpecker's beak, is a very imperfect organ, considering the purpose for which it is used. Yet, on
the principle that " similar functional requirements
frequently lead to the development of similar
structures in animals which are otherwise very
distinct "—as we see in the tubular tongue in

honey-eaters and humming birds—we might have expected to find in the Dendrocolaptidæ a better imitation of the woodpecker in so variable an organ as the beak, if not in the tongue.

Probably the oven-birds, and their nearest relations—generalized, hardy, builders of strong nests, and prolific—represent the parental form ; and when birds of this type had spread over the entire continent they became in different districts frequenters of marshes, forests, thickets and savannas. With altered life-habits the numerous divergent forms originated ; some, like Xiphorynchus, retaining a probing beak in a wonderfully modified form, attenuated in an extreme degree, and bent like a sickle ; others diverging more in the direction of nuthatches and woodpeckers.

This sketch of the Dendrocolaptidæ, necessarily slight and imperfect, is based on a knowledge of the habits of about sixty species, belonging to twenty-eight genera : from personal observation I am acquainted with less than thirty species. It is astonishing to find how little has been written about these most interesting birds in South America. One tree-creeper only, Furnarius rufus, the oven-bird *par excellence,* has been mentioned, on account of its wonderful architecture, in almost every general work of natural history published during the present century; yet the oven-bird does not surpass, or even equal in interest, many others in this family of nearly three hundred members.

CHAPTER XIX.

IN reading books of Natural History we meet with numerous instances of birds possessing the habit of assembling together, in many cases always at the same spot, to indulge in antics and dancing performances, with or without the accompaniment of music, vocal or instrumental; and by instrumental music is here meant all sounds other than vocal made habitually and during the more or less orderly performances; as, for instance, drumming and tapping noises; smiting of wings; and humming, whip-cracking, fan-shutting, grinding, scraping, and horn-blowing sounds, produced as a rule by the quills.

There are human dances, in which only one person performs at a time, the rest of the company looking on; and some birds, in widely separated genera, have dances of this kind. A striking example is the Rupicola, or cock-of-the-rock, of tropical South America. A mossy level spot of earth surrounded by bushes is selected for a dancing-place, and kept well cleared of sticks and stones; round this area the birds assemble, when a cock-bird, with vivid orange-scarlet crest and plumage, steps into it, and, with spreading wings and tail,

begins a series of movements as if dancing a
minuet; finally, carried away with excitement, he
leaps and gyrates in the most astonishing manner,
until, becoming exhausted, he retires, and another
bird takes his place.

In other species all the birds in a company unite
in the set performances, and seem to obey an impulse
which affects them simultaneously and in the same
degree; but sometimes one bird prompts the others
and takes a principal part.   One of the most curious
instances I have come across in reading is contained
in Mr. Bigg-Wither's *Pioneering in South Brazil.*
He relates that one morning in the dense forest
his attention was roused by the unwonted sound
of a bird singing—songsters being rare in that
district.   His men, immediately they caught the
sound, invited him to follow them, hinting that he
would probably witness a very curious sight.
Cautiously making their way through the dense
undergrowth, they finally came in sight of a small
stony spot of ground, at the end of a tiny glade ;
and on this spot, some on the stone and some on
the shrubs, were assembled a number of little birds,
about the size of tom-tits, with lovely blue plumage
and red top-knots.   One was perched quite still on
a twig, singing merrily, while the others were keeping time with wings and feet in a kind of dance,
and all twittering an accompaniment.   He watched
them for some time, and was satisfied that they
were having a ball and concert, and thoroughly enjoying themselves ; they then became alarmed, and
the performance abruptly terminated, the birds all
going off in different directions.   The natives told

him that these little creatures were known as the
" dancing birds."

This species was probably solitary, except when
assembling for the purpose of display; but in a
majority of cases, especially in the Passerine order,
the solitary species performs its antics alone, or
with no witness but its mate. Azara, describing a
small finch, which he aptly named *Oscilador*, says
that early and late in the day it mounts up vertically
to a moderate height; then flies off to a distance
of twenty yards, describing a perfect curve in its
passage; turning, it flies back over the imaginary
line it has traced, and so on repeatedly, appearing
like a pendulum swung in space by an invisible
thread.

Those who seek to know the cause and origin of
this kind of display and of song in animals are re-
ferred to Darwin's *Descent of Man* for an explanation.
The greater part of that work is occupied with a
laborious argument intended to prove that the love-
feeling inspires the animals engaged in these exhibitions, and that sexual selection, or the voluntary
selection of mates by the females, is the final cause
of all set musical and dancing performances, as well
as of bright and harmonious colouring, and of
ornaments.

The theory, with regard to birds is, that in the
love-season, when the males are excited and engage
in courtship, the females do not fall to the strongest
and most active, nor to those that are first in the
field; but that in a large number of species they
are endowed with a faculty corresponding to the
æsthetic feeling or taste in man, and deliberately

select males for their superiority in some æsthetic quality, such as graceful or fantastic motions, melody of voice, brilliancy of colour, or perfection of ornaments. Doubtless all birds were originally plain-coloured, without ornaments and without melody, and it is assumed that so it would always have been in many cases but for the action of this principle, which, like natural selection, has gone on accumulating countless small variations, tending to give a greater lustre to the species in each case, and resulting in all that we most admire in the animal world—the Rupicola's flame-coloured mantle, the peacock's crest and starry train, the joyous melody of the lark, and the pretty or fantastic dancing performances of birds.

My experience is that mammals and birds, with few exceptions—probably there are really *no* exceptions—possess the habit of indulging frequently in more or less regular or set performances, with or without sound, or composed of sound exclusively; and that these performances, which in many animals are only discordant cries and choruses, and uncouth, irregular motions, in the more aërial, graceful, and melodious kinds take immeasurably higher, more complex, and more beautiful forms. Among the mammalians the instinct appears almost universal; but their displays are, as a rule, less admirable than those seen in birds. There are some kinds, it is true, like the squirrels and monkeys, of arboreal habits, almost birdlike in their restless energy, and in the swiftness and certitude of their motions, in which the slightest impulse can be instantly expressed in graceful or fantastic action; others, like

the Chinchillidæ family, have greatly developed
vocal organs, and resemble birds in loquacity; but
mammals generally, compared with birds, are slow
and heavy, and not so readily moved to exhibitions
of the kind I am discussing.

The terrestrial dances, often very elaborate, of
heavy birds, like those of the gallinaceous kind, are
represented in the more volatile species by performances in the air, and these are very much more
beautiful; while a very large number of birds—
hawks, vultures, swifts, swallows, nightjars, storks,
ibises, spoonbills, and gulls—circle about in the
air, singly or in flocks. Sometimes, in serene
weather, they rise to a vast altitude, and float about
in one spot for an hour or longer at a stretch,
showing a faint bird-cloud in the blue, that does
not change its form, nor grow lighter and denser
like a flock of starlings; but in the seeming confusion there is perfect order, and amidst many
hundreds each swift- or slow-gliding figure keeps
its proper distance with such exactitude that no
two ever touch, even with the extremity of the long
wings, flapping or motionless :—such a multitude,
and such miraculous precision in the endless curving
motions of all the members of it, that the spectator
can lie for an hour on his back without weariness
watching this mystic cloud-dance in the empyrean.

The black-faced ibis of Patagonia, a bird nearly
as large as a turkey, indulges in a curious mad
performance, usually in the evening when feeding-
time is over. The birds of a flock, while winging
their way to the roosting-place, all at once seem
possessed with frenzy, simultaneously dashing

downwards with amazing violence, doubling about
in the most eccentric manner; and when close to
the surface rising again to repeat the action, all the
while making the air palpitate for miles around with
their hard, metallic cries.   Other ibises, also birds
of other genera, have similar aërial performances.

The displays of most ducks known to me take
the form of mock fights on the water; one exception is the handsome and loquacious whistling
widgeon of La Plata, which has a pretty aërial performance.   A dozen or twenty birds rise up until
they appear like small specks in the sky, and sometimes disappear from sight altogether ; and at that
great altitude they continue hovering in one spot,
often for an hour or longer, alternately closing and
separating; the fine, bright, whistling notes and
flourishes of the male curiously harmonizing with
the grave, measured notes of the female; and every
time they close they slap each other on the wings
so smartly that the sound can be distinctly heard,
like applauding hand-claps, even after the birds have
ceased to be visible.

The rails, active, sprightly birds with powerful
and varied voices, are great performers ; but owing
to the nature of the ground they inhabit and to
their shy, suspicious character, it is not easy to
observe their antics.   The finest of the Platan rails
is the ypecaha, a beautiful, active bird about the size
of the fowl. A number of ypecahas have their
assembling place on a small area of smooth, level
ground, just above the water, and hemmed in by
dense rush beds.   First, one bird among the rushes
emits a powerful cry, thrice repeated ; and this is a

note of invitation, quickly responded to by other birds from all sides as they hurriedly repair to the usual place. In a few moments they appear, to the number of a dozen or twenty, bursting from the rushes and running into the open space, and instantly beginning the performance. This is a tremendous screaming concert. The screams they utter have a certain resemblance to the human

Dance of Ypecaha Rails.

voice, exerted to its utmost pitch and expressive of extreme terror, frenzy, and despair. A long, piercing shriek, astonishing for its vehemence and power, is succeeded by a lower note, as if in the first the creature had well nigh exhausted itself: this double scream is repeated several times, and followed by other sounds, resembling, as they rise and fall, half smothered cries of pains and moans of anguish. Suddenly the unearthly shrieks are renewed in all their power. While screaming the birds rush from side to side, as if possessed with madness, the wings spread and vibrating, the long beak wide open and raised vertically. This exhibition lasts three or four minutes, after which the assembly peacefully breaks up.

The singular wattled, wing-spurred, and long-toed jacana has a remarkable performance, which seems specially designed to bring out the concealed

Wing-display of Jacanas.

beauty of the silky, greenish-golden wing-quills. The birds go singly or in pairs, and a dozen or fifteen individuals may be found in a marshy place feeding within sight of each other. Occasionally, in response to a note of invitation, they all in a moment leave off feeding and fly to one spot, and, forming a close cluster, and emitting short, excited, rapidly repeated notes, display their wings, like beautiful flags grouped loosely together: some hold the wings up vertically and motionless; others, half open and vibrating rapidly, while still others wave them up and down with a slow, measured motion.

In the ypecaha and jacana displays both sexes take part. A stranger performance is that of the spur-winged lapwing of the same region—a species resembling the lapwing of Europe, but a third larger, brighter coloured, and armed with spurs. The lapwing display, called by the natives its "dance," or "serious dance"—by which they mean square dance—requires three birds for its performance, and is, so far as I know, unique in this respect. The birds are so fond of it that they indulge in it all the year round, and at frequent intervals during the day, also on moonlight nights. If a person watches any two birds for some time— for they live in pairs—he will see another lapwing, one of a neighbouring couple, rise up and fly to them, leaving his own mate to guard their chosen ground; and instead of resenting this visit as an unwarranted intrusion on their domain, as they would certainly resent the approach of almost any other bird, they welcome it with notes and signs of pleasure. Advancing to the visitor, they place themselves behind it; then all three, keeping step, begin a rapid march, uttering resonant drumming notes in time with their movements; the notes of the pair behind being emitted in a stream, like a drum-roll, while the leader utters loud single notes at regular intervals. The march ceases; the leader elevates his wings and stands erect and motionless, still uttering loud notes; while the other two, with

puffed-out plumage and standing exactly abreast,
stoop forward and downward until the tips of their
beaks touch the ground, and, sinking their rhythmical voices to a murmur, remain for some time in
this posture. The performance is then over and
the visitor goes back to his own ground and mate,
to receive a visitor himself later on.

Dance of Spur-winged Lapwings.

In the Passerine order, not the least remarkable
displays are witnessed in birds that are not
accounted songsters, as they do not possess the
highly developed vocal organ confined to the sub-
order Oscines. The tyrant-birds, which represent
in South America the fly-catchers of the Old World,
all have displays of some kind; in a vast majority
of cases these are simply joyous, excited duets

between male and female, composed of impetuous and
more or less confused notes and screams, accompanied with beating of wings and other gestures.
In some species choruses take the place of duets,
while in others entirely different forms of display
have been developed. In one group—Cnipolegus—
the male indulges in solitary antics, while the silent,
modest-coloured female keeps in hiding. Thus, the
male of Cnipolegus Hudsoni, an intensely black-
plumaged species with a concealed white wing-band,
takes his stand on a dead twig on the summit of a
bush. At intervals he leaves his perch, displaying
the intense white on the quills, and producing, as
the wings are thrown open and shut alternately,
the effect of successive flashes of light. Then suddenly the bird begins revolving in the air about its
perch, like a moth wheeling round and close to the
flame of a candle, emitting a series of sharp clicks
and making a loud humming with the wings.
While performing this aërial waltz the black and
white on the quills mix, the wings appearing like a
grey mist encircling the body. The fantastic dance
over, the bird drops suddenly on to its perch
again ; and, until moved to another display, remains
as stiff and motionless as a bird carved out of jet.

The performance of the scissors-tail, another
tyrant-bird, is also remarkable. This species is
grey and white, with black head and tail and a
crocus-yellow crest. On the wing it looks like a
large swallow, but with the two outer tail-feathers
a foot long. The scissors-tails always live in pairs,
but at sunset several pairs assemble, the birds
calling excitedly to each other ; they then mount

upwards, like rockets, to a great height in the air, and, after wheeling about for a few moments, precipitate themselves downwards with amazing violence in a wild zigzag, opening and shutting the long tail-feathers like a pair of shears, and producing loud whirring sounds, as of clocks being wound rapidly up, with a slight pause after each turn of the key. This aërial dance over, they alight in separate couples on the tree tops, each couple joining in a kind of duet of rapidly repeated, castanet-like sounds.

The displays of the wood-hewers, or Dendrocolaptidæ, another extensive family, resemble those of the tyrant-birds in being chiefly duets, male and female singing excitedly in piercing or resonant voices, and with much action. The habit varies somewhat in the cachalote, a Patagonian species of the genus Homorus, about the size of the missel-thrush. Old and young birds live in a family together, and at intervals, on any fine day, they engage in a grand screaming contest, which may be heard distinctly at a distance of a mile and a half. One bird mounts on to a bush and calls, and instantly all the others hurry to the spot, and burst out into a chorus of piercing cries that sound like peals and shrieks of insane laughter. After the chorus, they all pursue each other wildly about among the bushes for some minutes.

In some groups the usual duet-like performances have developed into a kind of harmonious singing, which is very curious and pleasant to hear. This is pre-eminently the case with the oven-birds, as D'Orbigney first remarked. Thus, in the red oven-bird, the first bird, on the appearance of its mate flying to join it, begins to emit loud, measured notes, and sometimes a continuous trill, somewhat metallic in sound; but immediately on the other bird striking in this introductory passage is changed to triplets, strongly accented on the first note, in a *tempo vivace;* while the second bird utters loud single notes in the same time. While thus singing they stand facing each other, necks outstretched and tails expanded, the wings of the first bird vibrating rapidly to the rapid utterance, while those of the second bird beat measured time. The finale consists of three or four notes, uttered by the second bird alone, strong and clear, in an ascending scale, the last very piercing.

In the melodists proper the displays, in a majority of cases, are exclusively vocal, the singer sitting still on his perch. In the Troupials, a family of starling-like birds numbering about one hundred and forty species, there are many that accompany singing with pretty or grotesque antics. The male scream-ing cow-bird of La Plata, when perched, emits a hollow-sounding internal note that swells at the end into a sharp metallic ring, almost bell-like : this is uttered with wings and tail spread and depressed, the whole plumage being puffed out as in a strutting turkey-cock, while the bird hops briskly up and down on its perch as if dancing. The bell-like note of the male is followed by an impetuous scream from the female, and the dance ends. Another species, the common Argentine cow-bird of La Plata, when courting puffs out his glossy rich violet plumage, and, with wings vibrating, emits a succession of deep internal notes, followed by a set song in clear, ringing tones; and then, suddenly taking wing, he flies straight away, close to the surface, fluttering like a moth, and at a distance of twenty to thirty yards turns and flies in a wide circle round the female, singing loudly all the time, hedging her in with melody as it were.

Many songsters in widely different families possess the habit of soaring and falling alternately while singing, and in some cases all the aërial postures and movements, the swift or slow descent, vertical, often with oscillations, or in a spiral, and sometimes with a succession of smooth oblique lapses, seem to have an admirable correspondence with the changing and falling voice—melody and motion being united in a more intimate and beautiful way than in the most perfect and poetic forms of human dancing.

One of the soaring singers is a small yellow field-finch of La Plata—Sycalis luteola ; and this species, like some others, changes the form of its display with the seasons. It lives in immense flocks, and during the cold season it has, like most finches, only aërial pastimes, the birds wheeling about in a cloud, pursuing each other with lively chirpings. In August, when the trees begin to blossom, the flock betakes itself to a plantation, and, sitting on the branches, the birds sing in a concert of innumerable voices, producing a great volume of sound, as of a high wind when heard at a distance. Heard near, it is a great mass of melody; not a confused tangle of musical sounds as when a host of Troupials sing in concert, but the notes, although numberless, seem to flow smoothly and separately, producing an

effect on the ear similar to that which rain does on
the sight, when the sun shines on and lightens up the
myriads of falling drops all falling one way. In this
manner the birds sing for hours, without intermission,
every day. Then the passion of love infects them;
the pleasant choir breaks up, and its ten thousand
members scatter wide over the surrounding fields
and pasture lands. During courtship the male has
a feeble, sketchy music, but his singing is then accompanied with very charming love antics. His
circlings about the hen-bird; his numberless advances and retreats, and little soarings above her
when his voice swells with importunate passion ; his
fluttering lapses back to earth, where he lies prone
with outspread, tremulous wings, a suppliant at her
feet, his languishing voice meanwhile dying down to
lispings—all these apt and graceful motions seem to
express the very sickness of the heart. But the
melody during this emotional period is nothing.
After the business of pairing and nest-building is
over, his musical displays take a new and finer form.
He sits perched on a stalk above the grass, and at
intervals soars up forty or fifty yards high; rising,
he utters a series of long melodious notes; then he
descends in a graceful spiral, the set of the motionless wings giving him the appearance of a slowly-
falling parachute ; the voice then also falls, the notes
coming lower, sweeter, and more expressive until
he reaches the surface. After alighting the song
continues, the strains becoming longer, thinner, and
clearer, until they dwindle to the finest threads of
sound and faintest tinklings, as from a cithern
touched by fairy fingers. The great charm of the

song is in this slow gradation from the somewhat
throaty notes emitted by the bird when ascending
to the excessively attenuated sounds at the close.

In conclusion of this part I shall speak of one
species more—the white-banded mocking-bird of
Patagonia, which greatly excels all other songsters
known to me in the copiousness, variety and brilliant character of its music. Concealed in the
foliage this bird will sing by the half-hour, reproducing with miraculous fidelity the more or less
melodious set songs of a score of species — a
strange and beautiful performance ; but wonderful
as it seems while it lasts, one almost ceases to
admire this mimicking bird-art when the mocker,
as if to show by contrast his unapproachable superiority, bursts into his own divine song, uttered
with a power, abandon and joyousness resembling,
but greatly exceeding, that of the skylark " singing
at heaven's gate ; " the notes issuing in a continuous
torrent ; the voice so brilliant and infinitely varied,
that if " rivalry and emulation " have as large a
place in feathered breasts as some imagine all that
hear this surpassing melody might well languish
ever after in silent despair.

In a vast majority of the finest musical performances the same notes are uttered in the same
order, and after an interval the song is repeated
without any variation : and it seems impossible that
we could in any other way have such beautiful con-
trasts and harmonious lights and shades—the whole
song, so to speak, like a " melody sweetly played in
tune." This seeming impossibility is accomplished in
the mocking-bird's song : the notes never come in the

same order again and again, but, as if inspired, in
a changed order, with variations and new sounds :
and here again it has some resemblance to the skylark's song, and might be described as the lark's
song with endless variations and brightened and
spiritualized in a degree that cannot be imagined.

White-banded mocking-bird.

This mocking-bird is one of those species that
accompany music with appropriate motions. And
just as its song is, so to speak, inspired and an im-
provization, unlike any song the bird has ever
uttered, so its motions all have the same character
of spontaneity, and follow no order, and yet have a
grace and passion and a perfect harmony with the

music unparalleled among birds possessing a similar
habit. While singing he passes from bush to bush,
sometimes delaying a few moments on and at others
just touching the summits, and at times sinking out
of sight in the foliage : then, in an access of rap-
ture, soaring vertically to a height of a hundred
feet, with measured wing-beats, like those of a heron :
or, mounting suddenly in a wild, hurried zigzag,
then slowly circling downwards, to sit at last with
tail outspread fanwise, and vans, glistening white
in the sunshine, expanded and vibrating, or waved
languidly up and down, with a motion like that of
some broad-winged butterfly at rest on a flower.

I wish now to put this question : What relation
that we can see or imagine to the passion of love
and the business of courtship, have these dancing
and vocal performances in nine cases out of ten?
In such cases, for instance, as that of the scissors-
tail tyrant-bird, and its pyrotechnic evening displays,
when a number of couples leave their nests containing eggs and young to join in a wild aërial
dance : the mad exhibitions of ypecahas and ibises,
and the jacanas' beautiful exhibition of grouped
wings : the triplet dances of the spur-winged lapwing, to perform which two birds already mated are
compelled to call in a third bird to complete the
set : the harmonious duets of the oven-birds, and
the duets and choruses of nearly all the wood-
hewers, and the wing-slapping aërial displays of the
whistling widgeons—will it be seriously contended
that the female of this species makes choice of the

male able to administer the most vigorous and
artistic slaps ?

The believer in the theory would put all these
cases lightly aside, to cite that of the male cow-bird
practising antics before the female and drawing a
wide circle of melody round her; or that of the jet-
black, automaton-like, dancing tyrant-bird ; and
concerning this species he would probably say that
the plain-plumaged female went about unseen,
critically watching the dancing of different males,
to discover the most excellent performer according
to the traditional standard. And this was, in substance, what Darwin did. There are many species
in which the male, singly or with others, practises
antics or sings during the love-season before the
female ; and when all such cases, or rather those
that are most striking and bizarre, are brought
together, and when it is gratuitously asserted that
the females *do* choose the males that show off in the
best manner or that sing best, a case for sexual
selection seems to be made out. How unfair the
argument is, based on these carefully selected cases
gathered from all regions of the globe, and often
not properly reported, is seen when we turn from
the book to nature and closely consider the habits
and actions of all the species inhabiting any *one*
district. We see then that such cases as those
described and made so much of in the *Descent of
Man*, and cases like those mentioned in this chapter,
are not essentially different in character, but are
manifestations of one instinct, which appears to be
almost universal among the animals. The explanation I have to offer lies very much on the surface

and is very simple indeed, and, like that of Dr. Wallace[1] with regard to colour and ornaments, covers the whole of the facts. We see that the inferior animals, when the conditions of life are favourable, are subject to periodical fits of gladness, affecting them powerfully and standing out in vivid contrast to their ordinary temper. And we know what this feeling is—this periodic intense elation which even civilized man occasionally experiences when in perfect health, more especially when young. There are moments when he is mad with joy, when he cannot keep still, when his impulse is to sing and shout aloud and laugh at nothing, to run and leap and exert himself in some extravagant way. Among the heavier mammalians the feeling is manifested in loud noises, bellowings and screamings, and in lumbering, uncouth motions—throwing up of heels, pretended panics, and ponderous mock battles.

In smaller and livelier animals, with greater celerity and certitude in their motions, the feeling shows itself in more regular and often in more complex ways. Thus, Felidæ when young, and, in very agile, sprightly species like the Puma, throughout life, simulate all the actions of an animal hunting its prey—sudden, intense excitement of discovery, concealment, gradual advance, masked by interven-

---

[1] It is curious to find that Dr. Wallace's idea about colour has been independently hit upon by Ruskin. Of stones he writes in *Frondes Agrestis* :—" I have often had occasion to allude to the apparent connection of brilliancy of colour with vigour of life and purity of substance. This is pre-eminently the case in the mineral kingdom. The perfection with which the particles of any substance unite in crystallization, corresponds in that kingdom to the vital power in organic nature."

ing objects, with intervals of watching, when they
crouch motionless, the eyes flashing and tail waved
from side to side ; finally, the rush and spring, when
the playfellow is captured, rolled over on his back
and worried to imaginary death. Other species of
the most diverse kinds, in which voice is greatly
developed, join in noisy concerts and choruses;
many of the cats may be mentioned, also dogs and
foxes, capybaras and other loquacious rodents; and
in the howling monkeys this kind of performance
rises to the sublime uproar of the tropical forest at
eventide.

Birds are more subject to this universal joyous
instinct than mammals, and there are times when
some species are constantly overflowing with it ;
and as they are so much freer than mammals, more
buoyant and graceful in action, more loquacious,
and have voices so much finer, their gladness shows
itself in a greater variety of ways, with more regular
and beautiful motions, and with melody. But every
species, or group of species, has its own inherited
form or style of performance ; and, however rude
and irregular this may be, as in the case of the pretended stampedes and fights of wild cattle, that is
the form in which the feeling will always be expressed. If all men, at some exceedingly remote
period in their history, had agreed to express the
common glad impulse, which they now express in
such an infinite variety of ways or do not express
at all, by dancing a minuet, and minuet-dancing
had at last come to be instinctive, and taken to
spontaneously by children at an early period, just
as they take to walking " on their hind legs,"

man's case would be like that of the inferior
animals.

I was one day watching a flock of plovers, quietly
feeding on the ground, when, in a moment, all the
birds were seized by a joyous madness, and each
one, after making a vigorous peck at his nearest
neighbour, began running wildly about, each trying
in passing to peck other birds, while seeking by
means of quick doublings to escape being pecked in
turn. This species always expresses its glad impulse in the same way ; but how different in form
is this simple game of touch-who-touch-can from
the triplet dances of the spur-winged lapwings,
with their drumming music, pompous gestures, and
military precision of movement! How different
also from the aërial performance of another bird of
the same family—the Brazilian stilt—in which one is
pursued by the others, mounting upwards in a wild,
eccentric flight until they are all but lost to view ;
and back to earth again, and then skywards once
more ; the pursued bird when overtaken giving
place to another individual, and the pursuing pack
making the air ring with their melodious barking
cries ! How different again are all these from the
aërial pastimes of the snipe, in which the bird, in
its violent descent, is able to produce such wonderful, far-reaching sounds with its tail-feathers ! The
snipe, as a rule, is a solitary bird, and, like the
oscillating finch mentioned early in this paper, is
content to practise its pastimes without a witness.
In the gregarious kinds all perform together : for
this feeling, like fear, is eminently contagious, and the
sight of one bird mad with joy will quickly make

the whole flock mad. There are also species that
always live in pairs, like the scissors-tails already
mentioned, that periodically assemble in numbers
for the purpose of display. The crested screamer,
a very large bird, may also be mentioned : male and
female sing somewhat harmoniously together, with
voices of almost unparalleled power : but these
birds also congregate in large numbers, and a
thousand couples, or even several thousands, may
be assembled together : and, at intervals, both by
day and night, all sing in concert, their combined
voices producing a thunderous melody which seems
to shake the earth. As a rule, however, birds that
live always in pairs do not assemble for the purpose
of display, but the joyous instinct is expressed by
duet-like performances between male and female.
Thus, in the three South American Passerine
families, the tyrant-birds, wood-hewers, and ant-
thrushes, numbering together between eight and
nine hundred species, a very large majority appear
to have displays of this description.

In my own experience, in cases where the male
and female together, or assembled with others,
take equal parts in the set displays, the sexes are
similar, or differ little ; but where the female takes
no part in the displays the superiority of the male
in brightness of colour is very marked. One or two
instances bearing on this point may be given.

A scarlet-breasted troupial of La Plata perches
conspicuously on a tall plant in a field, and at intervals soars up vertically, singing, and, at the highest
ascending point, flight and song end in a kind of
aërial somersault and vocal flourish at the same

moment. Meanwhile, the dull-plumaged female is
not seen and not heard : for not even a skulking
crake lives in closer seclusion under the herbage—
so widely have the sexes diverged in this species.
Is the female, then, without an instinct so common ?
—has she no sudden fits of irrepressible gladness ?
Doubtless she has them, and manifests them down
in her place of concealment in lively chirpings and
quick motions—the simple, primitive form in which
gladness is expressed in the class of birds. In the
various species of the genus Cnipolegus, already
mentioned, the difference in the sexes is just as
great as in the case of the troupial : the solitary,
intensely black, statuesque male has, we have seen,
a set and highly fantastic performance; but on
more than one occasion I have seen four or five
females of one species meet together and have a
little simple performance all to themselves—in form
a kind of lively mock fight.

It might be objected that when a bird takes its
stand and repeats a set finished song at intervals
for an hour at a stretch, remaining quietly perched,
such a performance appears to be different in
character from the irregular and simple displays
which are unmistakably caused by a sudden glad
impulse. But we are familiar with the truth that
in organic nature great things result from small
beginnings—a common flower, and our own bony
skulls, to say nothing of the matter contained within
them, are proofs of it. Only a limited number of
species sing in a highly finished manner. Looking
at many species, we find every gradation, every
shade, from the simple joyous chirp and cry to the

most perfect melody. Even in a single branch of
the true vocalists we may see it—from the chirping
bunting, and noisy but tuneless sparrow, to linnet
and goldfinch and canary. Not only do a large
majority of species show the singing instinct, or
form of display, in a primitive, undeveloped state,
but in that state it continues to show itself in the
young of many birds in which melody is most highly
developed in the adult. And where the development has been solely in the male the female never
rises above that early stage ; in her lively chirpings
and little mock fights and chases, and other simple
forms which gladness takes in birds, as well as in
her plainer plumage, and absence of ornament, she
represents the species at some remote period. And
as with song so with antics and all set performances
aërial or terrestrial, from those of the whale and
the elephant to those of the smallest insect.

Another point remains to be noticed, and that is
the greater frequency and fulness in displays of all
kinds, including song, during the love season. And
here Dr. Wallace's colour and ornament theory
helps us to an explanation. At the season of courtship, when the conditions of life are most favourable
vitality is at its maximum, and naturally it is then
that the proficiency in all kinds of dancing-antics,
aërial and terrestrial, appears greatest, and that
melody attains its highest perfection. This applies
chiefly to birds, but even among birds there are
exceptions, as we have seen in the case of the field-
finch, *Sycalis luteola.* The love-excitement is
doubtless pleasurable to them, and it takes the
form in which keenly pleasurable emotions are

habitually expressed, although not infrequently
with variations due to the greater intensity of the
feeling. In some migrants the males arrive before
the females, and no sooner have they recovered
from the effects of their journey than they burst
out into rapturous singing; these are not love-strains,
since the females have not yet arrived, and pairing-
time is perhaps a month distant; their singing
merely expresses their overflowing gladness. The
forest at that season is vocal, not only with the
fine melody of the true songsters, but with hoarse
cawings, piercing cries, shrill duets, noisy choruses,
drummings, boomings, trills, wood-tappings—every
sound with which different species express the glad
impulse; and birds like the parrot that only exert
their powerful voices in screamings—because "they
can do no other"—then scream their loudest.
When courtship begins it has in many cases the
effect of increasing the beauty of the performance,
giving added sweetness, verve, and brilliance to the
song, and freedom and grace to the gestures and
motions. But, as I have said, there are exceptions.
Thus, some birds that are good melodists at other
times sing in a feeble, disjointed manner during
courtship. In Patagonia I found that several of
the birds with good voices—one a mocking bird—
were, like the robin at home, autumn and winter
songsters.

The argument has been stated very briefly: but
little would be gained by the mere multiplication of
instances, since, however many, they would be
selected instances—from a single district, it is true,
while those in the *Descent of Man* were brought

together from an immeasurably wider field ; but the
principle is the same in both cases, and to what I
have written it may be objected that, if, instead of
twenty-five, I had given a hundred cases, taking
them as they came, they might have shown a larger
proportion of instances like that of the cow-bird, in
which the male has a set performance practised
only during the love-season and in the presence of
the female.

It is, no doubt, true that all collections of facts
relating to animal life present nature to us somewhat as a " fantastic realm "—unavoidably so, in a
measure, since the writing would be too bulky, or
too dry, or too something inconvenient, if we did
not take only the most prominent facts that come
before us, remove them from their places, where
alone they can be seen in their proper relations to
numerous other less prominent facts, and rearrange
them patchwork-wise to make up our literature.
But I am convinced that any student of the subject
who will cast aside his books —supposing that they
have not already bred a habit in his mind of seeing
only " in accordance with verbal statement "—and
go directly to nature to note the actions of animals
for himself—actions which, in many cases, appear
to lose all significance when set down in writing—
the result of such independent investigation will be
a conviction that conscious sexual selection on the
part of the female is not the cause of music and
dancing performances in birds, nor of the brighter
colours and ornaments that distinguish the male.   It
is true that the females of some species, both in
the vertebrate and insect kingdoms, do exercise a

preference ; but in a vast majority of species the male
takes the female he finds, or that he is able to win
from other competitors ; and if we go to the reptile
class we find that in the ophidian order, which
excels in variety and richness of colour, there is no
such thing as preferential mating ; and if we go to
the insect class, we find that in butterflies, which
surpass all creatures in their glorious beauty, the
female gives herself up to the embrace of the first
male that appears, or else is captured by the
strongest male, just as she might be by a mantis or
some other rapacious insect.

CHAPTER XX.

BIOGRAPHY OF THE VIZCACHA.

(*Lagostomus Trichodactylus.*)

THE vizcacha is perhaps the most characteristic of
the South American Rodentia,[1] while its habits, in
some respects, are more interesting than those of
any other rodent known : it is, moreover, the most
common mammal we have on the pampas; and all
these considerations have induced me to write a
very full account of its customs. It is necessary to
add that since the following pages were written at
my home on the pampas a great war of extermination has been waged against this animal by the

---

[1] "According to Mr. Waterhouse, of all rodents the vizcacha
is most nearly related to marsupials; but in the points in which
it approaches this order its relations are general, that is, not to
any one marsupial species more than to another. As these points
of affinity are believed to be real and not merely adaptive, they
must be due in accordance with our view to inheritance from a
common progenitor. Therefore we must suppose either that all
rodents, including the vizcacha, branched off from some ancient
marsupial, which will naturally have been more or less intermediate in character with respect to all existing marsupials; or,
that both rodents and marsupials branched off from a common
progenitor. . . . On either view we must suppose that the
vizcacha has retained, by inheritance, more of the characters of
its ancient progenitor than have other rodents."—DARWIN ; *Origin
of Species.*

landowners, which has been more fortunate in its
results—or unfortunate if one's sympathies are with
the vizcacha—than the war of the Australians
against their imported rodent—the smaller and
more prolific rabbit.

The vizcachas on the pampas of Buenos Ayres
live in societies, usually numbering twenty or thirty

Vizcachas.

members.   The village, which is called Vizcachera, is
composed of a dozen or fifteen burrows or mouths ;
for one entrance often serves for two or more distinct
holes.   Often, where the ground is soft, there are
twenty or thirty or more burrows in an old vizcachera; but on stony, or " tosca " soil even an old
one may have no more than four or five burrows.
They are deep wide-mouthed holes, placed very
close together, the entire village covering an area

of from one hundred to two hundred square feet of ground.

The burrows vary greatly in extent ; and usually in a vizcachera there are several that, at a distance of from four to six feet from the entrance, open into large circular chambers. From these chambers other burrows diverge in all directions, some running horizontally, others obliquely downwards to a maximum depth of six feet from the surface : some of these burrows or galleries communicate with those of other burrows. A vast amount of loose earth is thus brought up, and forms a very irregular mound, fifteen to thirty inches above the surrounding level.

It will afford some conception of the numbers of these vizcacheras on the settled pampas when I say that, in some directions, a person might ride five hundred miles and never advance half a mile without seeing one or more of them. In districts where, as far as the eye can see, the plains are as level and smooth as a bowling-green, especially in winter when the grass is close-cropped, and where the rough giant-thistle has not sprung up, these mounds appear like brown or dark spots on a green surface. They are the only irregularities that occur to catch the eye, and consequently form an important feature in the scenery. In some places they are so near together that a person on horseback may count a hundred of them from one point of view.

The sites of which the vizcacha invariably makes choice to work on, as well as his manner of burrowing, adapt him peculiarly to live and thrive on the

open pampas.   Other burrowing species seem
always to fix upon some spot where there is a bank
or a sudden depression in the soil, or where there
is rank herbage, or a bush or tree, about the roots
of which to begin their kennel. They are averse
to commence digging on a clear level surface,
either because it is not easy for them where they
have nothing to rest their foreheads against while
scratching, or because they possess a wary instinct
that impels them to place the body in concealment
whilst working on the surface, thus securing the
concealment of the burrow after it is made.
Certain it is that where large hedges have been
planted on the pampas, multitudes of opossums,
weasels, skunks, armadillos, &c., come and make
their burrows beneath them ; and where there are
no hedges or trees, all these species make their
kennels under bushes of the perennial thistle, or
where there is a shelter of some kind.   The vizcacha,
on the contrary, chooses an open level spot, the
cleanest he can find to burrow on.   The first thing
that strikes the observer when viewing the vizcachera closely is the enormous size of the entrance
of the burrows, or, at least, of several of the central
ones in the mound ; for there are usually several
smaller outside burrows.   The pit-like opening to
some of these principal burrows is often four to six
feet across the mouth, and sometimes deep enough
for a tall man to stand up waist-deep in.   How
these large entrances can be made on a level surface
may be seen when the first burrow or burrows of
an incipient vizcachera are formed.   It is not
possible to tell what induces a vizcacha to be the

founder of a new community; for they increase
very slowly, and furthermore are extremely fond of
each other's society ; and it is invariably one
individual that leaves his native village to found a
new and independent one. If it were to have
better pasture at hand, then he would certainly
remove to a considerable distance ; but he merely
goes from forty to fifty or sixty yards off to begin
his work. Thus it is that in desert places, where
these animals are rare, a solitary vizcachera is never
seen; but there are always several close together,
though there may be no others on the surrounding
plain for leagues. When the vizcacha has made his
habitation, it is but a single burrow, with only
himself for an inhabitant, perhaps for many months.
Sooner or later, however, others join him : and
these will be the parents of innumerable generations ; for they construct no temporary lodging-
place, as do the armadillos and other species, but
their posterity continues in the quiet possession of
the habitations bequeathed to it; how long, it is
impossible to say. Old men who have lived all
their lives in one district remember that many of
the vizcacheras around them existed when they
were children. It is invariably a male that begins
a new village, and makes his burrow in the following
manner, though he does not always observe the
same method. He works very straight into the
earth, digging a hole twelve or fourteen inches wide,
but not so deep, at an angle of about 25° with the
surface. But after he has progressed inwards a
few feet, the vizcacha is no longer satisfied with
merely scattering away the loose earth he fetches

up, but cleans it away so far in a straight line from
the entrance, and scratches so much on this line
(apparently to make the slope gentler), that he
soon forms a trench a foot or more in depth, and
often three or four feet in length. Its use is, as I
have inferred, to facilitate the conveying of the
loose earth as far as possible from the entrance of
the burrow. But after a while the animal is unwilling that it should accumulate even at the end of
this long passage ; he therefore proceeds to make
two additional trenches, that form an acute, sometimes a right angle, converging into the first, so
that when the whole is completed it takes the form
of a capital Y.

These trenches are continually deepened and
lengthened as the burrow progresses, the angular
segment of earth between them scratched away,
until by degrees it has been entirely conveyed off,
and in its place is the one deep great unsymmetrical
mouth I have already described. There are soils
that will not admit of the animals working in this
manner. Where there are large cakes of "tosca"
near the surface, as in many localities on the
southern pampas, the vizcacha makes its burrow as
best he can, and without the regular trenches. In
earths that crumble much, sand or gravel, he also
works under great disadvantages.

The burrows are made best in the black and
red moulds of the pampas ; but even in such soils
the entrances of many burrows are made differently.
In some the central trench is wanting, or is so short
that there appear but two passages converging
directly into the burrow ; or these two trenches

may be so curved inwards as to form the segment of a circle. Many other forms may also be noticed, but usually they appear to be only modifications of the most common Y-shaped system.

As I have remarked that its manner of burrowing has peculiarly adapted the vizcacha to the pampas, it may be asked what particular advantage a species that makes a wide-mouthed burrow possesses over those that excavate in the usual way. On a declivity, or at the base of rocks or trees, there would be none; but on the perfectly level and shelterless pampas, the durability of the burrow, a circumstance favourable to the animal's preservation, is owing altogether to its being made in this way, and to several burrows being made together. The two outer trenches diverge so widely from the mouth that half the earth brought out is cast behind instead of before it, thus creating a mound of equal height about the entrance, by which it is secured from water during great rainfalls, while the cattle avoid treading over the great pit-like entrances. But the burrows of the dolichotis, armadillo, and other species, when made on perfectly level ground, are soon trod on and broken in by cattle; in summer they are choked up with dust and rubbish ; and, the loose earth having all been thrown up together in a heap on one side, there is no barrier to the water which in every great rainfall flows in and obliterates the kennel, drowning or driving out the tenant.

I have been minute in describing the habitations of the vizcacha, as I esteem the subject of prime importance in considering the zoology of this portion of America. The vizcacha does not benefit himself alone by his perhaps unique style of burrowing; but this habit has proved advantageous to several other species, and has been so favourable to two of our birds that they are among the most common species found here, whereas without these burrows they would have been exceedingly rare, since the natural banks in which they breed are scarcely found anywhere on the pampas. I refer to the Minera (Geositta cunicularia), which makes its breeding-holes in the bank-like sides of the vizcacha's burrow, and to the little swallow (Atticora cyanoleuca) which breeds in these excavations when forsaken by the Minera. Few old vizcacheras are seen without some of these little parasitical burrows in them.

Birds are not the only beings in this way related to the vizcachas : the fox and the weasel of the pampas live almost altogether in them. Several insects also frequent these burrows that are seldom found anywhere else. Of these the most interesting are :—a large predacious nocturnal bug, shining black, with red wings; a nocturnal Cicindela, a beautiful insect, with dark green striated wing-cases and pale red legs; also several diminutive wingless wasps. Of the last I have counted six species, most of them marked with strongly contrasted colours, black, red, and white. There are also other wasps that prey on the spiders found on the vizcachera. All these and others are so numerous on the mounds that dozens of them might there be collected any summer day; but if sought for in other situations they are exceedingly rare. If the dry mound of soft earth which the vizcacha elevates amidst a waste of humid, close-growing grass is not absolutely necessary to the existence of all these species, it supplies them with at least one favourable condition, and without doubt thereby greatly increases their numbers: they, too, whether predacious or preyed on, have so many relations with other outside species, and these again with still others, that it would be no mere fancy to say that probably hundreds of species are either directly or indirectly affected in their struggle for existence by the vizcacheras so abundantly sprinkled over the pampas.

In winter the vizcachas seldom leave their burrows till dark, but in summer come out before sunset ; and the vizcachera is then a truly interesting spectacle. Usually one of the old males first appears, and sits on some prominent place on the mound, apparently in no haste to begin his evening meal. When approached from the front he stirs not, but eyes the intruder with a bold indifferent stare. If the person passes to one side, he deigns not to turn his head.

Other vizcachas soon begin to appear, each one quietly taking up his station at his burrow's mouth, the females, known by their greatly inferior size and lighter grey colour, sitting upright on their haunches, as if to command a better view, and indicating by divers sounds and gestures that fear and curiosity struggles in them for mastery ; for they are always wilder and sprightlier in their motions than the males. With eyes fixed on the intruder, at intervals they dodge the head, emitting at the same time an internal note with great vehemence; and suddenly, as the danger comes nearer, they plunge simultaneously, with a startled cry, into their burrows. But in some curiosity is the strongest emotion; for, in spite of their fellow's contagious example, and already half down the entrance, again they start up to scrutinize the stranger, and will then often permit him to walk within five or six paces of them.

Standing on the mound there is frequently a pair of burrowing owls (Pholeoptynx cunicularia). These birds generally make their own burrows to breed in, or sometimes take possession of one of the lesser outside burrows of the village; but their favourite residence, when not engaged in tending their eggs or young, is on the vizcachera. Here a pair will sit all day; and I have often remarked a couple close together on the edge of the burrow; and when the vizcacha came out in the evening, though but a hand's breadth from them, they did not stir, nor did he notice them, so accustomed are these creatures to each other. Usually a couple of the little burrowing Geositta are also present. They are lively creatures, running with great rapidity about the mound and bare space that surrounds it, suddenly stopping and jerking their tails in a slow deliberate manner, and occasionally uttering their cry, a trill, or series of quick short clear notes, resembling somewhat the shrill excessive laughter of a child. Among the grave, stationary vizcachas, of which they take no heed, perhaps half a dozen or more little swallows (Atticora cyanoleuca) are seen, now clinging altogether to the bank-like entrance of a burrow, now hovering over it in a moth-like manner, as if uncertain where to alight, and anon sweeping about in circles, but never ceasing their low and sorrowful notes.

The vizcachera with all its incongruous inhabitants thus collected upon it is to a stranger one of the most novel sights the pampas afford.

The vizcacha appears to be a rather common species over all the extensive Argentine territory ; but they are so exceedingly abundant on the pampas inhabited by man, and comparatively so rare in the desert places I have been in, that I was at first much surprised at finding them so unequally distributed. I have also mentioned that the vizcacha is a tame familiar creature. This is in the pastoral districts, where they are never disturbed ; but in wild regions, where he is scarce, he is exceedingly wary, coming forth long after dark, and plunging into his burrow on the slightest alarm, so that it is a rare thing to get a sight of him. The reason is evident enough ; in desert regions the vizcacha has several deadly enemies in the larger rapacious mammals. Of these the puma or lion (Felis concolor) is the most numerous, as it is also the swiftest, most subtle, and most voracious ; for, as regards these traits, the jaguar (F. onca) is an inferior animal. To the insatiable bloody appetite of this creature nothing comes amiss ; he takes the male ostrich by surprise, and slays that wariest of wild things on his nest ; he captures little birds with the dexterity of a cat, and hunts for diurnal armadillos ; he comes unawares upon the deer and huanaco, and, springing like lightning on them, dislocates their necks before their

bodies touch the earth. Often after he has thus
slain them, he leaves their bodies untouched for the
Polyborus and vulture to feast on, so great a delight
does he take in destroying life. The vizcacha falls
an easy victim to this subtle creature; and it is not
to be wondered at that it becomes wild to excess,
and rare in regions hunted over by such an enemy,
even when all other conditions are favourable to its
increase. But as soon as these wild regions are
settled by man the pumas are exterminated, and the
sole remaining foe of the vizcacha is the fox, comparatively an insignificant one.

The fox takes up his residence in a vizcachera,
and succeeds, after some quarrelling (manifested in
snarls, growls, and other subterranean warlike
sounds), in ejecting the rightful owners of one of the
burrows, which forthwith becomes his. Certainly
the vizcachas are not much injured by being compelled to relinquish the use of one of their kennels for
a season or permanently; for, if the locality suits him,
the fox remains with them always. Soon they grow
accustomed to the unwelcome stranger; he is quiet
and unassuming in demeanour, and often in the
evening sits on the mound in their company, until
they regard him with the same indifference they do
the burrowing owl. But in spring, when the young
vizcachas are large enough to leave their cells, then
the fox makes them his prey; and if it is a bitch
fox, with a family of eight or nine young to provide
for, she will grow so bold as to hunt her helpless
quarry from hole to hole, and do battle with the old
ones, and carry off the young in spite of them, so
that all the young animals in the village are even-

tually destroyed. Often when the young foxes are large enough to follow their mother, the whole family takes leave of the vizcachera where such cruel havoc has been made to settle in another, there to continue their depredations. But the fox has ever a relentless foe in man, and meets with no end of bitter persecutions; it is consequently much more abundant in desert or thinly settled districts than in such as are populous, so that in these the check the vizcachas receive from the foxes is not appreciable.

The abundance of cattle on the pampas has made it unnecessary to use the vizcacha as an article of food. His skin is of no value; therefore man, the destroyer of his enemies, has hitherto been the greatest benefactor of his species. Thus they have been permitted to multiply and spread themselves to an amazing extent, so that the half-domestic cattle on the pampas are not nearly so familiar with man, or so fearless of his presence as are the vizcachas. It is not that they do him no injury, but because they do it indirectly, that they have so long enjoyed immunity from persecution. It is amusing to see the sheep-farmer, the greatest sufferer from the vizcachas, regarding them with such indifference as to permit them to swarm on his " run," and burrow within a stone's throw of his dwelling with impunity, and yet going a distance from home to persecute with unreasonable animosity a fox, skunk, or opossum on account of the small annual loss it inflicts on the poultry-yard. That the vizcacha has comparatively no adverse conditions to war with wherever man is settled is evident when we consider

its very slow rate of increase, and yet see them in
such incalculable numbers. The female has but one
litter in the year of two young, sometimes of three.
She becomes pregnant late in April, and brings
forth in September ; the period of gestation is, I
think, rather less than five months.

The vizcacha is about two years growing. A
full-sized male measures to the root of the tail
twenty-two inches, and weighs from fourteen to
fifteen pounds ; the female is nineteen inches in
length, and her greatest weight nine pounds. Probably it is a long-lived, and certainly it is a very hardy
animal. Where it has any green substance to eat
it never drinks water ; but after a long summer
drought, when for months it has subsisted on
bits of dried thistle-stalks and old withered grass,
if a shower falls it will come out of its burrows
even at noonday and drink eagerly from the pools.
It has been erroneously stated that vizcachas
subsist on roots. Their food is grass and seeds ;
but they may also sometimes eat roots, as the
ground is occasionally seen scratched up about the
burrows. In March, when the stalks of the perennial cardoon or Castile thistle (Cynara cardunculus)
are dry, the vizcachas fell them by gnawing about
their roots, and afterwards tear to pieces the great
dry flower-heads to get the seeds imbedded deeply
in them, of which they seem very fond. Large
patches of thistle are often found served thus, the
ground about them literally white with the silvery
bristles they have scattered. This cutting down
tall plants to get the seeds at the top seems very
like an act of pure intelligence ; but the fact is,

the vizcachas cut down every tall plant they can. I have seen whole acres of maize destroyed by them, yet the plants cut down were left untouched. If posts be put into the ground within range of their nightly rambles they will gnaw till they have felled them, unless of a wood hard enough to resist their chisel-like incisors.

The strongest instinct of this animal is to clear the ground thoroughly about its burrows; and it is this destructive habit that makes it necessary for cultivators of the soil to destroy all the vizcachas in or near their fields. On the uninhabited pampas, where the long grasses grow, I have often admired the vizcachera; for it is there the centre of a clean space, often of half an acre in extent, on which there is an even close-shaven turf : this clearing is surrounded by the usual rough growth of herbs and giant grasses. In such situations this habit of clearing the ground is eminently advantageous to them, as it affords them a comparatively safe spot to feed and disport themselves on, and over which they can fly to their burrows without meeting any obstruction, on the slightest alarm.

Of course the instinct continues to operate where it is no longer of any advantage. In summer, when the thistles are green, even when growing near the burrows, and the giant thistle (Carduus mariana) springs up most luxuriantly right on the mound, the vizcachas will not touch them, either disliking the strong astringent sap, or repelled by the thorns with which they are armed. As soon as they dry, and the thorns become brittle, they are levelled ; and afterwards, when the animal begins to drag them about and cut them up, as his custom is, he accidentally discovers and feasts on the seed : for vizcachas are fond of exercising their teeth on hard substances, such as sticks and bones, just as cats are of " sharpening their claws " on trees.

Another remarkable habit of the vizcacha, that of dragging to and heaping about the mouth of his burrow every stalk he cuts down, and every portable object that by dint of great strength he can carry, has been mentioned by Azara, Darwin, and others. On the level plains it is a useful habit; for as the vizcachas are continually deepening and widening their burrows, the earth thrown out soon covers up these materials, and so assists in raising the mound. On the Buenos-Ayrean pampas numbers of viz-cacheras would annually be destroyed by water in the great sudden rainfalls were the mounds less high. But this is only an advantage when the animals inhabit a perfectly level country subject to flooding rains ; for where the surface is unequal they invariably prefer high to low ground to burrow on, and are thus secured from destruction by water ; yet the instinct is as strong in such situations as on the level plains. The most that can be said of a habit apparently so obscure in its origin and uses is, that it appears to be part of the instinct of clearing the ground about the village. Every tall stalk the vizcacha cuts down, every portable object he finds, must be removed to make the surface clean and smooth ; but while encumbered with it he does not proceed further from his burrows, but invariably re-tires towards them, and so deposits it upon the mound. So well known is this habit, that whatever article is lost by night—whip, pistol, or knife—the loser next morning visits the vizcacheras in the vicinity, quite sure of finding it there. People also visit the vizcacheras to pick up sticks for firewood.

The vizcachas are cleanly in their habits; and the fur, though it has a strong earthy smell, is kept exceedingly neat. The hind leg and foot afford a very beautiful instance of adaptation. Propped by the hard curved tail, they sit up erect, and as firmly on the long horny disks on the undersides of the hind legs as a man stands on his feet. Most to be admired, on the middle toe the skin thickens into a round cushion, in which the curved teeth-like bristles are set; nicely graduated in length, so that " each particular hair " may come into contact with the skin when the animal scratches or combs itself. As to the uses of this appendage there can be no difference of opinion, as there is about the serrated claw in birds. It is quite obvious that the animal cannot scratch himself with his hind paw (as all mammals do) without making use of this natural comb. Then the entire foot is modified, so that this comb shall be well protected, and yet not be hindered from performing its office : thus the inner toe is pressed close to the middle one, and so depressed that it comes under the cushion of skin, and cannot possibly get before the bristles, or interfere with their coming against the skin in scratching, as would certainly be the case if this toe were free as the outer one.

Again, the vizcachas appear to form the deep trenches before the burrows by scratching the earth

violently backwards with the hind claws. Now
these straight, sharp, dagger-shaped claws, and
especially the middle one, are so long that the
vizcacha is able to perform all this rough work
without the bristles coming into contact with the
ground, and so getting worn by the friction. The
Tehuelcho Indians in Patagonia comb their hair with
a brush-comb very much like that on the vizcacha's
toe, but in their case it does not properly fulfil its
office, or else the savages make little use of it. Vizcachas have a remarkable way of dusting themselves :
the animal suddenly throws himself on his back,
and, bringing over his hind legs towards his head,
depresses them till his feet touch the ground. In
this strange posture he scratches up the earth with
great rapidity, raising a little cloud of dust, then
rights himself with a jerk, and, after an interval,
repeats the dusting. Usually they scratch a hole
in the ground to deposit their excrements in.
Whilst opening one of the outside burrows that had
no communication with the others, I once discovered
a vast deposit of their dung (so great that it must
have been accumulating for years) at the extremity.
To ascertain whether this be a constant, or only
a casual habit, it would be necessary to open up
entirely a vast number of vizcacheras. When a
vizcacha dies in his burrow the carcass is, after
some days, dragged out and left upon the mound.

The language of the vizcacha is wonderful for its
variety. When the male is feeding he frequently
pauses to utter a succession of loud, percussive, and
somewhat jarring cries ; these he utters in a leisurely
manner, and immediately after goes on feeding.

Often he utters this cry in a low grunting tone. One of his commonest expressions sounds like the violent hawking of a man clearing his throat. At other times he bursts into piercing tones that may be heard a mile off, beginning like the excited and quick-repeated squeals of a young pig, and growing longer, more attenuated, and quavering towards the end. After retiring alarmed into the burrows, he repeats at intervals a deep internal moan. All these, and many other indescribable guttural, sighing, shrill, and deep tones, are varied a thousand ways in strength and intonation, according to the age, sex, or emotions of the individual; and I doubt if there is in the world any other four-footed thing so loquacious, or with a dialect so extensive. I take great pleasure in going to some spot where they are abundant, and sitting quietly to listen to them; for they are holding a perpetual discussion all night long, which the presence of a human being will not interrupt.

At night, when the vizcachas are all out feeding, in places where they are very abundant (and in some districts they literally swarm) any very loud and sudden sound, as the report of a gun, or a clap of unexpected thunder, will produce a most extraordinary effect. No sooner has the report broken on the stillness of night than a perfect storm of cries bursts forth over the surrounding country. After eight or nine seconds there is in the storm a momentary lull or pause; and then it breaks forth again, apparently louder than before. There is so much difference in the tones of different animals that the cries of individuals close at hand may be distinguished amidst the roar of blended voices coming from a distance. It sounds as if thousands and tens of thousands of them were striving to express every emotion at the highest pitch of their voices; so that the effect is indescribable, and fills a stranger with astonishment. Should a gun be fired off several times, their cries become less each time; and after the third or fourth time it produces no effect. They have a peculiar, sharp, sudden, " far-darting " alarm-note when a dog is spied, that is repeated by all that hear it, and produces an instantaneous panic, sending every vizcacha flying to his burrow.

But though they manifest such a terror of dogs when out feeding at night (for the slowest dog can overtake them), in the evening, when sitting upon their mounds, they treat them with tantalizing contempt. If the dog is a novice, the instant he spies the animal he rushes violently at it; the vizcacha waits the charge with imperturbable calmness till his enemy is within one or two yards, and then disappears into the burrow. After having been foiled in this way many times, the dog resorts to stratagem : he crouches down as if transformed for the nonce into a Felis, and steals on with wonderfully slow and cautious steps, his hair bristling, tail hanging, and eyes intent on his motionless intended victim; when within seven or eight yards he makes a sudden rush, but invariably with the same disappointing result. The persistence with which the dogs go on hoping against hope in this unprofitable game, in which they always act the stupid part, is highly amusing, and is very interesting to the naturalist; for it shows that the native dogs on the pampas have developed a very remarkable instinct, and one that might be perfected by artificial selection; but dogs with the hunting habits of the cat would, I think, be of little use to man. When it is required to train dogs to hunt the nocturnal armadillo (Dasypus villosus), then this deep-rooted (and, it might be added, hereditary) passion for vizcachas is excessively annoying, and it is often necessary to administer hundreds of blows and rebukes before a dog is induced to track an armadillo without leaving the scent every few moments to make futile grabs at his old enemies.

The following instance will show how little suspicion of man the vizcachas have. A few years ago I went out shooting them on three consecutive evenings. I worked in a circle, constantly revisiting the same burrows, never going a greater distance from home than could be walked in four or five minutes. During the three evenings I shot sixty vizcachas dead; and probably as many more escaped badly wounded into their burrows; for they are hard to kill, and however badly wounded, if sitting near the burrow when struck, are almost certain to escape into it. But on the third evening I found them no wilder, and killed about as many as on the first. After this I gave up shooting them in disgust; it was dull sport, and to exterminate or frighten them away with a gun seemed an impossibility.

It is a very unusual thing to eat the vizcacha, most people, and especially the gauchos, having a silly unaccountable prejudice against their flesh. I

have found it very good, and while engaged writing
this chapter have dined on it served up in various
ways. The young animals are rather insipid, the
old males tough, but the mature females are excellent—the flesh being tender, exceedingly white,
fragrant to the nostrils, and with a very delicate
game-flavour.

Within the last ten years so much new land has
been brought under cultivation that farmers have
been compelled to destroy incredible numbers of
vizcachas: many large "estancieros" (cattle-
breeders) have followed the example set by the
grain-growers, and have had them exterminated
on their estates. Now all that Azara, on hearsay,
tells about the vizcachas perishing in their burrows,
when these are covered up, but that they can support life thus buried for a period of ten or twelve
days, and that during that time animals will
come from other villages and disinter them, unless
frightened off with dogs, is strictly true. Country
workmen are so well acquainted with these facts
that they frequently undertake to destroy all the
vizcacheras on an estate for so paltry a sum as ten-
pence in English money for each one, and yet will
make double the money at this work than they can
at any other. By day they partly open up, then
cover up the burrows with a great quantity of
earth, and by night go round with dogs to drive
away the vizcachas from the still open burrows
that come to dig out their buried friends. After all
the vizcacheras on an estate have been thus served,
the workmen are usually bound by previous agree-
ment to keep guard over them for a space of eight

or ten days before they receive their hire : for the animals covered up are then supposed to be all dead. Some of these men I have talked with have assured me that living vizcachas have been found after fourteen days—a proof of their great endurance. There is nothing strange, I think, in the mere fact of the vizcacha being unable to work his way out when thus buried alive; for, for all I know to the contrary, other species may, when their burrows are well covered up, perish in the same manner ; but it certainly is remarkable that other vizcachas should come from a distance to dig out those that are buried alive. In this good office they are exceedingly zealous; and I have frequently surprised them after sunrise, at a considerable distance from their own burrows, diligently scratching at those that had been covered up. The vizcachas are fond of each other's society, and live peaceably together; but their goodwill is not restricted to the members of their own little community; it extends to the whole species, so that as soon as night comes many animals leave their own and go to visit the adjacent villages. If one approaches a vizcachera at night, usually some of the vizcachas on it scamper off to distant burrows : these are neighbours merely come to pay a friendly visit. This intercourse is so frequent that little straight paths are formed from one vizcachera to another. The extreme attachment between members of different communities makes it appear less strange that they should assist each other : either the desire to see, as usual, their buried neighbours becomes intense enough to impel them to work their way to them; or cries of

distress from the prisoners reach and incite them
to attempt their deliverance. Many social species
are thus powerfully affected by cries of distress
from one of their fellows ; and some will attempt a
rescue in the face of great danger—the weasel and
the peccary for example.

Mild and sociable as the vizcachas are towards
each other, each one is exceedingly jealous of any
intrusion into his particular burrow, and indeed
always resents such a breach of discipline with the
utmost fury. Several individuals may reside in the
compartments of the same burrow ; but beyond
themselves not even their next-door neighbour is
permitted to enter ; their hospitality ends where it
begins, at the entrance. It is difficult to compel a
vizcacha to enter a burrow not his own ; even when
hotly pursued by dogs they often refuse to do so.
When driven into one, the instant their enemies
retire a little space they rush out of it, as if they
thought the hiding-place but little less dangerous
than the open plain. I have frequently seen vizcachas, chased into the wrong burrows, summarily
ejected by those inside : and sometimes they make
their escape only after being well bitten for their
offence.

I have now stated the most interesting facts I
have collected concerning the vizcacha : when others
rewrite its history they doubtless will, according to
the opportunities of observation they enjoy, be able
to make some additions to it, but probably none of
great consequence. I have observed this species
in Patagonia and Buenos Ayres only ; and as I have
found that its habits are considerably modified by

circumstances in the different localities where I have met with it, I am sure that other variations will occur in the more distant regions, where the conditions vary.

The most remarkable thing to be said about the vizcacha is, that although regarded by Mr. Waterhouse, and others who have studied its affinities, as one of the lowest of the rodents, exhibiting strong Marsupial characters, the living animal appears to be more intelligent than other rodents, not of South America only, but also of those of a higher type in other continents. A parallel case is, perhaps, to be found in the hairy armadillo, an extremely versatile and intelligent animal, although only an edentate. And among birds the ypecaha—a large La Plata rail—might also be mentioned as an example of what ought not to be; for it is a bold and intelligent bird, more than a match for the fowl, both in courage and in cunning; and yet it is one of the family which Professor Parker—from the point of view of the anatomist—characterizes as a " feeble-minded, cowardly group."

CHAPTER XXI.

THE DYING HUANACO.

LEST any one should misread the title to this chapter, I hasten to say that the huanaco, or guanaco as it is often spelt, is not a perishing species; nor, as things are, is it likely to perish soon, despite the fact that civilized men, Britons especially, are now enthusiastically engaged in the extermination of all the nobler mammalians :—a very glorious crusade, the triumphant conclusion of which will doubtless be witnessed by the succeeding generation, more favoured in this respect than ours. The huanaco, happily for it, exists in a barren, desolate region, in its greatest part waterless and uninhabitable to human beings; and the chapter-heading refers to a singular instinct of the dying animals, in very many cases allowed, by the exceptional conditions in which they are placed, to die naturally.

And first, a few words about its place in nature and general habits. The huanaco is a small camel —small, that is, compared with its existing relation —without a hump, and, unlike the camel of the Old World, non-specialized; doubtless it is a very ancient animal on the earth, and for all we know to the contrary, may have existed contemporaneously with some of the earliest known representatives of the

camel type, whose remains occur in the lower and
upper miocene deposits—Poëbrotherium, Protolabis,
Procamelus, Pliauchenia, and Macrauchenia. It
ranges from Tierra del Fuego and the adjacent islands, northwards over the whole of Patagonia, and
along the Andes into Peru and Bolivia. On the great
mountain chain it is both a wild and a domestic
animal, since the llama, the beast of burden of the
ancient Peruvians, is no doubt only a variety : but
as man's slave it has changed so greatly from the
original form that some naturalists have regarded
the llama as a distinct species, which, like the camel
of the East, exists only in a domestic state. It has
had time enough to vary, as it is more than probable
that the tamed and useful animal was inherited by
the children of the sun from races and nations that
came before them : and how far back Andean civilization extends may be inferred from the belief
expressed by the famous American archæologist,
Squiers, that the ruined city of Tiahuanaco, in the
vicinity of Lake Titicaca, is as old as Thebes and
the Pyramids.

It is, however, with the wild animal, the huanaco,
that I am concerned. A full-grown male measures
seven to eight feet in length, and four feet high
to the shoulder ; it is well clothed in a coat of
thick woolly hair, of a pale reddish colour, longest
and palest on the under parts. In appearance it is
very unlike the camel, in spite of the long legs and
neck ; in its finely-shaped head and long ears, and
its proud and graceful carriage, it resembles an
antelope rather than its huge and, from an æsthetic
point of view, deformed Asiatic relation. In habits

it is gregarious, and is usually seen in small herds, but herds numbering several hundreds or even a thousand are occasionally met with on the stony, desolate plateaus of Southern Patagonia; but the huanaco is able to thrive and grow fat where almost any other herbivore would starve. While the herd feeds one animal acts as sentinel, stationed on the hillside, and on the appearance of danger utters a shrill neigh of alarm, and instantly all take to flight. But although excessively shy and wary they are also very inquisitive, and have enough intelligence to know that a single horseman can do them no harm, for they will not only approach to look closely at him, but will sometimes follow him for miles. They are also excitable, and at times indulge in strange freaks. Darwin writes:—"On the mountains of Tierra del Fuego I have more than once seen a huanaco, on being approached, not only neigh and squeal, but prance and leap about in a most ridiculous manner, apparently in defiance as a challenge." And Captain King relates that while sailing into Port Desire he witnessed a chase of a huanaco after a fox, both animals evidently going at their greatest speed, so that they soon passed out of sight. I have known some tame huanacos, and in that state they make amusing intelligent pets, fond of being caressed, but often so frolicsome and mischievous as to be a nuisance to their master.

It is well known that at the southern extremity of Patagonia the huanacos have a dying place, a spot to which all individuals inhabiting the surrounding plains repair at the approach of death to deposit their bones. Darwin and Fitzroy first recorded this strange instinct in their personal narratives, and their observations have since been fully confirmed by others. The best known of these dying or burial-places are on the banks of the Santa Cruz and Gallegos rivers, where the river valleys are covered with dense primæval thickets of bushes and trees of stunted growth; there the ground is covered with the bones of countless dead generations. " The animals," says Darwin, " in most cases must have crawled, before dying, beneath and among the bushes." A strange instinct in a creature so preeminently social in its habits; a dweller all its life long on the open, barren plateaus and mountain sides! What a subject for a painter! The grey wilderness of dwarf thorn trees, aged and grotesque and scanty-leaved, nourished for a thousand years on the bones that whiten the stony ground at their roots; the interior lit faintly with the rays of the departing sun, chill and grey, and silent and motionless—the huanacos' Golgotha. In the long centuries, stretching back into a dim immeasurable past, so many of this race have journeyed hither from the mountain and the plain to suffer the sharp pang of death, that, to the imagination, something of it all seems to have passed into that hushed and mournful nature. And now one more, the latest pilgrim, has come, all his little strength spent in his struggle to penetrate the close thicket; looking old and gaunt and ghostly in the twilight; with long ragged hair; staring into the gloom out of death-dimmed sunken eyes. England has one artist who might show it to us on canvas, who would be able to catch the feeling of such a scene—of that mysterious, passionless tragedy of nature—I refer to J. M. Swan, the painter of the "Prodigal Son" and the "Lioness Defending her Cubs."

To his account of the animal's dying place and instinct, Darwin adds: " I do not at all understand the reason of this, but I may observe that the wounded huanacos at the Santa Cruz invariably walked towards the river."

It would, no doubt, be rash to affirm of any instinct that it is absolutely unique; but, putting aside some doubtful reports about a custom of the Asiatic elephant, which may have originated in the account of Sindbad the Sailor's discovery of an elephant's burial place, we have no knowledge of an instinct similar to that of the huanaco in any other animal. So far as we know, it stands alone and apart, with nothing in the actions of other species leading up, or suggesting any family like-ness to it. But what chiefly attracts the mind to it is its strangeness. It looks, in fact, less like an instinct of one of the inferior creatures than the superstitious observance of human beings, who have knowledge of death, and believe in a continued existence after dissolution; of a tribe that in past times had conceived the idea that the liberated spirit is only able to find its way to its future abode by starting at death from the ancient dying-place of the tribe or family, and thence moving westward, or skyward, or underground, over the well-worn immemorial track, invisible to material eyes.

But, although alone among animal instincts in its strange and useless purpose—for it is as absolutely useless to the species or race as to the dying individual

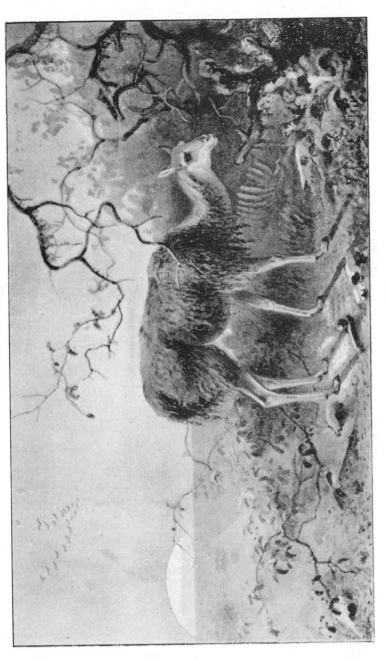

THE DYING HUANACO.

[Page 318.

—it is not the only useless instinct we know of: there are many others, both simple and complex ; and of such instincts we believe, with good reason, that they once played an important part in the life of the species, and were only rendered useless by changes in the condition of life, or in the organism, or in both. In other words, when the special conditions that gave them value no longer existed, the correlated and perfect instinct was not, in these cases, eradicated, but remained in abeyance and still capable of being called into activity by a new and false stimulus simulating the old and true. Viewed in this way, the huanaco's instinct might be regarded as something remaining to the animal from a remote past, not altogether unaffected by time perhaps; and like some ceremonial usage among men that has long ceased to have any significance, or like a fragment of ancient history, or a tradition, which in the course of time has received some new and false interpretation. The false interpretation, to continue the metaphor, is, in this case, that the *purpose* of the animal in going to a certain spot, to which it has probably never previously resorted, is to die there. A false interpretation, because, in the first place, it is incredible that an instinct of no advantage to the species in its struggle for existence and predominance should arise and become permanent; and, in the second place, it is equally incredible that it could ever have been to the advantage of the species or race to have a dying place. We must, then, suppose that there is in the sensations preceding death, when death comes slowly, some resemblance to the sensations experienced by the animal at a period when its curious instinct first took form and crystallized; these would be painful sensations that threatened life; and freedom from them, and safety to the animal, would only exist in a certain well-remembered spot. Further, we might assume that it was at first only the memory of a few individuals that caused the animals to seek the place of safety; that a habit was thus formed; that in time this traditional habit became instinctive, so that the animals, old and young, made their way unerringly to the place of refuge whenever the old danger returned. And such an instinct, slowly matured and made perfect to enable this animal to escape extinction during periods of great danger to mammalian life, lasting hundreds or even thousands of years, and destructive of numberless other species less hardy and adaptive than the generalized huanaco, might well continue to exist, to be occasionally called into life by a false stimulus, for many centuries after it had ceased to be of any advantage.

Once we accept this explanation as probable— namely, that the huanaco, in withdrawing from the herd to drop down and die in the ancient dying ground, is in reality only seeking an historically remembered place of refuge, and not of death—the action of the animal loses much of its mysterious character; we come on to firm ground, and find that we are no longer considering an instinct absolutely unique, with no action or instinct in any other animal leading up or suggesting any family likeness to it, as I said before. We find, in fact, that there is at least one very important and very well-known instinct in another class of creatures, which has a strong resemblance to that of the huanaco, as I have interpreted it, and which may even serve to throw a side light on the origin of the huanaco's instinct. I refer to a habit of some ophidians, in temperate and cold countries, of returning annually to hybernate in the same den.

A typical instance is that of the rattlesnake in the colder parts of North America. On the approach of winter these reptiles go into hiding, and it has been observed that in some districts a very large number of individuals, hundreds, and even thousands, will repair from the surrounding country to the ancestral den. Here the serpents gather in a mass to remain in a wholly or semi-torpid condition until the return of spring brings them out again, to scatter abroad to their usual summer haunts. Clearly in this case the knowledge of the hybernating den is not merely traditional—that is, handed down from generation to generation, through the young each year following the adults, and so forming the habit of repairing at certain seasons to a certain place; for the young serpent soon abandons its parent to lead an independent life; and on the approach of cold weather the hybernating den may be a long distance away, ten or twenty, or even thirty miles from the spot in which it was born. The annual return to the hybernating den is then a fixed unalterable instinct, like the autumnal migration of some birds to a warmer latitude. It is doubtless favourable to the serpents to hybernate in large numbers massed together; and the habit of resorting annually to the same spot once formed,

we can imagine that the individuals—perhaps a
single couple in the first place—frequenting some
very deep, dry, and well-sheltered cavern, safe from
enemies, would have a great advantage over others
of their race; that they would be stronger and
increase more, and spread during the summer
months further and further from the cavern on all
sides; and that the further afield they went the
more would the instinct be perfected; since all
the young serpents that did not have the instinct of returning unerringly to the ancestral refuge, and that, like the outsiders of their
race, to put it in that way, merely crept into the
first hole they found on the approach of the cold
season, would be more liable to destruction. Probably most snakes get killed long before a natural
decline sets in ; to say that not one in a thousand
dies of old age would probably be no exaggeration ;
but if they were as safe from enemies and accidents
as some less prolific and more highly-organized
animals, so that many would reach the natural term
of life, and death came slowly, we can imagine that
in such a heat-loving creature the failure of the
vital powers would simulate the sensations caused
by a falling temperature, and cause the old or sick
serpent, even in midsummer, to creep instinctively
away to the ancient refuge, where many a long
life-killing frost had been safely tided over in the
past.

The huanaco has never been a hybernating animal ; but we must assume that, like the crotalus of
the north, he had formed a habit of congregating
with his fellows at certain seasons at the same spot ;

further, that these were seasons of suffering to the animal—the suffering, or discomfort and danger, having in the first place given rise to the habit. Assuming again that the habit had existed so long as to become, like that of the reptile, a fixed, immutable instinct, a hereditary knowledge, so that the young huanacos, untaught by the adults, would go alone and unerringly to the meeting-place from any distance, it is but an easy step to the belief, that after the conditions had changed, and the refuges were no longer needed, this instinctive knowledge would still exist in them, and that they would take the old road when stimulated by the pain of a wound; or the miserable sensations experienced in disease; or during the decay of the life-energy, when the senses grow dim, and the breath fails, and the blood is thin and cold.

I presume that most persons who have observed animals a great deal have met with cases in which the animal has acted automatically, or instinctively, when the stimulus has been a false one. I will relate one such case, observed by myself, and which strikes me as being apposite to the question I am considering. It must be premised that this is an instance of an acquired habit; but this does not affect my argument, since I have all along assumed that the huanaco—a highly sagacious species in the highest class of vertebrates—first acquired a habit from experience of seeking a remembered refuge, and that such habit was the parent, as it were, or the first clay model, of the perfect and indestructible instinct that was to be.

It is not an uncommon thing in the Argentine

pampas—I have on two occasions witnessed it myself—for a riding-horse to come home, or to the
gate of his owner's house, to die. I am speaking of
riding-horses that are never doctored, nor treated
mercifully ; that look on their master as an enemy
rather than a friend ; horses that live out in the
open, and have to be hunted to the corral or enclosure, or roughly captured with a lasso as they run,
when their services are required. I retain a very vivid
recollection of the first occasion of witnessing an
action of this kind in a horse, although I was only a
boy at the time. On going out one summer evening
I saw one of the horses of the establishment standing unsaddled and unbridled leaning his head over
the gate. Going to the spot, I stroked his nose, and
then, turning to an old native who happened to be
near, asked him what could be the meaning of such
a thing. " I think he is going to die," he answered ;
" horses often come to the house to die." And next
morning the poor beast was found lying dead not
twenty yards from the gate ; although he had not
appeared ill when I stroked his nose on the previous
evening ; but when I saw him lying there dead, and
remembered the old native's words, it seemed to
me as marvellous and inexplicable that a horse
should act in that way, as if some wild creature—a
rhea, a fawn, or dolichotes—had come to exhale his
last breath at the gates of his enemy and constant
persecutor, man.

I now believe that the sensations of sickness and
approaching death in the riding-horse of the pampas resemble or similate the pains, so often experienced, of hunger, thirst and fatigue combined,

together with the oppressive sensations caused by
the ponderous native saddle, or recado, with its
huge surcingle of raw hide drawn up so tightly as
to hinder free respiration. The suffering animal
remembers how at the last relief invariably came,
when the twelve or fifteen hours' torture were over,
the toil and the want, and when the great iron
bridle and ponderous gear were removed, and he had
freedom and food and drink and rest. At the gate
or at the door of his master's house, the sudden
relief had always come to him ; and there does
he sometimes go in his sickness, his fear over-
mastered by his suffering, to find it again.

Discussing this question with a friend, who has
a subtle mind and great experience of the horse in
semi-barbarous countries, and of many other animals, wild and tame, in many regions of the globe,
he put forward a different explanation of the action
of the horse in coming home to die, which he thinks
simpler and more probable than mine. It is, that
a dying or ailing animal instinctively withdraws
itself from its fellows—an action of self-preservation in the individual in opposition to the well-
known instincts of the healthy animals, which
impels the whole herd to turn upon and persecute
the sickly member, thus destroying its chances of
recovery. The desire of the suffering animal is not
only to leave its fellows, but to get to some solitary
place where they cannot follow, or would never find
him, to escape at once from a great and pressing
danger. But on the pastoral pampas, where horses
are so numerous that on that level, treeless area they
are always and everywhere visible, no hiding-place

is discoverable. In such a case, the animal, goaded
by its instinctive fear, turns to the one spot that
horses avoid ; and although that spot has hitherto
been fearful to him, the old fear is forgotten in the
present and far more vivid one ; the vicinity of his
master's house represents a solitary place to him,
and he seeks it, just as the stricken deer seeks the
interior of some close forest, oblivious for the time,
in its anxiety to escape from the herd, of the dangers
lurking in it, and which he formerly avoided.

I have not set this explanation down merely
because it does credit to my friend's ingenuity, but
because it strikes me that it is the only alternative
explanation that can be given of the animal's action
in coming home to die. Another fact concerning
the ill-tamed and barbarously treated horses of the
pampas, which, to my mind, strengthens the view I
have taken, remains to be mentioned. It is not an
uncommon thing for one of these horses, after
escaping, saddled and bridled, and wandering about
for a night or night and day on the plains, to return
of its own accord to the house. It is clear that in a
case of this kind the animal comes home to seek
relief. I have known one horse that always had to
be hunted like a wild animal to be caught, and that
invariably after being saddled tried to break loose,
to return in this way to the gate after wandering
about, saddled and bridled, for over twenty hours in
uncomfortable freedom.

The action of the riding-horse returning to a
master he is accustomed to fly from, as from an
enemy, to be released of saddle and bridle, is, no
doubt more intelligent than that of the dying horse

coming home to be relieved from his sufferings, but the motive is the same in both cases; at the gate the only pain the animal has ever experienced has invariably begun, and there it has ended, and when the spur of some new pain afflicts him—new and yet like the old—it is to the well-remembered hated gate that it urges him.

To return to the huanaco. After tracing the dying instinct back to its hypothetical origin— namely, a habit acquired by the animal in some past period of seeking refuge from some kind of pain and danger at a certain spot, it is only natural to speculate a little further as to the nature of that danger and of the conditions the animal existed in.

If the huanaco is as old on the earth as its antique generalized form have led naturalists to suppose, we can well believe that it has survived not only a great many lost mammalian types, but many changes in the conditions of its life. Let us then imagine that at some remote period a change took place in the climate of Patagonia, and that it became colder and colder, owing to some cause affecting only that portion of the antarctic region ; such a cause, for instance, as a great accumulation of icebergs on the northern shores of the antarctic continent, extending century by century until a large portion of the now open sea became blocked up with solid ice. If the change was gradual and the snow became deeper each winter and lasted longer, an intelligent, gregarious, and exceedingly hardy and active animal like the huanaco, able to exist on the driest woody fibres, would stand the best chance of maintaining its existence in such altered conditions, and would form new habits to meet the new danger. One would be that at the approach of a period of deep snow and deadly cold, all the herds frequenting one place would gather together at the most favourable spots in the river valleys, where the vegetation is dense and some food could be had while the surrounding country continued covered with deep snow. They would, in fact, make choice of exactly such localities as are now used for dying places. There they would be sheltered from the cutting winds, the twigs and bark would supply them with food, the warmth from a great many individuals massed together would serve to keep the snow partially melted under foot, and would prevent their being smothered, while the stiff and closely interlaced branches would keep a roof of snow above them, and thus protected they would keep alive until the return of mild weather released them. In the course of many generations all weakly animals, and all in which the habit of seeking the refuge at the proper time was weak or uncertain in its action would perish, but their loss would be an advantage to the survivors.

It is worthy of remark that it is only at the southern extremity of Patagonia that the huanacos have dying places. In Northern Patagonia, and on the Chilian and Peruvian Andes no such instinct has been observed.

CHAPTER XXII.

THE STRANGE INSTINCTS OF CATTLE.

My purpose in this paper is to discuss a group of curious and useless emotional instincts of social animals, which have not yet been properly explained. Excepting two of the number, placed first and last in the list, they are not related in their origin; consequently they are here grouped together arbitrarily, only for the reason that we are very familiar with them on account of their survival in our domestic animals, and because they are, as I have said, useless; also because they resemble each other, among the passions and actions of the lower animals, in their effect on our minds. This is in all cases unpleasant, and sometimes exceedingly painful, as when species that rank next to ourselves in their developed intelligence and organized societies, such as elephants, monkeys, dogs, and cattle, are seen under the domination of impulses, in some cases resembling insanity, and in others simulating the darkest passions of man.

These instincts are :—

(1) The excitement caused by the smell of blood, noticeable in horses and cattle among our domestic animals, and varying greatly in degree, from an

emotion so slight as to be scarcely perceptible to the greatest extremes of rage or terror.

(2) The angry excitement roused in some animals when a scarlet or bright-red cloth is shown to them. So well known is this apparently insane instinct in our cattle that it has given rise to a proverb and metaphor familiar in a variety of forms to everyone.

(3) The persecution of a sick or weakly animal by its companions.

(4) The sudden deadly fury that seizes on the herd or family at the sight of a companion in extreme distress. Herbivorous mammals at such times will trample and gore the distressed one to death. In the case of wolves, and other savage-tempered carnivorous species, the distressed fellow is frequently torn to pieces and devoured on the spot.

To take the first two together. When we consider that blood is red; that the smell of it is, or may be, or has been, associated with that vivid hue in the animal's mind; that blood, seen and smelt is, or has been, associated with the sight of wounds and with cries of pain and rage or terror from the wounded or captive animal, there appears at first sight to be some reason for connecting these two instinctive passions as having the same origin —namely, terror and rage caused by the sight of a member of the herd struck down and bleeding, or struggling for life in the grasp of an enemy. I do not mean to say that such an image is actually present in the animal's mind, but that the inherited or instinctive passion is one in kind and in its work-

ing with the passion of the animal when experience
and reason were its guides.

But the more I consider the point the more am I
inclined to regard these two instincts as separate
in their origin, although I retain the belief that
cattle and horses and several wild animals are
violently excited by the smell of blood for the
reason just given—namely, their inherited memory
associates the smell of blood with the presence
among them of some powerful enemy that threatens
their life. To this point I shall return when dealing with the last and most painful of the instincts
I am considering.

The following incident will show how violently
this blood passion sometimes affects cattle, when
they are permitted to exist in a half-wild condition,
as on the pampas. I was out with my gun one day,
a few miles from home, when I came across a patch
on the ground where the grass was pressed or
trodden down and stained with blood. I concluded that some thievish gauchos had slaughtered
a fat cow there on the previous night, and, to
avoid detection, had somehow managed to carry
the whole of it away on their horses. As I walked
on, a herd of cattle, numbering about three hundred, appeared moving slowly on towards a small
stream a mile away; they were travelling in a thin
long line, and would pass the blood-stained spot
at a distance of seven to eight hundred yards,
but the wind from it would blow across their
track. When the tainted wind struck the leaders of
the herd they instantly stood still, raising their
heads, then broke out into loud excited bellowings;

and finally turning they started off at a fast trot, following up the scent in a straight line, until they arrived at the place where one of their kind had met its death. The contagion spread, and before long all the cattle were congregated on the fatal spot, and began moving round in a dense mass, bellowing continually.

It may be remarked here that the animal has a peculiar language on occasions like this ; it emits a succession of short bellowing cries, like excited exclamations, followed by a very loud cry, alternately sinking into a hoarse murmur, and rising to a kind of scream that grates harshly on the sense. Of the ordinary "cow-music" I am a great admirer, and take as much pleasure in it as in the cries and melody of birds and the sound of the wind in trees ; but this performance of cattle excited by the smell of blood is most distressing to hear.

The animals that had forced their way into the centre of the mass to the spot where the blood was, pawed the earth, and dug it up with their horns, and trampled each other down in their frantic excitement. It was terrible to see and hear them. The action of those on the border of the living mass in perpetually moving round in a circle with dolorous bellowings, was like that of the women in an Indian village when a warrior dies, and all night they shriek and howl with simulated grief, going round and round the dead man's hut in an endless procession.

The "bull and red rag" instinct, as it may be called, comes next in order.

It is a familiar fact that brightness in itself powerfully attracts most if not all animals. The higher mammalians are affected in the same way as birds and insects, although not in the same degree. This fact partly explains the rage of the bull. A scarlet flag fluttering in the wind or lying on the grass attracts his attention powerfully, as it does that of other animals; but though curious about the nature of the bright object, it does not anger him. His anger is excited—and this is the whole secret of the matter—when the colour is flaunted by a man; when it forces him to fix his attention on a man, i.e. an animal of another species that rules or drives him, and that he fears, but with only a slight fear, which may at any moment be overcome by his naturally bold aggressive disposition. Not only does the vivid colour compel him to fix his attention on the being that habitually interferes with his liberty, and is consequently regarded with unfriendly eyes, but it also produces the illusion on his mind that the man is near him, that he is approaching him in an aggressive manner : it is an insult, a challenge, which, being of so explosive a temper, he is not slow to accept.

On the pampas I was once standing with some gauchos at the gate of a corral into which a herd of half-wild cattle had just been driven. One of the men, to show his courage and agility, got off his horse and boldly placed himself in the centre of the open gate. His action attracted the attention of one of the nearest cows, and lowering her horns she began watching him in a threatening manner. He then suddenly displayed the scarlet lining of his poncho, and instantly she charged him furiously: with a quick movement to one side he escaped her horns, and after we had driven her back, resumed his former position and challenged her again in the same way. The experiment was repeated not less than half a dozen times, and always with the same result. The cattle were all in a savage temper, and would have instantly charged him on his placing himself before them on foot without the display of scarlet cloth, but their fear of the mounted men, standing with lassos in their hand on either side of him, kept them in check. But whenever the attention of any one individual among them was forcibly drawn to him by the display of vivid colour, and fixed on him alone, the presence of the horsemen was forgotten and fear was swallowed by rage.

It is a fact, I think, that most animals that exhibit angry excitement when a scarlet rag is flourished aggressively at them, are easily excited to anger at all times. Domestic geese and turkeys may be mentioned among birds : they do not fly at a grown person, but they will often fly at a child that challenges them in this way ; and it is a fact that they do not at any time fear a child very much and will sometimes attack him without being challenged. I think that the probability of the view I have taken is increased by another fact—namely, that the sudden display of scarlet colour sometimes affects timid animals with an extreme fear, just as, on the other hand, it excites those that are bold and aggressive to anger. Domestic sheep, for instance, that vary greatly in disposition in different races or breeds, and even in different individuals, may be affected in the two opposite ways, some exhibiting extreme terror and others only anger at a sudden display of scarlet colour by the shepherd or herder. The persecution of a sick animal by its companions comes next under consideration.

It will have been remarked, with surprise by some readers, no doubt, that I have set down as two different instincts this persecution of a sick or weakly individual by its fellows, and the sudden deadly rage that sometimes impels the herd to turn upon and destroy a wounded or distressed companion. It is usual for writers on the instincts of animals to speak of them as one : and I presume that they regard this sudden deadly rage of several individuals against a companion as merely an extreme form of the common persecuting instinct or impulse. They are not really one, but are as distinct in origin and character as it is possible for any two instincts to be. The violent and fatal impulse starts simultaneously into life and action, and is contagious, affecting all the members of the herd like a sudden madness. The other is neither violent nor contagious : the persecution is intermittent ; it is often confined to one or to a very few members of the herd, and seldom joined in by the chief member, the leader or head to whom all the others give way.

Concerning this head of the herd, or flock, or pack, it is necessary to say something more. Some gregarious animals, particularly birds, live together in the most perfect peace and amity ; and here no leader is required, because in their long association together as a species in flocks, they have attained to a oneness of mind, so to speak, which causes them to move or rest, and to act at all times harmoniously together, as if controlled and guided by an extraneous force. I may mention that the kindly instinct in animals, which is almost universal between male and female in the vertebrates, is most apparent in these harmoniously acting birds. Thus, in La Plata, I have remarked, in more than one species, that a lame or sick individual, unable to keep pace with the flock and find its food, has not only been waited for, but in some cases some of the flock have constantly attended it, keeping close to it both when flying and on the ground; and, I have no doubt, feeding it just as they would have fed their young.

Naturally among such kinds no one member is of more consideration than another. But among mammals such equality and harmony is rare. The instinct of one and all is to lord it over the others, with the result that one more powerful or domineering gets the mastery, to keep it thereafter as long as he can. The lower animals are, in this respect, very much like us; and in all kinds that are at all fierce-tempered the mastery of one over all, and of a few under him over the others, is most salutary; indeed, it is inconceivable that they should be able to exist together under any other system.

On cattle-breeding establishments on the pampas, where it is usual to keep a large number of fierce-tempered dogs, I have observed these animals a great deal, and presume that they are very much like feral dogs and wolves in their habits. Their quarrels are incessant; but when a fight begins the head of the pack as a rule rushes to the spot, whereupon the fighters separate and march off in different directions, or else cast themselves down and deprecate their tyrant's wrath with abject gestures and whines. If the combatants are both strong and have worked themselves into a mad rage before their head puts in an appearance, it may go hard with him : they know him no longer, and all he can do is to join in the fray ; then, if the fighters turn on him, he may be so injured that his power is gone, and the next best dog in the pack takes his place. The hottest contests are always between dogs that are well matched; neither will give place to the other, and so they fight it out; but from the foremost in strength and power down to the weakest there is a gradation of authority; each one knows just how far he can go, which companion he can bully when he is in a bad temper or wishes to assert himself, and to which he must humbly yield in his turn. In such a state the weakest one must always yield to all the others, and cast himself down, seeming to call himself a slave and worshipper of any other member of the pack that chooses to snarl at him, or command him to give up his bone with a good grace.

This masterful or domineering temper, so common among social mammals, is the cause of the persecution of the sick and weakly. When an animal begins to ail he can no longer hold his own; he ceases to resent the occasional ill-natured attacks made on him; his non-combative condition is quickly discovered, and he at once drops down to a place below the lowest; it is common knowledge in the herd that he may be buffeted with impunity by all, even by those that have hitherto suffered buffets but have given none. But judging from my own observation, this persecution is not, as a rule, severe, and is seldom fatal.

It is often the case that a sick or injured animal withdraws and hides himself from the herd; the instinct of the " stricken deer " this might be called. But I do not think that we need assume that the ailing individual goes away to escape the danger of being ill-used by his companions. He is sick and drooping and consequently unfit to be with the healthy and vigorous; that is the simplest and probably the true explanation of his action; although in some cases he might be driven from them by persistent rough usage. However peaceably gregarious mammals may live together, and however fond of each other's company they may be, they do not, as a rule, treat each other gently. Furthermore, their games are exceedingly rough and require that they shall be in a vigorous state of health to escape injury. Horned animals have no buttons to the sharp weapons they prod and strike each other with in a sportive spirit. I have often witnessed the games of wild and half-wild horses with astonishment; for it seemed that broken bones must result from the sounding kicks they freely bestowed on one another. This roughness itself would be a sufficient cause for the action of the individual, sick and out of tune and untouched by the glad contagion of the others, in escaping from them; and to leave them would be to its advantage (and to that of the race) since, if not fatally injured or sick unto death, its chances of recovery to perfect health would be thereby greatly increased.

It remains now to speak of that seemingly most cruel of instincts which stands last on my list. It is very common among gregarious animals that are at all combative in disposition, and still survives in our domestic cattle, although very rarely witnessed in England. My first experience of it was just before I had reached the age of five years. I was not at that early period trying to find out any of nature's secrets, but the scene I witnessed printed itself very vividly on my mind, so that I can recall it as well as if my years had been five-and-twenty ; perhaps better. It was on a summer's evening, and I was out by myself at some distance from the house, playing about the high exposed roots of some old trees ; on the other side of the trees the cattle, just returned from pasture, were gathered on the bare level ground. Hearing a great commotion among them, I climbed on to one of the high exposed roots, and, looking over, saw a cow on the ground, apparently unable to rise, moaning and bellowing in a distressed way, while a number of her companions were crowding round and goring her.

What is the meaning of such an instinct ? Darwin has but few words on the subject. " Can we believe," he says, in his posthumous *Essay on Instinct*, " when a wounded herbivorous animal returns to its own herd and is then attacked and gored, that this cruel and very common instinct is of any service to the species ? " At the same time, he hints that such an instinct might in some circumstances be useful, and his hint has been developed into the current belief among naturalists on the subject. Here it is, in Dr. Romanes' words : " We may readily imagine that the instinct displayed by many herbivorous animals of goring sick and wounded companions, is really of use in countries where the presence of weak members in a herd is a source of danger to the herd from the prevalence of wild beasts." Here it is assumed that the sick are set upon and killed, but this is not the fact ; sickness and decay from age or some other cause are slow things, and increase imperceptibly, so that the sight of a drooping member grows familiar to the herd, as does that of a member with some malformation, or unusual shade of colour, or altogether white, as in the case of an albino.

Sick and weak members, as we have seen, while subject to some ill-treatment from their companions (only because they can be ill-treated with impunity), do not rouse the herd to a deadly animosity ; the violent and fatal attack. is often as not made on a member in perfect health and vigour and unwounded, although, owing to some accident, in great distress, and perhaps danger, at the moment.

The instinct is, then, not only useless but actually detrimental ; and, this being so, the action of the herd in destroying one of its members is not even to be regarded as an instinct proper, but rather as an aberration of an instinct, a blunder, into which animals sometimes fall when excited to action in unusual circumstances.

The first thing that strikes us is that in these wild abnormal moments of social animals, they are acting in violent contradiction to the whole tenor of their lives; that in turning against a distressed fellow they oppose themselves to the law of their being, to the whole body of instincts, primary and secondary, and habits, which have made it possible for them to exist together in communities. It is, I think, by reflecting on the abnormal character of such an action that we are led to a true interpretation of this " dark saying of Nature."

Every one is familiar with Bacon's famous passage about the dog, and the noble courage which that animal puts on when " maintained by a man ; who is to him in place of a God, or *melior natura ;* which courage is manifestly such as that creature, without the confidence of a better nature than its own, could never attain." Not so. The dog is a social animal, and acts instinctively in concert with his fellows; and the courage he manifests is of the family, not the individual. In the domestic state the man he is accustomed to associate with and obey stands to him in the place of the controlling pack, and to his mind, which is canine and not human, *is* the pack. A similar " noble courage," greatly surpassing that exhibited on all other occasions, is displayed by an infinite number of mammals and birds of gregarious habits, when repelling the attacks of some powerful and dangerous enemy, or when they rush to the rescue of one of their captive fellows. Concerning this rage and desperate courage of social animals in the face of an enemy, we see (1) that it is excited by the distressed cries, or by the sight of a member of the herd or family flying from or struggling in the clutches of an enemy ; (2) that it affects animals when a number of individuals are together, and is eminently contagious, like fear, that communicates itself, quick as lightning, from one to another until all are in a panic, and like the joyous emotion that impels the members of a herd or flock to rush simultaneously into play.

Now, it is a pretty familiar fact that animals acting instinctively, as well as men acting intelligently, have at times their delusions and their illusions, and see things falsely, and are moved to action by a false stimulus to their own disadvantage. When the individuals of a herd or family are excited to a sudden deadly rage by the distressed cries of one of their fellows, or by the sight of its bleeding wounds and the smell of its blood, or when they see it frantically struggling on the ground, or in the cleft of a tree or rock, as if in the clutches of a powerful enemy, they do not turn on it to kill but to rescue it.

In whatever way the rescuing instinct may have risen, whether simply through natural selection or, as is more probable, through an intelligent habit becoming fixed and hereditary, its effectiveness depends altogether on the emotion of overmastering rage excited in the animal—rage against a tangible visible enemy, or invisible, and excited by the cries or struggles of a suffering companion ; clearly, then, it could not provide against the occasional rare accidents that animals meet with, which causes them to act precisely in the way they do when seized or struck down by an enemy. An illusion is the result of the emotion similar to the illusion produced by vivid expectation in ourselves, which has caused many a man to see in a friend and companion the adversary he looked to see, and to slay him in his false-seeing anger.

An illusion just as great, leading to action equally violent, but ludicrous rather than painful to witness, may be seen in dogs, when encouraged by a man to the attack, and made by his cries and gestures to expect that some animal they are accustomed to hunt is about to be unearthed or overtaken; and if, when they are in this disposition, he cunningly exhibits and sets them on a dummy, made perhaps of old rags and leather and stuffed with straw, they will seize, worry, and tear it to pieces with the greatest fury, and without the faintest suspicion of its true character.

That wild elephants will attack a distressed fellow seemed astonishing to Darwin, when he remembered the case of an elephant after escaping from a pit helping its fellow to escape also. But it is precisely the animals, high or low in the organic scale, that are social, and possess the instinct of helping each other, that will on occasions attack a fellow in misfortune—such an attack being no more than a blunder of the helping instinct.

Felix de Azara records a rather cruel experiment on the temper of some tame rats confined in a cage. The person who kept them caught the tail of one of the animals and began sharply pinching it, keeping his hand concealed under the cage. Its cries of pain and struggles to free itself greatly excited the other rats; and after rushing wildly round for some moments they flew at their distressed companion, and fixing their teeth in its throat quickly dispatched it. In this case if the hand that held the tail had been visible and in the cage, the bites would undoubtedly have been inflicted on it; but no enemy was visible; yet the fury and impulse to attack an enemy was present in the animals. In such circumstances, the excitement must be discharged—the instinct obeyed, and in the absence of any other object of attack the illusion is produced and it discharges itself on the struggling companion. It is sometimes seen in dogs, when three or four or five are near together, that if one suddenly utters a howl or cry of pain, when no man is near it and no cause apparent, the others run to it, and seeing nothing, turn round and attack each other. Here the exciting cause—the cry for help— is not strong enough to produce the illusion which is sometimes fatal to the suffering member; but each dog mistakingly thinks that the others, or one of the others, inflicted the injury, and his impulse is to take the part of the injured animal. If the cry for help—caused perhaps by a sudden cramp or the prick of a thorn—is not very sharp or intense, the other dogs will not attack, but merely look and growl at each other in a suspicious way.

To go back to Azara's anecdote. Why, it may be asked—and this question has been put to me in conversation—if killing a distressed companion is of no advantage to the race, and if something must be attacked—why did not these rats in this instance attack the cage they were shut in, and bite at the woodwork and wires? Or, in the case related by Mr. Andrew Lang in *Longman's Magazine* some time ago, in which the members of a herd of cattle in Scotland turned with sudden amazing fury on

one of the cows that had got wedged between two
rocks and was struggling with distressed bellowings
to free itself—why did they not attack the prisoning
rocks instead of goring their unfortunate comrade to
death? For it is well known that animals will, on
occasions, turn angrily upon and attack inanimate
objects that cause them injury or hinder their freedom
of action. And we know that this mythic faculty—the
mind's projection of itself into visible nature—survives in ourselves, that there are exceptional moments
in our lives when it comes back to us; no one, for
instance, would be astonished to hear that any man,
even a philosopher, had angrily kicked away or
imprecated a stool or other inanimate object against
which he had accidentally barked his shins. The
answer is, that there is no connection between these
two things—the universal mythic faculty of the
mind, and that bold and violent instinct of social
animals of rushing to the rescue of a stricken or
distressed companion, which has a definite, a narrow,
purpose—namely, to fall upon an enemy endowed
not merely with the life and intelligence common to
all things, including rocks, trees, and waters, but
with animal form and motion.

I had intended in this place to give other instances, observed in several widely-separated species,
including monkeys; but it is not necessary, as I
consider that all the facts, however varied, are
covered by the theory I have suggested—even a fact
like the one mentioned in this chapter of cattle
bellowing and madly digging up the ground where
the blood of one of their kind had been spilt:
also such a fact as that of wild cattle and other

animals caught in a trap or enclosure attacking and
destroying each other in their frenzy ; and the fact
that some fierce-tempered carnivorous mammals
will devour the companion they have killed. It is
an instinct of animals like wolves and peccaries to
devour the enemy they have overcome and slain :
thus, when the jaguar captures a peccary out of a
drove, and does not quickly escape with his prize
into a tree, he is instantly attacked and slain and
then consumed, even to the skin and bones. This
is the wolf's and the peccary's instinct; and the
devouring of one of their own companions is an
inevitable consequence of the mistake made in the
first place of attacking and killing it. In no other
circumstances, not even when starving, do they prey
on their own species.

If the explanation I have offered should seem a
true or highly probable one, it will, I feel sure,
prove acceptable to many lovers of animals, who,
regarding this seemingly ruthless instinct, not as
an aberration but as in some vague way advantageous to animals in their struggle for existence, are
yet unable to think of it without pain and horror ;
indeed, I know those who refuse to think of it at
all, who would gladly disbelieve it if they could.

It should be a relief to them to be able to look on
it no longer as something ugly and hateful, a blot
on nature, but as an illusion, a mistake, an unconscious crime, so to speak, that has for its motive
the noblest passion that animals know—that sublime courage and daring which they exhibit in
defence of a distressed companion. This fiery spirit
in animals, which makes them forget their own

safety, moves our hearts by its close resemblance to one of the most highly-prized human virtues; just as we are moved to intellectual admiration by the wonderful migratory instinct in birds that simulates some of the highest achievements of the mind of man. And we know that this beautiful instinct is also liable to mistakes—that many travellers leave us annually never to return. Such a mistake was undoubtedly the cause of the late visitation of Pallas' sand-grouse : owing perhaps to some unusual atmospheric or dynamic condition, or to some change in the nervous system of the birds, they deviated widely from their usual route, to scatter in countless thousands over the whole of Europe and perish slowly in climates not suited to them ; while others, overpassing the cold strange continent, sped on over colder, stranger seas, to drop at last like aerolites, quenching their lives in the waves.

Whether because it is true, as Professor Freeman and some others will have it, that humanity is a purely modern virtue ; or because the doctrine of Darwin, by showing that we are related to other forms of life, that our best feelings have their roots low down in the temper and instincts of the social species, has brought us nearer in spirit to the inferior animals, it is certain that our regard for them has grown, and is growing, and that new facts and fresh inferences that make us think more highly of them are increasingly welcome.

CHAPTER XXIII.

HORSE AND MAN.

THERE is no mode of progression so delightful as riding on horseback. Walking, rowing, bicycling are pleasant exercises in their way, but the muscular exertion and constant exercise of judgment they call for occupy the mind partly to the exclusion of other things; so that a long walk may sometimes be only a long walk and nothing more. In riding we are not conscious of exertion, and as for that close observation and accurate discernment necessary in traversing the ground with speed and safety, it is left to the faithful servant that carries us. Pitfalls, hillocks, slippery places, the thousand little inequalities of the surface that have to be measured with infallible eye, these disturb us little. To fly or go slowly at will, to pass unshaken over rough and smooth alike, fording rivers without being wet, and mounting hills without climbing, this is indeed unmixed delight. It is the nearest approach to bird-life we seem capable of, since all the monster bubbles and flying fabrics that have been the sport of winds from the days of Montgolfier downwards have brought us no nearer to it. The aeronaut gasping for breath above the clouds offers only a sad spectacle of the imbecility of science and man's shattered hopes. To the free inhabitants of air we can only liken the mounted Arab, vanishing, hawk-like, over the boundless desert.

In riding there is always exhilarating motion; yet, if the scenery encountered be charming, you are apparently sitting still, while, river-like, it flows toward and past you, ever giving place to fresh visions of beauty. Above all, the mind is free, as when one lies idly on the grass gazing up into the sky. And, speaking of myself, there is even more than this immunity from any tax on the understanding such as we require in walking; the rhythmic motion, the sensation as of flight, acting on the brain like a stimulus. That anyone should be able to think better lying, sitting, or standing, than when speeding along on horseback, is to me incomprehensible. This is doubtless due to early training and long use; for on those great pampas where I first saw the light and was taught at a tender age to ride, we come to look on man as a parasitical creature, fitted by nature to occupy the back of a horse, in which position only he has full and free use of all his faculties. Possibly the gaucho—the horseman of the pampas—is born with this idea in his brain; if so, it would only be reasonable to suppose that its correlative exists in a modification of structure. Certain it is that an intoxicated gaucho lifted on to the back of his horse is perfectly safe in his seat. The horse may do his best to rid himself of his burden; the rider's legs—or posterior arms as they might appropriately be called—retain their iron grip, notwithstanding the fuddled brain.

The gaucho is more or less bow-legged ; and, of
course, the more crooked his legs are, the better
for him in his struggle for existence. Off his
horse his motions are awkward, like those of certain
tardigrade mammals of arboreal habits when removed from their tree. He waddles in his walk ;

Gaucho.

his hands feel for the reins ; his toes turn inwards
like a duck's. And here, perhaps, we can see why
foreign travellers, judging him from their own
standpoint, invariably bring against him the charge
of laziness. On horseback he is of all men most
active. His patient endurance under privations

that would drive other men to despair, his laborious days and feats of horsemanship, the long journeys he performs without rest or food, seem to simple dwellers on the surface of the earth almost like miracles. Deprive him of his horse, and he can do nothing but sit on the ground cross-legged, or *en cuclillas*,—on his heels. You have, to use his own figurative language, cut off his feet.

Darwin in his earlier years appears not to have possessed the power of reading men with that miraculous intelligence always distinguishing his researches concerning other and lower orders of beings. In the *Voyage of a Naturalist*, speaking of this supposed indolence of the gauchos, he tells that in one place where workmen were in great request, seeing a poor gaucho sitting in a listless attitude, he asked him why he did not work. The man's answer was that *he was too poor to work!* The philosopher was astonished and amused at the reply, but failed to understand it. And yet, to cne acquainted with these lovers of brief phrases, what more intelligible answer could have been returned? The poor fellow simply meant to say that his horses had been stolen—a thing of frequent occurrence in that country, or, perhaps, that some minion of the Government of the moment had seized them for the use of the State.

To return to the starting point, the pleasures of riding do not flow exclusively from the agreeable sensations attendant on flight-like motion ; there is also the knowledge, sweet in itself, that not a mere cunningly fashioned machine, like that fabled horse of brass " on which the Tartar king did ride,"

sustains us ; but a something with life and thought,
like ourselves, that feels what we feel, understands
us, and keenly participates in our pleasures. Take,
for example, the horse on which some quiet old
country gentleman is accustomed to travel; how
soberly and evenly he jogs along, picking his way
over the ground. But let him fall into the hands
of a lively youngster, and how soon he picks up a
frisky spirit ! Were horses less plastic, more the
creatures of custom than they are, it would always
be necessary, before buying one, to inquire into the
disposition of its owner.

When I was thirteen years old I was smitten
with love for a horse I once saw—an untamable-
looking brute, that rolled his eyes, turbulently,
under a cloud of black mane tumbling over his
forehead. I could not take my sight off this proud,
beautiful creature, and I longed to possess him
with a great longing. His owner—a worthless
vagabond, as it happened—marked my enthusiastic
admiration, and a day or two afterwards, having
lost all his money at cards, he came to me, offering
to sell me the horse. Having obtained my father's
consent, I rushed off to the man with all the money
I possessed—about thirty or thirty-five shillings, I
believe. After some grumbling, and finding he
could get no more, he accepted the money. My
new possession filled me with unbounded delight,
and I spent the time caressing him and leading him
about the grounds in search of succulent grasses
and choice leaves to feed him on. I am sure this
horse understood and loved me, for, in spite of
that savage look, which his eyes never quite lost,

he always displayed a singular gentleness towards me. He never attempted to upset me, though he promptly threw—to my great delight, I must confess—anyone else who ventured to mount him. Probably the secret of his conduct was that he hated the whip. Of this individual, if not of the species, the celebrated description held true :—" The horse is a docile animal, but if you flog him he will not do so." After he had been mine a few days, I rode on him one morning to witness a cattle-marking on a neighbouring estate. I found thirty or forty gauchos on the ground engaged in catching and branding the cattle. It was rough, dangerous work, but apparently not rough enough to satisfy the men, so after branding an animal and releasing him from their lassos, several of the mounted gauchos would, purely for sport, endeavour to knock it down as it rushed away, by charging furiously on to it. As I sat there enjoying the fun, my horse stood very quietly under me, also eagerly watching the sport. At length a bull was released, and, smarting from the fiery torture, lowered his horns and rushed away towards the open plain. Three horsemen in succession shot out from the crowd, and charged the bull at full speed; one by one, by suddenly swerving his body round, he avoided them, and was escaping scot-free. At this moment my horse—possibly interpreting a casual touch of my hand on his neck, or some movement of my body, as a wish to join in the sport—suddenly sprang forward and charged on the flying bull like a thunderbolt, striking him full in the middle of his body, and hurling him with a tremendous shock to earth. The stricken beast rolled violently over, while my horse stood still as a stone watching him. Strange to say, I was not unseated, but, turning round, galloped back, greeted by a shout of applause from the spectators—the only sound of that description I have ever had the privilege of listening to. They little knew that my horse had accomplished the perilous feat without his rider's guidance. No doubt he had been accustomed to do such things, and, perhaps, for the moment, had forgotten that he had passed into the hands of a new owner—one of tender years. He never voluntarily attempted an adventure of that kind again; he knew, I suppose, that he no longer carried on his back a reckless dare-devil, who valued not life. Poor Picáso! he was mine till he died. I have had scores of horses since, but never one I loved so well.

With the gauchos the union between man and horse is not of so intimate a nature as with the Indians of the pampas. Horses are too cheap, where a man without shoes to his feet may possess a herd of them, for the closest kind of friendship to ripen. The Indian has also less individuality of character. The immutable nature of the conditions he is placed in, and his savage life, which is a perpetual chase, bring him nearer to the level of the beast he rides. And probably the acquired sagacity of the horse in the long co-partnership of centuries has become hereditary, and of the nature of an instinct. The Indian horse is more docile, he understands his master better; the slightest touch of the hand on his neck, which seems to have

developed a marvellous sensitiveness, is sufficient
to guide him. The gaucho labours to give his
horse " a silken mouth," as he aptly calls it; the
Indian's horse has it from birth. Occasionally the
gaucho sleeps in the saddle; the Indian can die
on his horse. During frontier warfare one hears
at times of a dead warrior being found and removed
with difficulty from the horse that carried him out
of the fight, and about whose neck his rigid fingers
were clasped in death. Even in the gaucho
country, however, where, I grieve to confess, the
horse is not deservedly esteemed, there are very
remarkable instances of equine attachment and
fidelity to man, and of a fellowship between horse
and rider of the closest kind. One only I will
relate.

When Rosas, that man of " blood and iron," was
Dictator of the Argentine country—a position which
he held for a quarter of a century—deserters from
the army were inexorably shot when caught, as they
generally were. But where my boyhood was spent
there was a deserter, a man named Santa Anna,
who for seven years, without ever leaving the neighbourhood of his home, succeeded in eluding his pursuers by means of the marvellous sagacity and
watchful care exercised by his horse. When taking
his rest on the plain—for he seldom slept under a
roof—his faithful horse kept guard. At the first
sight of mounted men on the horizon he would fly
to his master, and, seizing his cloak between his
teeth, rouse him with a vigorous shake. The hunted
man would start up, and in a moment man and
horse would vanish into one of the dense reed-beds

abounding in the place, and where no man could follow. I have not space to tell more about this horse; but at last, in the fulness of time, when the figs were ripe—literally as well as figuratively, for it happened in the autumn of the year—the long tyrannous rule ended, and Santa Anna came out of the reed-beds, where he had lived his wild-animal life, to mix with his fellows. I knew him some years later. He was a rather heavy-looking man, with little to say, and his reputation for honesty was not good in the place; but I dare say there was something good in him.

Students of nature are familiar with the modifying effects of new conditions on man and brute. Take, for example, the gaucho: he must every day traverse vast distances, see quickly, judge rapidly, be ready at all times to encounter hunger and fatigue, violent changes of temperature, great and sudden perils. These conditions have made him differ widely from the peasant of the Peninsula ; he has the endurance and keen sight of a wolf, is fertile in expedients, quick in action, values human life not at all, and is in pain or defeat a Stoic. Unquestionably the horse he rides has also suffered a great change. He differs as much from the English hunter, for instance, as one animal can well differ from another of the same species. He never pounds the earth and wastes his energies in vain parade. He has not the dauntless courage that performs such brilliant feats in the field, and that often as not attempts the impossible. In the chase he husbands all his strength, carrying his head low, and almost grazing the ground with his hoofs, so that he is not a showy animal. Con-

stant use, or the slow cumulative process of natural
selection, has served to develop a keenness of sense
almost preternatural. The vulture's eye, with all the
advantage derived from the vulture's vast elevation
above the scene surveyed, is not so far-reaching as
the sense of smell in the pampa horse. A common
phenomenon on the pampas is a sudden migration
of the horses of a district to some distant place.
This occurs in seasons of drought, when grass or
water fails. The horses migrate to some district
where, from showers having fallen or other circumstances, there is a better supply of food and drink.
A slight breeze blowing from the more favoured
region, which may be forty or fifty miles away, or
even much further, is enough to start them off. Yet,
during the scorching days of midsummer, very little
moisture or smell of grass can possibly reach them
from such a distance.

Another phenomenon, even more striking, is
familiar to every frontiersman. For some reason,
the gaucho horse manifests the greatest terror at an
Indian invasion. No doubt his fear is, in part at
any rate, an associate feeling, the coming of the
Indians being always a time of excitement and commotion, sweeping like a great wave over the country ;
houses are in flames, families flying, cattle being
driven at frantic speed to places of greater safety.
Be this as it may, long before the marauders reach
the settlement (often when they are still a whole
day's journey from it) the horses take the alarm
and come wildly flying in : the contagion quickly
spreads to the horned cattle, and a general stampede
ensues. The gauchos maintain that the horses *smell*

the Indians. I believe they are right, for when passing a distant Indian camp, from which the wind blew, the horses driven before me have suddenly taken fright and run away, leading me a chase of many miles. The explanation that ostriches, deer, and other fleet animals driven in before the invaders might be the cause of the stampede cannot be accepted, since the horses are familiar with the sight of these animals flying from their gaucho hunters.

There is a pretty fable of a cat and dog lying in a dark room, aptly illustrating the fine senses of these two species. " Listen ! I heard a feather drop ! " said the dog. " Oh, no ! " said the cat, "it was a needle ; I saw it." The horse is not commonly believed to have senses keen as that, and a dog tracing his master's steps over the city pavement is supposed to be a feat no other animal can equal. No doubt the artificial life a horse lives in England, giving so little play to many of his most important faculties, has served to blunt them. He is a splendid creature ; but the noble bearing, the dash and reckless courage that distinguish him from the modest horse of the desert, have not been acquired without a corresponding loss in other things. When ridden by night the Indian horse—and sometimes the same habit is found in the gaucho's animal—drops his head lower and lower as the darkness increases, with the danger arising from the presence of innumerable kennels concealed in the grass, until his nose sweeps the surface like a foxhound's. That this action is dictated by a powerful instinct of self-preservation is plain ; for, when I have attempted to forcibly drag the animal's head up, he has answered such an experiment by taking the bit in his teeth, and violently pulling the reins out of my hand. His miraculous sense of smell measures the exact position of every hidden kennel, every treacherous spot, and enables him to pass swiftly and securely over it.

On the desert pampa the gaucho, for a reason that he knows, calls the puma the " friend of man." The Arab gives this designation to his horse ; but in Europe, where we do not associate closely with the horse, the dog naturally takes the foremost place in our affections. The very highest praise yet given to this animal is probably to be found in Bacon's essay on Atheism. " For take an example of a dog," he says, " and mark what a generosity and courage he will put on when he finds himself maintained by a man, who is to him in place of a god, or *melior natura*, which courage is manifestly such as that creature, without the confidence of a better nature than its own, could never attain! " Can we not say as much of the horse? The very horses that fly terror-stricken from the smell of an Indian will, when "maintained by a man," readily charge into a whole host of yelling savages.

I once had a horse at home, born and bred on the place, so docile that whenever I required him I could go to him where the horses were at pasture, and, though they all galloped off at my approach, he would calmly wait to be caught. Springing on to his back, I would go after the other horses, or gallop home with only my hand on his neck to guide him. I did not often ride him, as he was slow and lazy, but with timid women and children he was a favourite; he was also frequently used for farm work, in or out of harness, and I could shoot from his back. In the peach season he would roam about the plantation, getting the fruit, of which he was very fond, by tugging at the lower branches of the trees and shaking it down in showers. One intensely dark night I was riding home on this horse. I came through a road with a wire fence on each side, two miles in length, and when I had got nearly to the end of this road my horse suddenly stopped short, uttering a succession of loud terrified snorts. I could see nothing but the intense blackness of the night before me, and tried to encourage him to go on. Touching him on the neck, I found his hair wet with the sudden profuse sweat of extreme fear. The whip made no impression on him. He continued to back away, his eyes apparently fixed on some object of horror just before him, while he trembled to such a degree that I was shaken in the saddle. He attempted several times to wheel round and run away, but I was determined not to yield to him, and continued the contest. Suddenly, when I was beginning to despair of getting home by that road, he sprang forward, and regularly charged the (to me) invisible object before him, and in another moment, when he had apparently passed it, taking the bit between his teeth he almost flew over the ground, never pausing till he brought me to my own door. When I dismounted his terror seemed gone, but he hung his head in a dejected manner, like a horse that has been under the saddle all day. I have never witnessed another such instance of almost maddening fear. His terror and apprehension were like what we can imagine a man experiencing at sight of a ghost in some dark solitary place.

Yet he did not forcibly carry me away from it, as he
might so easily have done; but, finding himself
maintained by a "nature superior to his own," he
preferred to face it. I have never met in the dog
a more striking example of this noblest kind of
brute courage. The incident did not impress me
very much at the moment, but when I came to reflect
that my sight was mere blindness compared with
that of my horse, and that it was not likely his
imagination clothed any familiar natural object
with fantastic terrors, it certainly did impress me
very deeply.

I am loth to finish with my subject, in which, to
express myself in the manner of the gauchos, I
have passed over many matters, like good grass and
fragrant herbs the galloping horse sniffs at but cannot stay to taste; and especially loth to conclude
with this last incident, which has in it an element
of gloom. I would rather first go back for a few moments to my original theme—the pleasures of riding,
for the sake of mentioning a species of pleasure my
English reader has probably never tasted or even
heard of. When riding by night on the pampas, I
used to enjoy lying back on my horse till my head
and shoulders rested well on his back, my feet also
being raised till they pressed against his neck; and
in this position, which practice can make both safe
and comfortable, gaze up into the starry sky. To
enjoy this method of riding thoroughly, a sure-footed
unshod horse with perfect confidence in his rider is
necessary; and he must be made to go at a swift
and smooth pace over level grassy ground. With
these conditions the sensation is positively delightful.
Nothing of earth is visible, only the vast circle of

the heavens glittering with innumerable stars; the muffled sound of the hoofs on the soft sward becomes in fancy only the rushing of the wings of our Pegasus, while the enchanting illusion that we are soaring through space possesses the mind. Unfortunately, however, this method of riding is impracticable in England. And, even if people with enthusiasm enough could be found to put it in practice by importing swift light-footed Arabian or pampa horses, and careering about level parks on dark starry nights, probably a shout of derision would be raised against so undignified a pastime.

Apropos of dignity, I will relate, in conclusion, an incident in my London life which may possibly interest psychologists. Some time ago in Oxford Street I got on top of an omnibus travelling west. My mind was preoccupied, I was anxious to get home, and, in an absent kind of way, I became irritated at the painfully slow rate of progress. It was all an old familiar experience, the deep thought, lessening pace, and consequent irritation. The indolent brute I imagined myself riding was, as usual, taking advantage of his rider's abstraction; but I would soon "feelingly persuade" him that I was not so far gone as to lose sight of the difference between a swinging gallop and a walk. So, elevating my umbrella, I dealt the side of the omnibus a sounding blow, very much to the astonishment of my fellow-passengers. So overgrown are we with usages, habits, tricks of thought and action springing from the soil we inhabit; and when we have broken away and removed ourselves far from it, so long do the dead tendrils still cling to us!

CHAPTER XXIV.

WE can imagine what the feelings of a lapidary
would be—an enthusiast whose life is given to the
study of precious stones, and whose sole delight is
in the contemplation of their manifold beauty—if a
stranger should come in to him, and, opening his
hand, exhibit a new unknown gem, splendid as ruby
or as sapphire, yet manifestly no mere variety of
any familiar stone, but differing as widely from all
others as diamond from opal or cat's-eye; and then,
just when he is beginning to rejoice in that strange
exquisite loveliness, the hand should close and the
stranger, with a mocking smile on his lips, go forth
and disappear from sight in the crowd. A feeling
such as that would be is not unfrequently experienced by the field naturalist whose favoured lot it
is to live in a country not yet " thoroughly worked
out," with its every wild inhabitant scientifically
named, accurately described, and skilfully figured in
some colossal monograph. One swift glance of the
practised eye, ever eagerly searching for some new
thing, and he knows that here at length is a form
never previously seen by him; but his joy is perhaps only for a few moments, and the prize is
snatched from sight for ever. The lapidary might

have some doubts; he might think that the
stranger had, after all, only mocked him with the
sight of a wonderful artificial gem, and that a close
examination would have proved its worthlessness;
but the naturalist can have no doubts : if he is an
enthusiast, well acquainted with the fauna of his
district, and has good eyesight, he knows that there
is no mistake ; for there it is, the new strange
form, photographed by instantaneous process on his
mind, and there it will remain, a tantalizing image,
its sharp lines and fresh colouring unblurred by
time.

Walking in some open forest glade, he may look
up just in time to see a great strange butterfly—a
blue Morpho, let us say, wandering in some far
country where this angel insect is unknown—passing athwart his vision with careless, buoyant flight,
the most sylph-like thing in nature, and all blue
and pure like its aërial home, but with a more
delicate and wonderful brilliance in its cerulean
colour, giving such unimaginable glory to its broad
airy wings; and then, almost before his soul has
had time to feel its joy, it may soar away unloitering
over the tall trees, to be seen no more.

But the admiration, the delight, and the desire
are equally great, and the loss just as keenly felt,
whether the strange species seen happens to be one
surpassingly beautiful or not. Its newness is to the
naturalist its greatest attraction. How beautiful
beyond all others seems a certain small unnamed
brown bird to my mind! So many years have
passed and its image has not yet grown dim; yet I
saw it only for a few moments, when it hopped out

from the thick foliage and perched within two or three yards of me, not afraid, but only curious; and after peering at me first with one eye and then the other, and wiping its small dagger on a twig, it flew away and was seen no more. For many days I sought for it, and for years waited its reappearance, and it was more to me than ninety and nine birds which I had always known ; yet it was very modest, dressed in a brown suit, very pale on the breast and white on the throat, and for distinction a straw-coloured stripe over the eye—that ribbon which Queen Nature bestows on so many of her feathered subjects, in recognition, I suppose, of some small and common kind of merit. If I should meet with it in a collection I should know it again ; only, in that case it would look plain and homely to me—this little bird that for a time made all others seem unbeautiful.

Even a richer prize may come in sight for a brief period—one of the nobler mammalians, which are fewer in number, and bound to earth like ourselves, and therefore so much better known than the wandering children of air. In some secluded spot, resting amidst luxuriant herbage or forest undergrowth, a slight rustling makes us start, and, lo ! looking at us from the clustering leaves, a strange face ; the leaf-like ears erect, the dark eyes round with astonishment, and the sharp black nose twitching and sniffing audibly, to take in the unfamiliar flavour of a human presence from the air, like the pursed-up and smacking lips of a wine-drinker tasting a new vintage. No sooner seen than gone, like a dream, a phantom, the quaint

furry face to be thereafter only an image in
memory.

Sometimes the prize may be a very rich one, and
actually within reach of the hand—challenging the
hand, as it were, to grasp it, and yet presently slip
away to be seen no more, although it may be sought
for day after day, with a hungry longing comparable to that of some poor tramp who finds a
gold doubloon in the forest, and just when he is
beginning to realize all that it means to him drops
it in the grass and cannot find it again. There is
not the faintest motion in the foliage, no rustle of
any dry leaf, and yet we know that something has
moved—something has come or has gone ; and,
gazing fixedly at one spot, we suddenly see that it
is still there, close to us, the pointed ophidian head
and long neck, not drawn back and threatening,
but sloping forward, dark and polished as the green
and purple weed-stems springing from marshy soil,
and with an irregular chain of spots extending
down the side.   Motionless, too, as the stems it is ;
but presently the tongue, crimson and glistening,
darts out and flickers, like a small jet of smoke and
flame, and is withdrawn ; then the smooth serpent
head drops down, and the thing is gone.

How I saw and lost the noble wrestling frog has
been recounted in Chapter IV. : other tantalizing
experiences of the same kind remain to be told in
the present chapter, which is not intended for the
severe naturalist, but rather for such readers as
may like to hear something about the pains and
pleasures of the seeker as well as the result of the
seeking.

One of my earliest experiences of seeing and losing relates to a humming-bird—a veritable "jewel of ornithology." I was only a boy at the time, but already pretty well acquainted with the birds of the district I lived in, near La Plata River, and among them were three species of the humming-bird. One spring day I saw a fourth—a wonderful little thing, only half as big as the smallest of the other three—the well-known Phaïthornis splendens —and scarcely larger than a bumble-bee. I was within three feet of it as it sucked at the flowers,

A lost Humming-bird.

suspended motionless in the air, the wings appearing formless and mist-like from their rapid vibratory motion, but the rest of the upper plumage was seen distinctly as anything can be seen. The head and neck and upper part of the back were emerald green, with the metallic glitter usually seen in the burnished scale-like feathers of these small birds; the lower half of the back was velvet-black; the tail and tail-coverts white as snow. On two other occasions, at intervals of a few days, I saw this brilliant little stranger, always very near, and tried without success to capture it, after which it disappeared from the plantation. Four years later I saw it once again not far from the same place. It was late in summer, and I was out walking on the level plain where the ground was carpeted with short grass, and nothing else grew there except a solitary stunted cardoon thistle-bush with one flower on its central stem above the grey-green artichoke-like leaves. The disc of the great thorny blossom was as broad as that of a sunflower, purple in colour, delicately frosted with white ; on this flat disc several insects were feeding—flies, fireflies, and small wasps—and I paused for a few minutes in my walk to watch them. Suddenly a small misty object flew swiftly downwards past my face, and paused motionless in the air an inch or two above the rim of the flower. Once more my lost humming-bird, which I remembered so well ! The exquisitely graceful form, half circled by the misty moth-like wings, the glittering green and velvet-black mantle, and snow-white tail spread open like a fan—there it hung like a beautiful bird-shaped gem suspended by an invisible gossamer thread. One—two—three moments passed, while I gazed, trembling with rapturous excitement, and then, before I had time to collect my faculties and make a forlorn attempt to capture it with my hat, away it flew, gliding so swiftly on the air that form and colour were instantly lost, and in appearance it was only an obscure grey line traced rapidly along the low sky and fading quickly out of sight. And that was the last I ever saw of it.

The case of this small " winged gem," still wandering nameless in the wilds, reminds me of yet

another bird seen and lost, also remarkable for its
diminutive size. For years I looked for it, and
when the wished-for opportunity came, and it was
in my power to secure it, I refrained; and Fate
punished me by never permitting me to see it again.
On several occasions while riding on the pampas I
had caught glimpses of this minute bird flitting up
mothlike, with uncertain tremulous flight, and again
dipping into the weeds, tall grass, or thistles. Its
plumage was yellowish in hue, like sere dead herbage, and its extremely slender body looked longer
and slimmer than it was, owing to the great length
of its tail, or of the two middle tail-feathers. I
knew that it was a Synallaxis—a genus of small
birds of the Woodhewer family. Now, as I have
said in a former chapter, these are wise little birds,
more interesting—I had almost said more beautiful
—in their wisdom, or wisdom-simulating instincts,
than the quatzel in its resplendent green, or the
cock-of-the-rock in its vivid scarlet and orange
mantle. Wrens and mocking-birds have melody
for their chief attraction, and the name of each
kind is, to our minds, also the name of a certain
kind of sweet music; we think of swifts and
swallows in connection with the mysterious migratory instinct; and humming-birds have a glittering
mantle, and the miraculous motions necessary to
display its ever-changing iridescent beauty. In
like manner, the homely Dendrocolaptidæ possess
the genius for building, and an account of one of
these small birds without its nest would be like a
biography of Sir Christopher Wren that made no
mention of his works. It was not strange then,

that when I saw this small bird the question rose
to my mind, What kind of nest does it build?

One morning in the month of October, the great
breeding-time for birds in the Southern Hemisphere,
while cautiously picking my way through a bed of
cardoon bushes, the mysterious little creature flitted
up and perched among the clustering leaves quite
near to me. It uttered a feeble grasshopper-like
chirp; and then a second individual, smaller, paler-
coloured, and if possible shyer than the first, showed
itself for two or three seconds, after which both
birds dived once more into concealment. How glad
I was to see them! for here they were, male and
female, in a suitable spot in my own fields, where
they evidently meant to breed. Every day after
that I paid them one cautious visit, and by waiting
from five to fifteen minutes, standing motionless
among the thistles, I always succeeded in getting
them to show themselves for a few moments. I
could easily have secured them then, but my wish
was to discover their nesting habits; and after
watching for some days, I was rewarded by finding
their nest ; then for three days more I watched it
slowly progressing towards completion, and each
time I approached it one of the small birds would
flit out to vanish into the herbage. The structure
was about six inches long, and not more than two
inches in diameter, and was placed horizontally on
a broad stiff cardoon leaf, sheltered by other leaves
above. It was made of the finest dry grass loosely
woven, and formed a simple perfectly straight tube,
open at both ends. The aperture was so small that
I could only insert my little finger, and the bird

could not, of course, have turned round in so narrow
a passage, and so always went in at one end and
left by the other. On visiting the spot on the
fourth day I found, to my intense chagrin, that the
delicate fabric had been broken and thrown down
by some animal ; also, that the birds had utterly

Small Spine-tail and Nest.

vanished—for I sought them in vain, both there and
in every weedy and thistly spot in the neighbourhood. The bird without the nest had seemed a
useless thing to possess ; now, for all my pains, I
had only a wisp of fine dry grass in my hand, and
no bird. The shy, modest little creature, dwelling

violet-like amidst clustering leaves, and even when
showing itself still " half-hidden from the eye," was
thereafter to be only a tantalizing image in memory.
Still, my case was not so hopeless as that of the
imagined lapidary ; for however rare a species may
be, and near to its final extinction, there must
always be many individuals existing, and I was
cheered by the thought that I might yet meet with
one at some future time.   And, even if this particular species was not to gladden my sight again,
there were others, scores and hundreds more, and
at any moment I might expect to see one shining, a
living gem, on Nature's open extended palm.

Sometimes it has happened that an animal would
have been overlooked or passed by with scant
notice, to be forgotten, perhaps, but for some singular action or habit which has instantly given it
a strange importance, and made its possession
desirable.

I was once engaged in the arduous and monotonous task of driving a large number of sheep a distance of two hundred and fifty miles, in excessively
hot weather, when sheep prefer standing still to
travelling.   Five or six gauchos were with me, and
we were on the southern pampas of Buenos Ayres,
near to a long precipitous stony sierra which rose
to a height of five or six hundred feet above the
plain.   Who that has travelled for eighteen days on
a dead level in a broiling sun can resist a hill ?
That sierra was more sublime to us than Conon-
dagua, than Illimani.

Leaving the sheep, I rode to it with three of the
men ; and after securing our horses on the lower

slope, we began our laborious ascent. Now the gaucho when taken from his horse, on which he lives like a kind of parasite, is a very slow-moving creature, and I soon left my friends far behind. Coming to a place where ferns and flowering herbage grew thick, I began to hear all about me sounds of a character utterly unlike any natural sound I was acquainted with—innumerable low clear voices tinkling or pealing like minute sweet-toned, resonant bells—for the sounds were purely metallic and perfectly bell-like. I was completely ringed round with the mysterious music, and as I walked it rose and sank rhythmically, keeping time to my steps. I stood still, and immediately the sounds ceased. I took a step forwards, and again the fairy-bells were set ringing, as if at each step my foot touched a central meeting point of a thousand radiating threads, each thread attached to a peal of little bells hanging concealed among the herbage. I waited for my companions, and called their attention to the phenomenon, and to them also it was a thing strange and perplexing. " It is the bell-snake ! " cried one excitedly. This is the rattle-snake ; but although at that time I had no experience of this reptile, I knew that he was wrong. Yet how natural the mistake ! The Spanish name of " bell-snake " had made him imagine that the whirring sound of the vibrating rattles, resembling muffled cicada music, is really bell-like in character. Eventually we discovered that the sound was made by grasshoppers ; but they were seen only to be lost, for I could not capture one, so excessively shy and cunning had the perpetual ringing of their own

little tocsins made them.　And presently I had to
return to my muttons ; and afterwards there was no
opportunity of revisiting the spot to observe so
singular a habit again and collect specimens.　It
was a very slender grasshopper, about an inch and
a half long, of a uniform, tawny, protective colour
—the colour of an old dead leaf.　It also possessed
a protective habit common to most grasshoppers, of
embracing a slender vertical stem with its four fine
front legs, and moving cunningly round so as to
keep the stem always in front of it to screen itself
from sight.　Only other grasshoppers are silent
when alarmed, and the silence and masking action
are related, and together prevent the insect from
being detected.　But this particular species, or race,
or colony, living on the sides of the isolated sierra,
had acquired a contrary habit, resembling a habit
of gregarious birds and mammals.　For this informing sound (unless it mimicked some *warning-sound,*
as of a rattlesnake, which it didn't) could not possibly be beneficial to individuals living alone, as
grasshoppers generally do, but, on the contrary,
only detrimental; and such a habit was therefore
purely for the public good, and could only have
arisen in a species that always lived in communities.

On another occasion, in the middle of the hot
season, I was travelling alone across-country in a
locality which was new to me, a few leagues east of
La Plata River, in its widest part.　About eleven
o'clock in the morning I came to a low-lying level
plain where the close-cropped grass was vivid green,
although elsewhere all over the country the vegeta-

tion was scorched and dead, and dry as ashes. The
ground being so favourable, I crossed this low
plain at a swinging gallop, and in about thirty
minutes' time. In that half-hour I saw a vast
number of snakes, all of one kind, and a species
new to me ; but my anxiety to reach my destina-
tion before the oppressive heat of the afternoon
made me hurry on. So numerous were the snakes
in that green place that frequently I had as many
as a dozen in sight at one time. It looked to me
like a coronella—harmless colubrine snakes—but
was more than twice as large as either of the two
species of that genus I was already familiar with.
In size they varied greatly, ranging from two to
fully five feet in length, and the colour was dull
yellow or tan, slightly lined and mottled with shades
of brown. Among dead or partially withered grass
and herbage they would have been undistinguishable
at even a very short distance, but on the vivid
green turf they were strangely conspicuous, some
being plainly visible forty or fifty yards away ; and
not one was seen coiled up. They were all lying
motionless, stretched out full length, and looking
like dark yellow or tan-coloured ribbons, thrown on
to the grass. It was most unusual to see so many
snakes together, although not surprising in the circumstances. The December heats had dried up all
the watercourses and killed the vegetation, and
made the earth hard and harsh as burnt bricks ; and
at such times snakes, especially the more active non-
venomous kinds, will travel long distances, in their
slow way, in search of water. Those I saw during
my ride had probably been attracted by the mois-

ture from a large area of country; and although
there was no water, the soft fresh grass must have
been grateful to them. Snakes are seen coiled up
when they are at home; when travelling and far
afield, they lie as a rule extended full length, even
when resting—and they are generally resting.
Pausing at length, before quitting this green plain,
to give my horse a minute's rest, I got off and
approached a large snake; but when I was quite
twelve yards from it, it lifted its head, and, turning
deliberately round, came rather swiftly at me. I
retreated, and it followed, until, springing on to my
horse, I left it, greatly surprised at its action, and
beginning to think that it must be venomous. As
I rode on the feeling of surprise increased, conquering haste; and in the end, seeing more snakes,
I dismounted and approached the largest, when
exactly the same thing occurred again, the snake
rousing itself and coming angrily at me when I was
still (considering the dull lethargic character of the
deadliest kinds) at an absurd distance from it.
Again and again I repeated the experiment, with the
same result. And at length I stunned one with a
blow of my whip to examine its mouth, but found
no poison-fangs in it.

I then resumed my journey, expecting to meet
with more snakes of the same kind at my destina-
tion; but there were none, and very soon business
called me to a distant place, and I never met with
this species afterwards. But when I rode away
from that green spot, and was once more on the
higher, desolate, wind-swept plain surrounding it—
a rustling sea of giant thistles, still erect, although

dead, and red as rust, and filling the hot blue sky
with silvery down—it was with a very strange
feeling. The change from the green and living to
the dead and dry and dusty was so great! There
seemed to be something mysterious, extra-natural,
in that low level plain, so green and fresh and
snaky, where my horse's hoofs had made no sound
—a place where no man dwelt, and no cattle
pastured, and no wild bird folded its wing. And
the serpents there were not like others—the
mechanical coiled-up thing we know, a mere bone-
and-muscle man-trap, set by the elements, to spring
and strike when trodden on : but these had a high
intelligence, a lofty spirit, and were filled with a
noble rage and astonishment that any other kind of
creature, even a man, should venture there to disturb
their sacred peace. It was a fancy, born of that
sense of mystery which the unknown and the
unusual in nature wakes in us—an obsolescent
feeling that still links us to the savage. But the
simple fact was wonderful enough, and that has
been set down simply and apart from all fancies.
If the reader happens not to be a naturalist, it is
right to tell him that a naturalist cannot exaggerate
consciously; and if he be capable of unconscious
exaggeration, then he is no naturalist. He should
hasten " to join the innumerable caravan that
moves " to the fantastic realms of romance. Looking at the simple fact scientifically, it was a case of
mimicry—the harmless snake mimicking the fierce
threatening gestures and actions proper to some
deadly kind. Only with this difference : the
venomous snake, of all deadly things in nature, is

the slowest to resentment, the most reluctant to
enter into a quarrel ; whereas in this species angry
demonstrations were made when the intruder was
yet far off, and before he had shown any hostile
intentions.

My last case—the last, that is, of the few I have
selected—relates to a singular variation in the
human species. On this occasion I was again
travelling alone in a strange district on the southern
frontier of Buenos Ayres. On a bitterly cold midwinter day, shortly before noon, I arrived, stiff and
tired, at one of those pilgrims' rests on the pampas
—a wayside *pulperia,* or public house, where the
traveller can procure anything he may require or
desire, from a tumbler of Brazilian rum to make
glad his heart, to a poncho, or cloak of blue cloth
with fluffy scarlet lining, to keep him warm o'
nights ; and, to speed him on his way, a pair of
cast-iron spurs weighing six pounds avoirdupois,
with rowels eight inches in diameter, manufactured
in this island for the use of barbarous men beyond
the sea. The wretched mud-and-grass building was
surrounded by a foss crossed by a plank draw-
bridge ; outside of the enclosure twelve or fourteen
saddled horses were standing, and from the loud
noise of talk and laughter in the bar I conjectured
that a goodly company of rough frontiersmen were
already making merry at that early hour. It was
necessary for me to go in among them to see the
proprietor of the place and ask permission to visit
his kitchen in order to make myself a " tin of coffee,"
that being the refreshment I felt inclined for.
When I went in and made my salutation, one man

wheeled round square before me, stared straight
into my eyes, and in an exceedingly high-pitched
reedy or screechy voice and a sing-song tone returned my " good morning," and bade me call for
the liquid I loved best at his expense. I declined
with thanks, and in accordance with gaucho
etiquette added that I was prepared to pay for his
liquor. It was then for him to say that he had
already been served and so let the matter drop, but
he did not do so : he screamed out in his wild
animal voice that he would take gin. I paid for
his drink, and would, I think, have felt greatly
surprised at his strange insolent behaviour, so unlike that of the usually courteous gaucho, but this
thing affected me not at all, so profoundly had his
singular appearance and voice impressed me ; and
for the rest of the time I remained in the place I
continued to watch him narrowly. Professor
Huxley has somewhere said, " A variation frequently
occurs, but those who notice it take no care about
noting down the particulars." That is not a failing
of mine, and this is what I noted down while the
man's appearance was still fresh in memory. He
was about five feet eleven inches in height—very
tall for a gaucho—straight and athletic, with exceedingly broad shoulders, which made his round
head look small ; long arms and huge hands. The
round flat face, coarse black hair, swarthy reddish
colour, and smooth hairless cheeks seemed to show
that he had more Indian than Spanish blood in him,
while his round black eyes were even more like
those of a rapacious animal in expression than in the
pure-blooded Indian. He also had the Indian or

half-breed's moustache, when that natural ornament
is permitted to grow, and which is composed of
thick bristles standing out like a cat's whiskers.
The mouth was the marvellous feature, for it was
twice the size of an average mouth, and the two lips
were alike in thickness. This mouth did not smile,
but snarled, both when he spoke and when he
should have smiled; and when he snarled the whole
of his teeth and a part of the gums were displayed.
The teeth were not as in other human beings—
incisors, canines, and molars : they were all exactly
alike, above and below, each tooth a gleaming white
triangle, broad at the gum where it touched its
companion teeth, and with a point sharp as the
sharpest-pointed dagger. They were like the teeth
of a shark or crocodile. I noticed that when he
showed them, which was very often, they were not
set together as in dogs, weasels, and other savage
snarling animals, but apart, showing the whole
terrible serration in the huge red mouth.

After getting his gin he joined in the boisterous
conversation with the others, and this gave me an
opportunity of studying his face for several minutes,
all the time with a curious feeling that I had put
myself into a cage with a savage animal of horrible
aspect, whose instincts were utterly unknown to
me, and were probably not very pleasant. It was
interesting to note that whenever one of the others
addressed him directly, or turned to him when speaking, it was with a curious expression, not of fear,
but partly amusement and partly something else
which I could not fathom. Now, one might think
that this was natural enough purely on account of

the man's extraordinary appearance. I do not think that a sufficient explanation; for however strange a man's appearance may be, his intimate friends and associates soon lose all sense of wonder at his strangeness, and even forget that he is unlike others. My belief is that this curiosity, or whatever it was they showed in their faces, was due to something in his character—a mental strangeness, showing itself at unexpected times, and which might flash out at any moment to amuse or astonish them. There was certainly a correspondence between the snarling action of the mouth and the dangerous form of the teeth, perfect as that in any snarling animal; and such animals, it should be remembered, snarl not only when angry and threatening, but in their playful moods as well. Other and more important correspondences or correlations might have existed; and the voice was certainly unlike any human voice I have ever heard, whether in white, red, or black man. But the time I had for observation was short, the conversation revealed nothing further, and by-and-by I went away in search of the odorous kitchen, where there would be hot water for coffee, or at all events cold water and a kettle, and materials for making a fire—to wit, bones of dead cattle, "buffalo chips," and rancid fat.

I have never been worried with the wish or ambition to be a head-hunter in the Dyak sense, but on this one occasion I did wish that it had been possible, without violating any law, or doing anything to a fellow-creature which I should not like done to myself, to have obtained possession of this man's head, with its set of unique and terrible teeth. For

how, in the name of Evolution, did he come by
them, and by other physical peculiarities—the
snarling habit and that high-pitched animal voice,
for instance—which made him a being different
from others—one separate and far apart? Was
he, so admirably formed, so complete and well-
balanced, merely a freak of nature, to use an old-
fashioned phrase—a sport, or spontaneous individual
variation—an experiment for a new human type,
imagined by Nature in some past period, inconceivably long ago, but which she had only now, too
late, found time to carry out? Or rather was he
like that little hairy maiden exhibited not long ago
in London, a reproduction of the past, the mystery
called reversion—a something in the life of a species
like memory in the life of an individual, the memory
which suddenly brings back to the old man's mind
the image of his childhood? For no dream-monster
in human form ever appeared to me with so strange
and terrible a face; and this was no dream but
sober fact, for I saw and spoke with this man;
and unless cold steel has given him his quietus,
or his own horse has crushed him, or a mad bull
gored him—all natural forms of death in that wild
land—he is probably still living and in the prime
of life, and perhaps at this very moment drink-
ing gin at some astonished traveller's expense
at that very bar where I met him. The old
Palæolithic man, judging from the few remains we
have of him, must have had an unspeakably savage
and, to our way of thinking, repulsive and horrible
aspect, with his villainous low receding forehead,
broad nose, great projecting upper jaw, and retreat-

ing chin; to meet such a man face to face in Piccadilly would frighten a nervous person of the present time. But his teeth were not unlike our own, only very much larger and more powerful, and well adapted to their work of masticating the flesh, underdone and possibly raw, of mammoth and rhinoceros. If, then, this living man recalls a type of the past, it is of a remoter past, a more primitive man, the volume of whose history is missing from the geological record. To speculate on such a subject seems idle and useless; and when I coveted possession of that head it was not because I thought that it might lead to any fresh discovery. A lower motive inspired the feeling. I wished for it only that I might bring it over the sea, to drop it like a new apple of discord, suited to the spirit of the times, among the anthropologists and evolutionists generally of this old and learned world. Inscribed, of course, " To the most learned," but giving no locality and no particulars. I wished to do that for the pleasure—not a very noble kind of pleasure, I allow—of witnessing from some safe hiding-place the stupendous strife that would have ensued—a battle more furious, lasting and fatal to many a brave knight of biology, than was ever yet fought over any bone or bony fragment or fabric ever picked up, including the celebrated cranium of the Neanderthal.

APPENDIX.

THE PUMA, OR LION OF AMERICA.

THE following passage occurs in an article on "The
Naturalist in La Plata," by the late Professor Romanes,
which appeared in the *Nineteenth Century*, May, 1893.
After quoting the account of the puma's habits and character
given in the book, the writer says:—"I have received
corroboration touching all these points from a gentleman
who, when walking alone and unarmed on the skirts of a
forest, was greatly alarmed by a large puma coming out to
meet him. Deeming it best not to stand, he advanced to
meet the animal, which thereupon began to gambol around
his feet and rub against his legs, after the manner of an
affectionate cat. At first he thought these movements must
have been preliminary to some peculiar mode of attack, and
therefore he did not respond, but walked quietly on, until
the puma suddenly desisted and re-entered the forest. This
gentleman says that, until the publication of Mr. Hudson's
book, he had always remained under the impression that
that particular puma must have been insane."

MUSIC AND DANCING IN NATURE.

I have found among my papers the following mislaid note
on the subject of sportive displays of mammalians, which
should have been used on page 281, where the subject is
briefly treated:—Most mammalians are comparatively silent
and live on the ground, and not having the power to escape

easily, which birds have, and being more persecuted by man, they do not often disport themselves unrestrainedly in his presence; it is difficult to watch any wild animal without the watcher's presence being known or suspected. Nevertheless, their displays are not so rare as we might imagine. I have more than once detected species, with which I was, or imagined myself to be, well acquainted, disporting themselves in a manner that took me completely by surprise. While out tinamou shooting one day in autumn, near my own home in La Plata, I spied a troop of about a dozen weasels racing madly about over a vizcacha village—the mound and group of pit-like burrows inhabited by a community of vizcachas. These weasels were of the large common species, Galictis barbara, about the size of a cat; and were engaged in a pastime resembling a complicated dance, and so absorbed were they on that occasion that they took no notice of me when I walked up to within nine or ten yards of them, and stood still to watch the performance. They were all swiftly racing about and leaping over the pits, always doubling quickly back when the limit of the mound was reached, and although apparently carried away with excitement, and crossing each other's tracks at all angles, and this so rapidly and with so many changes of direction that I became confused when trying to keep any one animal in view, they never collided nor even came near enough to touch one another. The whole performance resembled, on a greatly magnified scale and without its beautiful smoothness and lightning swiftness, the fantastic dance of small black water-beetles, frequently seen on the surface of a pool or stream, during which the insects glide about in a limited area with such celerity as to appear like black curving lines traced by flying invisible pens; and as the lines everywhere cross and intersect, they form an intricate pattern on the surface. After watching the weasel dance for some minutes, I stepped up to the mound, whereupon the animals became alarmed and rushed pell-mell into the burrows, but only to reappear in a few seconds, thrusting up their long ebony-black necks and flat grey-capped heads, snarling and chattering at me, glaring with fierce, beady eyes.

THE STRANGE INSTINCTS OF CATTLE.

In November and December, 1893, a short correspondence appeared in the *Field* on the curious subject of " Dogs burying their dead." It arose through a letter from a Mr. Gould, of Albany, Western Australia, relating the following incident :—

A settler shot a bitch from a neighbouring estate that had formed the habit of coming on to his land to visit and play with his dog. The dog, finding his companion dead, was observed to dig a large hole in the ground, into which he dragged the carcase ; but he did not cover it with earth. The writer wished to know if any reader of the *Field* had met with a similar case. Some notes, which I contributed in reply to this letter, bear on one of the subjects treated in the chapter on " strange instincts," namely, the instinct of social animals to protect and shield their fellows ; and for this reason I have thought it best to reproduce them in this place.

I remember on one occasion watching at intervals, for an entire day, a large and very savage dog keeping watch over the body of a dead bitch that had been shot. He made no attempt to bury the dead animal, but he never left it. He was observed more than once trying to drag the body away, doubtless with the intention of hiding it ; not succeeding in these attempts, he settled down by its side again, although it was evident that he was suffering greatly from thirst and heat. It was at last only with the greatest trouble that the people of the house succeeded in getting the body away and burying it out of his sight.

Another instance, more to the point, occurred at my own house on the pampas, and I was one of several persons who witnessed it. A small, red, long-haired bitch—a variety of the common native cur—gave birth to four or five pups. A peon was told to destroy them, and, waiting until the bitch was out of sight, he carried them off to the end of the orchard, some 400 or 500 yards from the house, and threw them into a pool of water which was only two to three feet deep. The bitch passed the rest of the day in rushing frantically about, searching for her young, and in the evening, a little after dark, actually succeeded in finding them, although they were lying at the bottom of the pool. She got them all out, and carried them, one by one, to another part of the grounds, where she passed the night with them, uttering at intervals the most piercing cries. In the morning she carried them to still another spot, where there was a soft mould, and then dug a hole large and deep enough to bury them all, covering them over with the loose earth. Her task done, she returned to the house to sleep all day, but when night came again the whole piteous performance was repeated: the pups were dug up, and she passed the long, piercingly cold night—for it was in the depth of winter—trying to keep them warm, and uttering, as before, distressing cries. Yet a third time the whole thing was repeated; but after the third night, when the dog came home to sleep, the dead pups were taken out of the ground and buried at a distance.

Such an action as this strikes one with astonishment only because we have the custom of burying our dead, and are too ready at all times to regard the dog as human-like. But the explanation of the action in this case is to be found in the familiar fact that very many animals, including the dog, have the habit or instinct of burying or concealing the thing they wish to leave in safety. Thus, the dog buries the bone it does not want to eat, and when hungry digs it up again. When a dog buries or hides the dead body of the she dog it was attached to, or the she dog buries her dead young, it is with the same motive—namely, to conceal the animal that cannot be roused, and that it would not be safe to leave exposed.

It is plain to all who observe their actions that the lower animals have no comprehension of death. In the case of two animals that are accustomed to play or to be much together, if one dies, or is killed, and its body left, the other will come to sniff at, touch, and at last try to rouse it; but finding all attempts vain, it will at length go away to seek companionship elsewhere. In cases where the attachment is much stronger, the dead body may be watched over for an indefinite period. A brother of mine once related to me a very pathetic incident which occurred at an estancia on the pampas where he was staying. A large portion of the land was a low, level, marshy plain, partly overgrown with reeds and rushes; and one day, in this wilderness, a little boy of eight or nine, from the estancia, lost himself. A small dog, his invariable attendant, had gone out with him, but did not return. Seven days later the poor boy was found, at a great distance from the house, lying on the grass, where he had died of exhaustion. The dog was lying coiled up at his side, and appeared to be sleeping; but, when spoken to, he did not stir, and was presently found to be dead too. The dog could have gone back at any moment to the estancia, but his instinct of attachment overcame all others; he kept guard over his little master, who slept so soundly and so long, until he, too, slept in the same way.

A still more remarkable case of this kind was given in one of my books, of a gaucho, accompanied by his dog, who was chased and overtaken by a troop of soldiers during one of the civil wars in Uruguay. Suspecting him of being a spy, or, at all events, an enemy, his captors cut his throat, then rode away, calling to the dog to follow them; but the animal refused to leave his dead master's side. Returning to the spot a few days later, they saw the body of the man they had killed surrounded by a large number of vultures, which the dog, in a frenzy of excitement, was occupied in keeping at a respectable distance. It was observed that the dog, after making one of his sallies, driving the birds away with furious barkings, would set out at a run to a small stream

not far from the spot; but when half way to it he would
look back, and, seeing the vultures advancing once more to
the corpse, would rush back to protect it. The soldiers
watched him for some time with great interest, and once
more they tried in vain to get him to follow them. Two
days afterwards they revisited the spot, to find the dog
lying dead by the side of his dead master. I had this story
from the lips of one of the witnesses.

In all such cases, whether the dog watches over, conceals,
or buries a dead body, he is doubtless moved by the same
instinct which leads him to safeguard the animal he is
attached to—another dog or his human master. But, as
the dead animal is past help, it is, of course, a blunder of
the instinct; and the blunder must be of very much less
frequent occurrence among wild than among domestic
animals. In a state of nature, when a gregarious animal
dies, he dies, as a rule, alone; his body is not seen by his
former companions, and he is not missed. When he dies by
violence—which is the common fate—the body is carried off
or devoured by the killer. This being the usual order, there
is no instinct, except in a very few species, relating to the
disposal of the dead among mammals and other vertebrates,
such as is found in ants and other social insects. There are
a few mammalians that live together in small communities,
in a habitation made to last for many generations, in which
such an instinct would appear necessary, and it accordingly
exists, but is very imperfect. This is the case with the
vizcacha, the large rodent of the pampas, which lives with
its fellows, to the number of twenty or thirty, in a cluster of
huge burrows. When a vizcacha dies in a burrow, the body
is dragged out and thrown on to the mound among the mass
of rubbish collected on it—but not until he has been dead a
long time, and there is nothing left of him but the dry bones
held together by the skin. In that condition the other
members of the community probably cease to look on him as
one of their companions who has fallen into a long sleep; he
is no more than so much rubbish, which must be cleared out

of an old disused burrow. Probably the beaver possesses some rude instinct similar to that of the vizcacha.

Apropos of animals burying their treasures (or connections) for safety, it is worth mentioning that the skunk of the pampas occasionally buries her young in the kennel, when hunger compels her to go out foraging. I had often heard of this habit of the female skunk from the gauchos, and one day had the rare good fortune to witness an animal engaged in obliterating her own kennel. The senses of the skunk are so defective that one is able at times to approach very near to without alarming them. In this instance I sat on my horse at a distance of twenty yards, and watched the animal at work, drawing in the loose earth with her fore feet until the entrance to the kennel was filled up to within three inches of the surface; then, dropping into the shallow cavity, she pressed the loose mould down with her nose. Her task finished, she trotted away, and the hollow in the soil, when I examined it closely, looked only like the mouth of an ancient choked-up burrow. The young inhabit a circular chamber, lined with fine dry grass, at the end of a narrow passage from 3 ft. to 5 ft. long, and no doubt have air enough to serve them until their parent returns; but I believe the skunk only buries her young when they are very small.

INDEX.

A CATALOG OF SELECTED
DOVER BOOKS
IN ALL FIELDS OF INTEREST

A CATALOG OF SELECTED DOVER
BOOKS IN ALL FIELDS OF INTEREST

DRAWINGS OF REMBRANDT, edited by Seymour Slive. Updated Lippmann, Hofstede de Groot edition, with definitive scholarly apparatus. All portraits, biblical sketches, landscapes, nudes. Oriental figures, classical studies, together with selection of work by followers. 550 illustrations. Total of 630pp. 9⅛ × 12¼.
21485-0, 21486-9 Pa., Two-vol. set $25.00

GHOST AND HORROR STORIES OF AMBROSE BIERCE, Ambrose Bierce. 24 tales vividly imagined, strangely prophetic, and decades ahead of their time in technical skill: "The Damned Thing," "An Inhabitant of Carcosa," "The Eyes of the Panther," "Moxon's Master," and 20 more. 199pp. 5⅜ × 8½. 20767-6 Pa. $3.95

ETHICAL WRITINGS OF MAIMONIDES, Maimonides. Most significant ethical works of great medieval sage, newly translated for utmost precision, readability. Laws Concerning Character Traits, Eight Chapters, more. 192pp. 5⅜ × 8½.
24522-5 Pa. $4.50

THE EXPLORATION OF THE COLORADO RIVER AND ITS CANYONS, J. W. Powell. Full text of Powell's 1,000-mile expedition down the fabled Colorado in 1869. Superb account of terrain, geology, vegetation, Indians, famine, mutiny, treacherous rapids, mighty canyons, during exploration of last unknown part of continental U.S. 400pp. 5⅜ × 8½. 20094-9 Pa. $6.95

HISTORY OF PHILOSOPHY, Julián Marías. Clearest one-volume history on the market. Every major philosopher and dozens of others, to Existentialism and later. 505pp. 5⅜ × 8½. 21739-6 Pa. $8.50

ALL ABOUT LIGHTNING, Martin A. Uman. Highly readable non-technical survey of nature and causes of lightning, thunderstorms, ball lightning, St. Elmo's Fire, much more. Illustrated. 192pp. 5⅜ × 8½. 25237-X Pa. $5.95

SAILING ALONE AROUND THE WORLD, Captain Joshua Slocum. First man to sail around the world, alone, in small boat. One of great feats of seamanship told in delightful manner. 67 illustrations. 294pp. 5⅜ × 8½. 20326-3 Pa. $4.95

LETTERS AND NOTES ON THE MANNERS, CUSTOMS AND CONDITIONS OF THE NORTH AMERICAN INDIANS, George Catlin. Classic account of life among Plains Indians: ceremonies, hunt, warfare, etc. 312 plates. 572pp. of text. 6⅛ × 9¼. 22118-0, 22119-9 Pa. Two-vol. set $15.90

ALASKA: The Harriman Expedition, 1899, John Burroughs, John Muir, et al. Informative, engrossing accounts of two-month, 9,000-mile expedition. Native peoples, wildlife, forests, geography, salmon industry, glaciers, more. Profusely illustrated. 240 black-and-white line drawings. 124 black-and-white photographs. 3 maps. Index. 576pp. 5⅜ × 8½. 25109-8 Pa. $11.95

ILLUSTRATED DICTIONARY OF HISTORIC ARCHITECTURE, edited by Cyril M. Harris. Extraordinary compendium of clear, concise definitions for over 5,000 important architectural terms complemented by over 2,000 line drawings. Covers full spectrum of architecture from ancient ruins to 20th-century Modernism. Preface. 592pp. 7½ × 9⅜. 24444-X Pa. $14.95

THE NIGHT BEFORE CHRISTMAS, Clement Moore. Full text, and woodcuts from original 1848 book. Also critical, historical material. 19 illustrations. 40pp. 4⅝ × 6. 22797-9 Pa. $2.50

THE LESSON OF JAPANESE ARCHITECTURE: 165 Photographs, Jiro Harada. Memorable gallery of 165 photographs taken in the 1930's of exquisite Japanese homes of the well-to-do and historic buildings. 13 line diagrams. 192pp. 8⅜ × 11¼. 24778-3 Pa. $8.95

THE AUTOBIOGRAPHY OF CHARLES DARWIN AND SELECTED LETTERS, edited by Francis Darwin. The fascinating life of eccentric genius composed of an intimate memoir by Darwin (intended for his children); commentary by his son, Francis; hundreds of fragments from notebooks, journals, papers; and letters to and from Lyell, Hooker, Huxley, Wallace and Henslow. xi + 365pp. 5⅜ × 8. 20479-0 Pa. $5.95

WONDERS OF THE SKY: Observing Rainbows, Comets, Eclipses, the Stars and Other Phenomena, Fred Schaaf. Charming, easy-to-read poetic guide to all manner of celestial events visible to the naked eye. Mock suns, glories, Belt of Venus, more. Illustrated. 299pp. 5¼ × 8¼. 24402-4 Pa. $7.95

BURNHAM'S CELESTIAL HANDBOOK, Robert Burnham, Jr. Thorough guide to the stars beyond our solar system. Exhaustive treatment. Alphabetical by constellation: Andromeda to Cetus in Vol. 1; Chamaeleon to Orion in Vol. 2; and Pavo to Vulpecula in Vol. 3. Hundreds of illustrations. Index in Vol. 3. 2,000pp. 6⅛ × 9¼. 23567-X, 23568-8, 23673-0 Pa., Three-vol. set $37.85

STAR NAMES: Their Lore and Meaning, Richard Hinckley Allen. Fascinating history of names various cultures have given to constellations and literary and folkloristic uses that have been made of stars. Indexes to subjects. Arabic and Greek names. Biblical references. Bibliography. 563pp. 5⅜ × 8½. 21079-0 Pa. $7.95

THIRTY YEARS THAT SHOOK PHYSICS: The Story of Quantum Theory, George Gamow. Lucid, accessible introduction to influential theory of energy and matter. Careful explanations of Dirac's anti-particles, Bohr's model of the atom, much more. 12 plates. Numerous drawings. 240pp. 5⅜ × 8½. 24895-X Pa. $4.95

CHINESE DOMESTIC FURNITURE IN PHOTOGRAPHS AND MEASURED DRAWINGS, Gustav Ecke. A rare volume, now affordably priced for antique collectors, furniture buffs and art historians. Detailed review of styles ranging from early Shang to late Ming. Unabridged republication. 161 black-and-white drawings, photos. Total of 224pp. 8⅜ × 11¼. (Available in U.S. only) 25171-3 Pa. $12.95

VINCENT VAN GOGH: A Biography, Julius Meier-Graefe. Dynamic, penetrating study of artist's life, relationship with brother, Theo, painting techniques, travels, more. Readable, engrossing. 160pp. 5⅜ × 8½. (Available in U.S. only) 25253-1 Pa. $3.95

CHRISTMAS CUSTOMS AND TRADITIONS, Clement A. Miles. Origin, evolution, significance of religious, secular practices. Caroling, gifts, yule logs, much more. Full, scholarly yet fascinating; non-sectarian. 400pp. 5⅜ × 8½.
23354-5 Pa. $6.50

THE HUMAN FIGURE IN MOTION, Eadweard Muybridge. More than 4,500 stopped-action photos, in action series, showing undraped men, women, children jumping, lying down, throwing, sitting, wrestling, carrying, etc. 390pp. 7⅞ × 10⅝.
20204-6 Cloth. $19.95

THE MAN WHO WAS THURSDAY, Gilbert Keith Chesterton. Witty, fast-paced novel about a club of anarchists in turn-of-the-century London. Brilliant social, religious, philosophical speculations. 128pp. 5⅜ × 8½.
25121-7 Pa. $3.95

A CEZANNE SKETCHBOOK: Figures, Portraits, Landscapes and Still Lifes, Paul Cezanne. Great artist experiments with tonal effects, light, mass, other qualities in over 100 drawings. A revealing view of developing master painter, precursor of Cubism. 102 black-and-white illustrations. 144pp. 8¾ × 6⅝.
24790-2 Pa. $5.95

AN ENCYCLOPEDIA OF BATTLES: Accounts of Over 1,560 Battles from 1479 B.C. to the Present, David Eggenberger. Presents essential details of every major battle in recorded history, from the first battle of Megiddo in 1479 B.C. to Grenada in 1984. List of Battle Maps. New Appendix covering the years 1967–1984. Index. 99 illustrations. 544pp. 6½ × 9¼.
24913-1 Pa. $14.95

AN ETYMOLOGICAL DICTIONARY OF MODERN ENGLISH, Ernest Weekley. Richest, fullest work, by foremost British lexicographer. Detailed word histories. Inexhaustible. Total of 856pp. 6½ × 9¼.
21873-2, 21874-0 Pa., Two-vol. set $17.00

WEBSTER'S AMERICAN MILITARY BIOGRAPHIES, edited by Robert McHenry. Over 1,000 figures who shaped 3 centuries of American military history. Detailed biographies of Nathan Hale, Douglas MacArthur, Mary Hallaren, others. Chronologies of engagements, more. Introduction. Addenda. 1,033 entries in alphabetical order. xi + 548pp. 6½ × 9¼. (Available in U.S. only)
24758-9 Pa. $11.95

LIFE IN ANCIENT EGYPT, Adolf Erman. Detailed older account, with much not in more recent books: domestic life, religion, magic, medicine, commerce, and whatever else needed for complete picture. Many illustrations. 597pp. 5⅜ × 8½.
22632-8 Pa. $8.95

HISTORIC COSTUME IN PICTURES, Braun & Schneider. Over 1,450 costumed figures shown, covering a wide variety of peoples: kings, emperors, nobles, priests, servants, soldiers, scholars, townsfolk, peasants, merchants, courtiers, cavaliers, and more. 256pp. 8⅜ × 11¼.
23150-X Pa. $7.95

THE NOTEBOOKS OF LEONARDO DA VINCI, edited by J. P. Richter. Extracts from manuscripts reveal great genius; on painting, sculpture, anatomy, sciences, geography, etc. Both Italian and English. 186 ms. pages reproduced, plus 500 additional drawings, including studies for *Last Supper, Sforza* monument, etc. 860pp. 7⅞ × 10¾. (Available in U.S. only) 22572-0, 22573-9 Pa., Two-vol. set $25.90

CATALOG OF DOVER BOOKS

AMERICAN CLIPPER SHIPS: 1833–1858, Octavius T. Howe & Frederick C. Matthews. Fully-illustrated, encyclopedic review of 352 clipper ships from the period of America's greatest maritime supremacy. Introduction. 109 halftones. 5 black-and-white line illustrations. Index. Total of 928pp. 5⅜ × 8½.
25115-2, 25116-0 Pa., Two-vol. set $17.90

TOWARDS A NEW ARCHITECTURE, Le Corbusier. Pioneering manifesto by great architect, near legendary founder of "International School." Technical and aesthetic theories, views on industry, economics, relation of form to function, "mass-production spirit," much more. Profusely illustrated. Unabridged translation of 13th French edition. Introduction by Frederick Etchells. 320pp. 6⅛ × 9¼. (Available in U.S. only)
25023-7 Pa. $8.95

THE BOOK OF KELLS, edited by Blanche Cirker. Inexpensive collection of 32 full-color, full-page plates from the greatest illuminated manuscript of the Middle Ages, painstakingly reproduced from rare facsimile edition. Publisher's Note. Captions. 32pp. 9⅜ × 12¼.
24345-1 Pa. $4.95

BEST SCIENCE FICTION STORIES OF H. G. WELLS, H. G. Wells. Full novel The Invisible Man, plus 17 short stories: "The Crystal Egg," "Aepyornis Island," "The Strange Orchid," etc. 303pp. 5⅜ × 8½. (Available in U.S. only)
21531-8 Pa. $4.95

AMERICAN SAILING SHIPS: Their Plans and History, Charles G. Davis. Photos, construction details of schooners, frigates, clippers, other sailcraft of 18th to early 20th centuries—plus entertaining discourse on design, rigging, nautical lore, much more. 137 black-and-white illustrations. 240pp. 6⅛ × 9¼.
24658-2 Pa. $5.95

ENTERTAINING MATHEMATICAL PUZZLES, Martin Gardner. Selection of author's favorite conundrums involving arithmetic, money, speed, etc., with lively commentary. Complete solutions. 112pp. 5⅜ × 8½. 25211-6 Pa. $2.95

THE WILL TO BELIEVE, HUMAN IMMORTALITY, William James. Two books bound together. Effect of irrational on logical, and arguments for human immortality. 402pp. 5⅜ × 8½. 20291-7 Pa. $7.50

THE HAUNTED MONASTERY and THE CHINESE MAZE MURDERS, Robert Van Gulik. 2 full novels by Van Gulik continue adventures of Judge Dee and his companions. An evil Taoist monastery, seemingly supernatural events; overgrown topiary maze that hides strange crimes. Set in 7th-century China. 27 illustrations. 328pp. 5⅜ × 8½. 23502-5 Pa. $5.95

CELEBRATED CASES OF JUDGE DEE (DEE GOONG AN), translated by Robert Van Gulik. Authentic 18th-century Chinese detective novel; Dee and associates solve three interlocked cases. Led to Van Gulik's own stories with same characters. Extensive introduction. 9 illustrations. 237pp. 5⅜ × 8½.
23337-5 Pa. $4.95

Prices subject to change without notice.
Available at your book dealer or write for free catalog to Dept. GI, Dover Publications, Inc., 31 East 2nd St., Mineola, N.Y. 11501. Dover publishes more than 175 books each year on science, elementary and advanced mathematics, biology, music, art, literary history, social sciences and other areas.